Mislabeled as Disabled

The Educational Abuse of Struggling
Learners and How **We** Can Fight It

"In this extraordinary and deeply disturbing book, Buzzy Hettleman, a long-time warrior for struggling learners in our schools, tells us about the children trapped in the flawed systems we provide for them. He lays out in painstaking and shocking detail the enormity of this crime, and what needs to be done to remedy this broken system. Everyone who cares about the education of all of our children should read this book."

Robert E. Slavin, Director, Center for Research and Reform in Education, Johns Hopkins University (from the Introduction)

"Kalman R. Hettleman is a marvel, an experienced policymaker and political activist with an unrivaled understanding of how and why some schools work and others don't. In this book, he reveals what is actually going on in our nation's special education programs and why we can't seem to give struggling students the help they need and deserve."

Jay Mathews, Washington Post education columnist

"Kalman (Buzzy) Hettleman's book is a masterpiece. Based on his own experience in the field as well as policy research, it brilliantly analyzes the policies and politics that have contributed to the failure of educational reform efforts on behalf of students with disabilities and other struggling learners. Frontline practitioners, parents and policymakers should embrace his proposals for reform."

Donald D. Deshler, University of Kansas Distinguished Professor Emeritus of Special Education and Founder, Center for Research on Learning

"Some will be uncomfortable with Hettleman's premise for the book. But none can quibble with his unflinching and dogged commitment to students identified with a disability, and his fierce passion and insights in fighting battles for all struggling learners who deserve the best instruction possible."

Edward J. Kame'enui, Professor Emeritus, University of Oregon and Founding Director, National Center for Special Education Research, Institute of Education Sciences, U.S. Department of Education

Mislabeled as Disabled

The Educational Abuse of Struggling Learners and How **We** Can Fight It

Kalman R. Hettleman

Radius Book Group
New York

Distributed by Radius Book Group
A Division of Diversion Publishing Corp.
443 Park Avenue South, Suite 1004
New York, NY 10016
www.RadiusBookGroup.com

For more information, email info@radiusbookgroup.com.

Library of Congress Control Number: 2018961075

First edition:
Hardcover ISBN: 978-1-63576-639-4
Trade Paperback ISBN: 978-1-63576-634-9
eBook ISBN: 978-1-63576-640-0

Manufactured in the United States of America
10 9 8 7 6 5 4 3 2 1

Cover design by Charles Hames
Interior design by Scribe Inc.

To all the devoted parents and teachers I have worked with, who know the system must change and will answer a call to action to bring it about.

And to Myra, who everyday makes it possible for me to try to do my part in the struggle.

Contents

Introduction xi

Preface xv

Part I. The Indictment

  1 A Preview of Coming Infractions 3

  2 The Big Lie—How Struggling Learners Are
Illegally Placed in Special Education 22

  3 Underachievement and the Big Cover Up 41

Part II. The Right Instruction at the Right Time

  4 RTI to the Rescue of Struggling Learners 57

  5 Special Education Is Not Special Enough 81

Part III. Who's to Blame?

  6 Show Teachers the Money 103

  7 Mismanagement of Classroom Instruction 116

Part IV. The Possibilities and Politics of Reform

  8 The Folly of Reliance on State and Local Reform 141

  9 A Civil Right to End the Wrongs and the
Reinvention of Special Education 146

10 A Political Call to Action:
Parents—Unite and Fight! 157

Notes 181

Index 207

Acknowledgments 217

About the Author 219

Introduction

Robert E. Slavin
*Director, Center for Research
and Reform in Education,
Johns Hopkins University*

This book by Kalman "Buzzy" Hettleman is a true crime detective story. The victims are millions of children who are denied effective education. For reasons not of their own making, they live in a wasteland between general and special education. They are called struggling readers, or struggling learners, or students at risk, or students who are disabled. Behind their backs they are called "dummies" or much worse things. But we put far too much effort into deciding what to call these students, far too little into teaching them.

Struggling readers start off in life like anyone else. They are beautiful, as all children are. They love to learn, and grow rapidly in language and understanding of the world around them, as all children do. They are natural scientists, full of curiosity and excitement about learning, as all children are. A very small number of children suffer serious disabilities, such as visual or hearing impairment or severe cognitive problems that are apparent to anyone. But the problems of struggling learners are only apparent from 9:00 to 3:00 on school days. During school hours, they comprise the clear majority of students who are found eligible for some form of special education. Other struggling learners may not receive special education, but are in the lowest reading groups, the lowest-performing classes, and/or the lowest-achieving schools. It is not inconsequential that struggling learners are far more likely than other students to be from disadvantaged or minority families, but these demographic facts do not explain how they become struggling learners, as much as they explain why their problems are rarely solved.

The damage done to children who have preventable or treatable learning problems, and to our school systems and society, need hardly be enumerated. Students who fail in school lose the enthusiasm they came with, and begin to act out (wouldn't you?). They see success in school as out of their reach, so they seek success in other avenues, including anti-social behaviors. Our neglect breeds a self-perpetuating class of under-achieving and often alienated citizens, composed largely of once-promising, once-motivated young people failed by our schools.

Now that we have established who the victims are, what is the crime? In any human population, there is bound to be variation. Some kids are faster runners than others, some have great musical or artistic skills, and some do not. Aren't learning skills just the same? Where is the crime here?

To understand the situation, consider the state of medicine in ages past. Millions of children used to die in childbirth, or of measles, tuberculosis, typhoid, polio, malaria, infections, smallpox, and so on. Childhood mortality was just seen as God's will.

Now imagine that we decided today, despite all the medical advances made mostly in the 20th century, to stop trying to prevent or cure childhood illnesses. Parents who could afford medical care could buy it, but those who could not—well, too bad. Millions of disadvantaged children would needlessly die, but is that murder? Would it be a crime?

I think most people would agree that withholding proven treatments and causing millions of unnecessary illnesses or even deaths would be a moral outrage. A crime by any definition, if not on the law books.

Returning to education, we are in exactly the same position. We have proven programs and practices that are known to be able to prevent school failure or to successfully solve problems that arise despite vigorous attempts at prevention. There are many programs, especially for elementary schools, known to improve reading and math learning, learning for students in general, and for struggling learners in specific. Then there are one-to-small group and one-to-one tutoring approaches able to ensure that virtually every student who has a reading or math problem can get off to a good start and keep up in these crucial subjects. Proven approaches have been known for at least a decade, and more of them are validated in high-quality, rigorous research every year. These programs can be expensive, but their costs are trivial compared to what we spend on education in general, and even more so when you consider the costs of special education and retentions in grade.

Allowing so many students to fail, when their failure could have been effectively prevented or quickly remediated, is a crime, by any definition. At best, it is a shortsighted misallocation of public funds. When you consider the effects on individual children, what word fits better than "crime"?

Now that we've established the crime and the victims, let's consider the perpetrators. The problem here is that there are so many. But let me start with who they are *not*.

- It's not teachers, who work heroically in a deeply flawed system to do the best they can to rescue those children they can rescue.
- It's not principals or other administrators, who work as hard as the teachers within the same flawed system.
- It's not the parents, who send to school the best kids they have.
- It's not the kids, who do their best until they finally begin to understand that their best is not going to be good enough.

The crimes against struggling learners are not perpetrated by evil people. Quite the contrary, they are people who truly care about making things better. But they are people who do not know, or choose not to know, that outcomes could be far better for struggling learners. They are people who imagine that simple solutions, such as more money, or new federal or state regulations, or higher standards for teachers, or charter schools, or copying Finland or Singapore, are all we need to do. More money and other structural and regulatory changes will certainly be needed to solve the problem of struggling learners, but these structural changes are not enough in themselves if we neglect proven instructional programs and practices.

The most important "perpetrator" is not anyone in particular. It is *complacency*. Everyone says they wish schools were better, and they are concerned about struggling learners and disadvantaged students in an abstract way, but their own kids' schools are pretty good, and their own kids are doing ok, so they do not put their passion into other peoples' schools.

So we've identified the victims, the crime, and the perpetrator. Here's how this story should end:

"Complacency! Come out with your hands up! We've got you surrounded. You know your rights, so we're going to read you your responsibilities:

- You will commit yourself to caring about struggling learners enough to ensure that they are no longer struggling learners.
- You will find out what programs have been proven to prevent failures in reading and math, and will commit to applying these as broadly as possible to ensure success for every child in your care.
- You will create conditions in schools to support learning about, implementing, and evaluating proven programs until the problem of struggling readers is solved."

In this extraordinary and deeply disturbing book, Buzzy Hettleman, a long-time warrior for struggling learners in our schools, tells us about the children trapped in the flawed systems we provide for them. He lays out in painstaking and shocking detail the enormity of this crime, and what needs to be done to remedy this broken system.

Everyone who cares about the education of all of our children should read this book and then take action to solve these problems. We must urgently do this before another generation of children eager to learn is victimized by a system willing to do everything for them except to give them proven instruction, and make certain it works.

Baltimore, Maryland
September 30, 2018

Preface

Kenny, when I first met him, was in the 10th grade at a public high school in Baltimore. He was a 16-year-old low-income African-American who lived in a poor inner city neighborhood. The high school he attended required high grades and test scores for admission. He liked video games and to hang with friends. He had a girlfriend, and didn't like school very much.

So far, no big surprises. Kenny sounds like a teenager who, if you've watched Homicide or The Wire, was better off than many peers in a city like Baltimore. But there's more you need to know about him.

Kenny was reading at a kindergarten grade level.

Let that sink in. Though in the 10th grade and in a selective high school, Kenny barely knew the names and sounds of the 26 letters of the alphabet and how to read words like cat, bat and rat.

How could that be? He had good attendance. And unlike many peers, he had never been a behavior problem. So why was he never taught to read? And how in the world, since he couldn't read at all, could he do high school work and pass his courses?

This book will answer these questions. But for now, let's try to imagine how Kenny felt. It's not easy, but let's try to put ourselves in the shoes of a 10th grader who is not severely disabled, yet, in his own mind and in the eyes of his classmates, is a big "dummy."

We can better imagine how his parents felt. Heartbroken and in utter despair, knowing that their son had gone from kindergarten to 10th grade without being taught to read. Knowing that their son was totally unprepared for college or a good job. Knowing that their son hid his pain and frustration but suffered deeply from self-awareness of his academic failings.

And while this probably doesn't occur to you, how do you think his teachers felt? I'd say sad, empathic, determined to help him as much as they could and, more than anything else, helpless. Many had sought additional aid for Kenny at various points but were rebuffed by the "system."

This book exposes the "system." It is the tragic tale of Kenny and tens of millions of other schoolchildren who are never taught basic skills in reading, writing and math. In these pages, you will learn how and why this amounts to the crime of educational abuse by public school systems across the U.S. Most of the victims, like Kenny, are poor and minority and concentrated in large urban school systems. But you will be shocked at how many struggling learners in suburbs and rural areas, from rich and middle class homes, in red and blue states, are also victimized.

It's educational abuse because school systems could do much better than they're doing, even with limited resources. This means, more than anything else, timely assistance when children first struggle to learn to read. The framework for this is called "Response to Intervention" or RTI. RTI sounds abstract, but it's real, we know how to do it, and it can make all the difference in the world to Kenny and other struggling learners. It can also make all the difference in the world to parents who suffer alongside their children.

I hope this Preface grabs your attention, but even more I hope it makes your blood start to boil. If so, you will begin to understand my own state of mind as I wrote the book. I am a policy wonk and have churned out over the years innumerable articles and reports, laden with detailed analyses, policy proposals and footnotes. I have said, only half-kiddingly, that my literary ambition was to write the great American memo.

Still, I want this book to be more than policy diagnoses and prescriptions and a call to action. I want it also to be a memoir of sorts, chronicling my journey through decades of work to improve public schools. Over that time, I have represented pro bono over 200 struggling learners, chiefly in Baltimore but also elsewhere in Maryland. I have developed and advocated for policy reforms in Maryland and nationally.

And I have done some good on both fronts. The greatest reward has been making a difference in an individual child's life, and easing the anguish of parents who had felt forsaken. But overall, most days and weeks and years I've felt a lot of frustration and anger.

It's bad enough that I have seen hundreds of students and families victimized. But the frustration and anger are compounded because I know that they suffer needlessly. Needless it is, because despite the seeming intractability of problems related to poverty, race and public schools, we do have the ways and means to reform K-12 education in our country. As a nation, we also have the will. If Americans are united in these troubled times behind any national mission, it is to improve public schools.

Well, if we know the way and have the will, what's holding us up? There is no simple answer in this book or anywhere else. But there are attainable reforms, and there is no acceptable excuse for our national inaction.

And so my frustration and anger seep through these pages. Obviously you don't have to look farther than the book's title to get that message. I have been advised by respected colleagues to tone it down. The term "educational abuse," they say, will turn off readers, particularly educators. But I have resisted that advice. The abuse ruins the lives of children and torments their parents. Just ask Kenny and his family. I want readers to know the truth and feel what I feel daily in my work: their pain.

You'll learn the origins of the abuse, why so many students like Kenny are mislabeled as disabled, and what can be done about it. At the same time, despite all the sad stories and daunting obstacles, I hope you'll come to share my optimism about the possibilities for significant change. There is hope if, as a nation, we understand what's at stake, and unite and fight for what is right.

Before fully getting underway, there are several cross-cutting issues of great importance that I want to point out. The first is fear that my blunt accusation of educational abuse—though I stand by it, as I've already said—may be misunderstood. Specifically, that it may be taken as an indictment of teachers. That is farthest from my mind and the opposite of my belief.

Frontline teachers are heroes of mine and they should be yours. This book is dedicated to them. The overwhelming majority are dedicated and able; yet, they are underpaid and undervalued by our society as whole. You may know that already. But what you probably don't realize is the extent to which they are hung out to dry by their own leaders in the upper ranks of national, state and local educational agencies. Throughout the book, I try to make clear the distinction between the rank and file of teachers, who are the very good guys, and the educational establishment as later defined. It's the latter that bears—along with all of the rest of us—a share of the responsibility for our nation's failure to provide an adequate education to millions of children, predominantly from poor and minority families.

Another concern has to do with how "special education" is portrayed. Special education is as complex, misunderstood and woeful as any aspect of K-12 schooling, and a thrust of the book is on those students in special education who don't belong there. I call them the "mainly mislabeled." However, special education is usually better for students who are *truly disabled*. They have severe disabilities, most of which, though not all, include significant cognitive impairment. Students with these severe disabilities belong in truly "special" education. And they are not victims of the educational abuse at the center of the book.

They—despite all my criticisms of special education—have been relatively well served by it. The exclusion and sheer neglect that gave rise to the initial federal law governing students with disabilities in 1975 are long gone. To be sure, there is some over-identification of students with severe disabilities. Some of it is even purposeful because schools are held to lower standards for the achievement of these students. Still, for those who are truly disabled, expectations and services should be substantially raised. This is far more likely to happen if, as advocated in the book, there is a reinvention of special education so it serves only students who are truly disabled. We should go back to the future since that's what the original federal law intended.

Let me now say a few preliminary words about what I bring to my role as education reform crusader. For about 20 years, I have participated in over 500 meetings with school based staff who determine the Individualized Education Programs (IEPs) of students in special education. From this experience in the trenches and policy research, I have written four published reports that spell out the inadequacies and illegalities in the system nationwide. At the same time, I have worked to reform policy on the inside as a member of the Baltimore City school board and as an outside advocate. I have been the chief architect of a nationally recognized reform that raises the bar for expectations and academic progress of students in special education (though it has not yet been well implemented). Hopefully, this work on the ground outweighs the fact that I have no professional educational credentials.

Finally, this book is dedicated not just to teachers but to the hundreds of parents of struggling learners, inside and outside of special education, who I have represented over the years. Whatever their family composition and income level, their love for their children and their David-like determination to fight the school system Goliath are awe-inspiring. These parents don't give up, and we dare not either.

To that end, I hope the book informs, engages and, yes, enrages you. So much so that we are more determined than ever to take political action and bring about reform. To borrow from Dr. Martin Luther King, Jr., let's work together so that the arc of public education once again bends toward justice for all our schoolchildren.

PART I

....

THE INDICTMENT

Chapter 1

····································

Preview of Coming Infractions

Usually it's the teaching that's disabled, not the students.[1]

Millions of American schoolchildren are victims of educational abuse. These children are struggling learners who fall behind early in learning to read, write and compute. They almost never catch up. Many become mislabeled as disabled and, let's tell it like it is, "dumped" into a special education system that for them is deplorably ineffective. In the Preface, you saw what happened to Kenny. Most struggling learners are doomed to fail in school and to suffer lifelong harm.

This doesn't have to happen. This book will show that better instruction—better instruction that we already know about—will enable the great majority of all struggling learners to succeed. And the fact that many of them are poor and minority children is not a credible alibi for our national failure. We all—including educators and policymakers—need to learn this lesson. Parents, especially, must, first, be informed about the educational abuse and, second, mobilize to lead the battle to bring about reform.

Because we know what to do but don't do it, the charge of educational abuse is not rhetorical overkill. The legal definition of criminal child abuse varies from state to state. But in every state it is a crime when someone abuses, neglects or fails to take proper care of a child. And these crimes do not require an intent to harm.[2] It is more than enough that there is injury and gross negligence. If a child dies or is harmed because a caretaker fails to seek medical care, it is abuse. So when struggling learners are denied the right educational medicine, and when as a result they face bleak economic and social futures and are educationally and emotionally scarred for the rest of their lives, is there any doubt they are the victims of abuse?

Our nation should stand indicted. We desperately need a jarring wake-up call to action, and this book tries to sound the alarm. This Chapter overviews the content of the book, framed at the outset by the case of Marcus. Marcus, another student I represented as an advocate, is much younger than Kenny, and is another tragic example of how the educational abuse happens.

MEET MARCUS

Marcus is African-American and his Mom is a low-income single parent. He has a low-average IQ, but it is well within the range that would enable him, if taught using research-based instruction, to earn passing grades. Yet, when his Mom first came to see me, she tearfully told me that *although he was in the 6th grade, he was reading at a kindergarten level.*

He fell behind as soon as he entered kindergarten, falling further behind in the first and second grades. Still, the school did not substantially alter his instruction. He was provided minimal extra assistance and repeated the second grade.

In the third grade, he was referred for eligibility for special education, but the school special education team found "no suspected disability." Although he was already about two years behind his peers, the team found that he had not fallen far enough behind to warrant special education.

A year later, when Marcus was by then about four years behind his same-age peers in reading (and not much better off in math), he was found eligible for special education under the classification of Specific Learning Disability. However, the special education that he got was not very special. He still was not prescribed research-based interventions. He was mainly given the same dumbed-down work over and over again. The gap between his performance level and enrolled grade level widened farther.

All the while, gradually from the second grade on, his behavior deteriorated. He argued or fought with classmates. He often refused to do his classwork or homework. He talked back to teachers. He faked illnesses to keep from going to school, crying that he didn't want to go. When Mom contacted me, the school, based on his behavior, was ready to change his designated disability from Learning Disability to Emotional Disability and put him in a segregated program for emotionally and behaviorally disturbed students. The school still had no significant plan to improve his reading instruction.

If he was in any way emotionally disturbed, it was not because of an underlying mental health condition. Rather, he was disturbed—unmotivated, upset and acting out—because he was so far behind his peers and unable to keep up with classwork. He wasn't "disturbed" at home, only at school.

I was able to prevent him from being mislabeled with an Emotional Disability and placed in an even more segregated special education program. Instead, his Individual Educational Program (IEP) was revised so that he received 45 minutes of one on one tutoring. four days per week. No miracle has occurred. He is still behind and struggling. Yet, his reading level and his behavior have significantly improved. For sure, when he is in the 10th grade, he will not be in the same dire straits as Kenny.

Still, Marcus, like Kenny, deserved a lot better. Suppose each of them had been given evidence-based small group instruction and one-to-one tutoring as necessary. They could have caught up and kept up with classmates. And under the law they should have received this instructional assistance.

This book will peel away the layers of illegalities and injustices that caused both of them, instead, to be abused by the Baltimore public school system. It will show how and why millions of other struggling learners nationwide are similarly victimized.

We begin by defining the several groups of struggling learners who populate these pages.

WHO ARE THE STRUGGLING LEARNERS?

Marcus and Kenny wound up being found eligible for special education. But the focus of the book is less on how to reform special education, as bad as it is for struggling learners, and more about keeping children out of special education in the first place. Stated another way, this book is not mainly about students with actual disabilities. It's about struggling learners who don't receive timely evidence-based instructional interventions in general education and as a result perform far below their grade level, especially in reading.

Many of them are mislabeled as disabled and found eligible for services in special education. But not all. Most struggling learners remain in general education without any special education services.[3] So which struggling learners become eligible for special education and which don't? Our school systems are so broken that it is nearly impossible to tell.

Practice nationwide is a maze of varying interpretations and methods of determining eligibility for special education.[4] There are huge variations from state to state, from school district to school district, from school to school, and even from classroom to classroom. Two experts have noted that the sorting process is "barely more accurate than a flip of the coin."[5]

Both classes of struggling learners are victimized. Most of those who remain in general education without any special education services fail to meet proficiency standards. But it is the struggling learners who are mislabeled as disabled and wind up in special education who are wronged the most. Chapter 5 details how special education, despite its lofty aims and legal promises, is not nearly special enough. Students who receive special education services continue to fall further and further behind. It seems almost inconceivable but most students in so-called "special" education would have fared better academically if they had remained in general education without any special education services.[6] And they would also have been spared the stigma and segregation that students in special education endure.

This leads us to another threshold delineation that is equally essential.

THE DIFFERENCE BETWEEN "MAINLY MISLABELED" AND "TRULY DISABLED" STUDENTS IN SPECIAL EDUCATION

The "Big Lie," exposed in Chapter 2, is that the over six million students in special education nationally are actually disabled. In fact, the overwhelming majority aren't disabled in the true sense of a medical disability. Under federal law they should not even qualify as students with disabilities.

The "Big Truth" is that except for students with the most severe disabilities, struggling learners should not be referred to special education *unless they have first received adequate instruction in general education alone.* But this law is violated every day. Astonishingly, as many as three-quarters of all students are found eligible for special education because this legal (and common sense) requirement is ignored in school systems large or small and urban, suburban or rural.

Yet, we do almost nothing about it. A fundamental reason is that educators fail to distinguish between the two relatively distinct populations of students who receive special education services. First, there are students with severe disabilities who are not able to meet the same academic standards as non-disabled peers. Most of them have significant cognitive disabilities. Let's call them the Truly Disabled. Second, there are struggling learners who do not have severe disabilities and are able to meet the standards with the right supports. Let's call them the Mainly Mislabeled.

The line, to be sure, is not exact.[7] Disability classifications under the federal Individuals with Disabilities Act (IDEA) are imprecise educationally as well as clinically. True disabilities lie along continuums. And there are large variations nationwide in the percentages of students with disabilities, ranging from 17.5 percent in Massachusetts to 8.6 percent in Texas.[8] Variations are even larger in the percentages within the various disability classifications. For example, the percentage of students in special education classified as having a Specific Learning Disability is 60.4 percent in Iowa and 18.6 percent in Kentucky.[9]

Still, the differences are distinct enough to guide policy and practice. The Every Student Succeeds Act (ESSA), like its predecessor the No Child Left Behind Act, mandates that all states and school districts must be held accountable for ensuring that all students, including all students in special education, are held to the same academic standards. Yet, at the same time, ESSA and IDEA draw a distinction and allow states to develop alternate assessments based on less-demanding alternate academic standards for the Truly Disabled.[10]

The Truly Disabled

The Truly Disabled students, as a general rule, "will have been identified as disabled during infancy and early childhood and preschool years, frequently by health-care professionals or early childhood education specialists, and they will already have begun receiving intervention services before they enter elementary school."[11] A large majority of these students have significant cognitive abilities. Others suffer predominately from deafness, blindness and physical disabilities.

It is these students who are the public face of special education. Their disabilities tend to be physically visible, arousing instant recognition and empathy—for example students with multiple physical disabilities or with Down syndrome. The heroic struggles of these students (and their parents who fight long battles to get appropriate services for them under IDEA) are often featured in the media.

Yet, the public prominence of these students masks an astonishing surprise: These students comprise only about 15 to 20 percent of all students who are found eligible for special educations.[12]

The Mainly Mislabeled

The remaining students in special education—those who do not have severe disabilities—are predominantly struggling learners who are mislabeled as disabled. They comprise the very large majority of all students in special education who are found eligible under the disability classifications of Specific Learning Disability, Speech or Language Impairments, Other Health Impairment (mainly attention deficit disorders), Emotional Disability, and, in some instances, Autism. *They generally have the cognitive ability to meet state standards if they receive proper instruction. But their instruction falls far short.*

A "dream team" of the nation's leading experts on reading estimated that about 70 percent of struggling learners wind up unnecessarily and wrongfully in special education.[13] The National Center on Educational Outcomes, the leading research organization on accountability for the achievement of students with disabilities, has found that "The vast majority of special education students (80–85 percent) can meet the same achievement standards as other students if they are given specially designed instruction, appropriate access, supports and accommodations, as required by IDEA."[14]

Arne Duncan, when U.S. secretary of education under President Obama, bravely took up the cause of these struggling learners. He said, "No belief is more damaging in education than the misperception that children with disabilities cannot really and shouldn't be challenged to reach the same high standards as all children."[15] Yet, his position was widely ridiculed. Policymakers and many educators rolled their eyes in disbelief. Mr. Duncan, they thought, must be living in educational la-la land. How can these students be expected to meet the same academic standards as non-disabled peers? They are disabled, aren't they?

No, most of them aren't, as stated above. Chapter 2 will further unravel how they become mislabeled as disabled, and dispatched illegally to inferior instruction and stigma and segregation in special education. But let me jump ahead and preview the most powerful and insidious cause for the mislabeling: simple expediency.

Expediency is the mother of special education invention. When general education teachers are overwhelmed by too many struggling learners who are far behind their peers and impede instruction and class management, they turn in desperation to special education. Dumping these students in special education is their lifeline to keep the whole class from sinking. That makes things better for general education teachers and other students, but the plight of students who are mislabeled as disabled only gets much worse.

Baltimore—surprise, surprise, since my city is otherwise a poster child for urban decay, including its deficient schools—is a national pioneer in trying to improve instruction in special education. But alas, implementation of the policy is lagging, as admitted in Chapter 5.

THE ROAD TO REFORM

Is it really possible to rescue struggling learners in general education and special education from school failure? Right now—in general education or special education—struggling learners are likely to die slow academic deaths. Here's a sample of the national data that tells the catastrophic tale.[16]

Struggling Learners in General Education (That Is, Those Students Who Don't Receive Any Special Education Services) Nationwide

In the fourth grade, only 30% of students in general education alone achieved proficiency in reading and 35% in math. In the eighth grade, the numbers are 34% in reading and 27% in math.

Struggling Learners in Special Education (That Is, Those Students Who Do Receive Special Education Services) Nationwide
In the fourth grade, only 10% of students in special education achieved proficiency in reading and 14% in math. In the eighth grade, the numbers are 8% in reading and 7% for math.

And the scores are not improving.

If you can bear it, there's more data in Chapter 3. And believe it or not, the data is even worse than it looks. Chapter 3 reveals how school systems shamelessly inflate test scores and cover up much of the damage done to struggling learners. In both general education and special education, struggling learners pass from grade to grade only because of blatant grade inflation. If they don't later drop out, as alarming numbers do, their high school graduation diplomas are usually bogus; most struggling learners have not learned anywhere near enough to be legitimately college or career ready.

So the road to school reform begins in the academic pits. Then it must surmount steep hurdles if it is to get anywhere. Most daunting of all, from their first day in pre-kindergarten or kindergarten, many struggling learners carry in their backpacks all the disadvantages of impoverished families and neighborhoods. Do we in fact know how to deliver the classroom teaching that will enable them and other struggling learners to succeed? It wouldn't be fair to level the harsh charge of educational abuse without offering credible evidence that our schools can do much better than they do. Outspoken advocates like me should put up or shut up, and in Chapter 4, I take on the challenge. It can be done. Here's a preview of how.

The Right Instruction at the Right Time
Let me beat skeptics to the punch. Yes, there is no simple answer or quick fix. Education reforms are forever coming and going without reversing the academic misfortunes of struggling learners, especially students who are poor and minority. But one basic strategy with transformative potential has been grossly neglected.

It's called Response to Intervention (RTI). RTI, as explored in Chapter 4, is a framework for timely identification of struggling learners and interventions. It incorporates:

- Assessment as early as pre-kindergarten and kindergarten to dis-cover students who are falling behind developmentally appropriate milestones in learning the basic skills of reading, writing and math.
- Evidence—based instruction to address their skill deficits.
- Progress monitoring to determine whether the extra instruction is working.
- More progressively intensive instructional interventions if stu-dents don't stay on pace to achieve age-appropriate standards.

It's hard to dispute the logic of the process. Students get the right medi-cine as soon and in the necessary dosage as they need it. If done right RTI, as we'll see in Chapter 4, will literally cause most so-called special education disabilities to disappear.

But logic and evidence alone have never been enough to cure the deep ills of public schools. As we will see in later chapters, there are formidable obstacles that stand in the way of effective implementation of RTI on a nationwide scale. Nonetheless, I've always taken heart from the famous children's story I've read to four sons and eight grandchildren: *The Little Engine That Could*. RTI could be the engine that, against mountainous odds, carries struggling students to new heights of achievement.

So far, however, the RTI engine is stuck in the station awaiting a national go-signal. RTI has not been implemented, much less succeeded, on a large scale in any large school system. Yet, to borrow from G.K. Ches-terton's lament about the absence of Christian ideals, RTI has not been tried and found wanting; it has been found difficult, and left untried. To end the educational abuse of millions of American schoolchildren, that must change.

WHO ARE TO BLAME FOR THE ABSENCE OF RTI AND THE EDUCATIONAL ABUSE?

Why is RTI stuck in the station? And who are mainly responsible for the tragic fate of struggling learners? In Chapters 6 and 7 I line up the usual, and some unusual, suspects in two large groupings: "All of Us" and "Edu-cators." All of Us are the policymakers, parents and the general public who don't put up the money for world-class public schools. We don't provide classroom teachers with the small pupil-teacher ratios, training and other classroom supports to fuel the engine of RTI.

We also do very little these days to address the conditions of poverty and inequality that cause the learning deficits of so many struggling learners. All the while, we are bogged down in ideological education wars that detour reform from its main destination: classroom instruction.

Educators, too, must share the blame with the rest of us. Educators violate federal laws governing eligibility for special education, resist the use of evidence-based best instructional practices, and don't manage well the money they have. It is painful to say but educators who labor valiantly and deserve our gratitude are sometimes their own worst enemies.

Let me repeat, because it is so crucial, a point introduced in the Preface: my anxiety that my criticisms of Educators may be misunderstood. An indictment of the universe of individual teachers and other school professionals is farthest from my mind. Throughout the book I strive to make clear that general education and special education teachers and other personnel who are integral to special education (primarily psychologists, social workers, speech and language pathologists, and occupational therapists) care deeply and work tirelessly. Yet they work under inadequate conditions—such as excessive class sizes and caseloads, weak curricula, woeful training and far too little supervisory support—that undermine their professionalism.

They are betrayed by what the famed educator E. D. Hirsch called "the controlling system of ideas that currently prevents needed changes from being contemplated or understood."[17] The controllers of these ideas and protectors of the status quo are found in the upper ranks of what, in Chapter 7, I describe as the "education establishment." The education establishmentarians include federal and state regulators, teachers colleges, and national associations of K-12 education professions. Chapter 7 will show how they, albeit unwittingly, contribute to the educational abuse that harms students and inflicts collateral damage on teachers.

Don't be fooled, however. Many if not most frontline teachers know they're being let down by the forces that be. But they are afraid to speak up because of fear of retribution. Innumerable times, school staff have stopped me in hallways and told me privately (several with tears in their eyes) that they agreed that the child I was representing needed more services. But they were afraid to say so. Several teachers or other staff have gone even farther, calling me in the evening to tip me off that a student is being egregiously under-served and harmed, and hoping I will take on the case.

I should be charged with teacher-abuse myself if throughout the book, I do not do everything possible to make clear that frontline teachers are victimized too. The wrongdoing is institutional, not individual. And the most fundamental root cause of all the wrongdoing—by All of Us as well as Educators—is low expectations.

Our society in general harbors low expectations for struggling learners, particularly those who are poor and minority. The unjustified low expectations become self-fulfilling prophecies of failure, and we then tend to blame the victims. I have witnessed time and time again that when low-income students struggle to learn to read, schools attribute the poor performance to poor homes rather than poor instruction. Later in the book, you'll meet Devon who I represented when he was in fourth grade and reading at kindergarten level. In his case, the school's main defense was that his single parent Mom had not made him try harder in school or helped him enough with homework. I have virtually never heard any school attribute a student's low achievement to inadequate instruction. Blaming the victim is rampant.

One proof of this is too telling to hold for a later chapter. In a scholarly study, 50 school psychologists, who play a key role in determining eligibility for special education, were asked how often they found that the child's learning problems were due primarily to inappropriate teaching practices. "The answer," the study reported, "was none." The surveyed psychologists admitted "that informal school policy (or 'school culture') dictates that conclusions be limited to child and family factors."[18]

True, educational and economic family circumstances are potent influences. But demography is not destiny. Effective instruction—particularly early identification and intervention delivered via RTI—can overcome disadvantaged circumstances. And, therefore, "blaming the victim" is wrongful and abusive educational malpractice.

WHAT SHOULD WE DO NEXT? WHAT ARE THE POSSIBILITIES AND POLITICS OF REFORM?

How do we get from here—the abuse of struggling learners and a badly broken system of special education—to where we want to go, particularly aboard the engine of RTI? Chapters 8 to 10 explore pathways through the political thicket. No reform route is a sure thing. Some recommendations are more long-shot and long-term than others. But there is one underlying certainty.

The Feds Must Lead the Way

The path out of the K-12 wilderness will have to be blazed by the federal government. This seems counter-intuitive if not outright crazy. Isn't our country's love affair with state and local control of public schools as torrid as ever? Wasn't the aggressive federal role in the No Child Left Behind Act snuffed out with the law's repeal? And in the era of Donald Trump, aren't the national political winds blowing in the direction of a shrunken federal presence in all domestic policies?

Yes, yes, yes. Nonetheless, consider the alternatives. First, don't expect reform from within. There is little to no reason to believe that the education establishment will turn on itself and expose its own deep shortcomings. Habits of mind—including low expectations and the tendency to blame the victims—are hard to shake. And educators are taught not to rock the bureaucratic boat: to get along, go along with the way things are.

Second, don't expect state and local governments to be profiles in leadership either. Chapter 8 describes the folly of faith in state and local action to end abusive practices that disproportionately harm children in poverty. Historically, the U.S. has sometimes risen above deference to state and local control to ensure civil rights and an economic safety net for its neediest citizens. But it takes time and is usually a last resort. Winston Churchill famously said, "You can always count on Americans to do the right thing after they've tried everything else."

This is what has happened with basic rights in public K-12 education. *Brown v. Board of Education* and desegregation did not occur until 1954. It was the case with the first federal aid targeted to assist low-income students, the Elementary and Secondary Education Act of 1965; President Lyndon B. Johnson, a former school teacher, proclaimed "I deeply believe that no law I have signed or will ever sign means more to the future of America." And it was the case with the first federal law establishing the rights of students with disabilities, enacted in 1975; that law was primarily intended to guarantee a "free and appropriate" education to students with severe disabilities who were excluded from public schools altogether or warehoused in inferior schools.

In these landmark instances, the feds had to step in because state and local school systems were not willing or able to provide equal educational opportunity. Now, the feds must step in again to stop the nationwide educational abuse of struggling learners.

A new generation of federal actions is ready to be born. At their core lies the principle that the right to succeed in school—to be prepared for higher education, jobs and civic participation—is a fundamental civil right. That right lies waiting to be recognized in the U.S. Constitution and almost all state constitutions. It just hasn't been enforced. And students who are mislabeled as disabled and other struggling learners are the scarred poster children who prove it.

Chapter 9 contends that the best road to reform runs through the White House and Congress. The Every Student Succeeds Act (ESSA) could be amended to guarantee students the right to adequate instruction that will enable them to meet state academic standards. At the same time, loopholes and ambiguities in IDEA could be replaced with unequivocal definitions that separate the Truly Disabled from the Mainly Mislabeled. Amendments to ESSA and IDEA—if followed by monitoring with teeth in it—could go a long way toward reducing the underachievement and eliminating the educational abuse of struggling learners.

None of these federal reforms rules out creative initiatives and professional judgments by state and local educators. Amendments to ESSA and IDEA would only delineate the basic right to an adequate education and standards by which state and local educators can be held accountable. That is, when it comes to guaranteeing the rights of schoolchildren, the feds would prescribe *what* must be done; states and locals can go their own ways in figuring out *how* to do it.

The Reinvention of Special Education

The amendments to ESSA and IDEA could also lay the foundation for reinvention of special education altogether, as spelled out in Chapter 9. The big idea is that special education would be exclusively reserved for students who are Truly Disabled. Actually, as Chapter 2 tells, it would be less reinvention and more restoration of what special education was supposed to be in the first place. As Margaret J. McLaughlin, a professor at the University of Maryland and special education policy expert, has put it, let's

> alter the current construct of "disability" under the IDEA and take special education policy back to its roots as an educational law that pertains only to students with clear and evident disabilities. . . . This could focus the resources on those students most in need of specialized long term education and related services as opposed to having special education programs provide compensatory services for students whose only "disability" has been poor or insufficient general education.[19]

If special education were re-engineered along these lines, it would no longer be possible for general education to dump struggling learners into special education. At the same time the mission of general education could be fortified with the money and management to provide RTI-like interventions for all struggling learners.

Equally important, the truly disabled students would benefit dramatically from having special education all to themselves. Fewer disability classifications and students (recall that students who are severely disabled constitute only about 15 to 20 percent of all current students in special education) would enable classroom instruction and related services to be more specialized. Teachers would be better trained. The system could be held more accountable.

And last but hardly least, there would be more money for services for the students who are truly disabled. In the realpolitik of public education (discussed in Chapter 10), there is competition over policy attention and scarce dollars between the political constituencies for students with severe disabilities and other students in special education. Bottom line, the current system in which so many students are mislabeled as disabled "robs the genuinely handicapped of funds and services they need. . . ."[20]

Resort to the Courts

The speed at which the nation undertakes reinvention or other legislative and administrative reforms will be accelerated by class action lawsuits in the tradition of *Brown v. Board of Education.* Four decades of school finance litigation, asserting a constitutional right to adequate school funding, may be running out of steam. However, there are several trailblazing lawsuits that claim a "right to read" for struggling learners under the U.S. Constitution. Reading is a proxy for the right to an adequate education in its entirety. Literacy is the indispensable foundation not just for success in school but for economic and social well-being.

One pending class action filed in Berkeley, California is based on alleged violations of IDEA, similar to those identified in this book. They include the failure to provide "appropriate RTI" defined as "intensive early and research-based intervention."[21]

Another broader suit has arisen in Detroit. Brought in U.S. district court in 2016, it claims that students in general and special education "have been denied access to literacy by being deprived of evidence-based literacy instruction and by being subject to school conditions that prevent them from learning."[22] The denial, according to the class action complaint, violates the Due Process and Equal Protection clauses of the 14th amendment of the U.S. Constitution. While the lower court recently dismissed the suit, an appeal is likely.

These suits, and copycat ones sure to follow, face long roads and uncertain futures. But they build on the legacy of historic civil rights cases on behalf of poor and minority families and children. And there are grounds for optimism. Lawrence Tribe, a celebrated constitutional law scholar at Harvard University, expects the Detroit case to make history "much as Brown v. Board of Education did."[23] At the least, the "right to read" cases will raise public awareness of educational abuse and generate political pressure for reform.

Chapter 10 lays out political strategies and tactics for the struggle ahead.

PARENTS AND TEACHERS UNITE!

For any reform action to succeed at the federal, state or local levels, All of Us must get our political act together. But who can be counted on to put on the pressure and lead the charge?

Parents

This book seeks to be a guide for parents in understanding the causes of educational abuse of their children who are struggling learners and the possibilities for reform. But it also comes with a big homework assignment. And that is for parents to unite with teachers and lead the fight for reform.

You would think that the parents of struggling learners who are victimized in general education and special education would constitute a large pool of volunteers ready to enlist in the political battle. After all, struggling learners comprise as many as half or more of all public school students. Yet, no such movement exists and it won't be as easy as you might imagine to mobilize one.

One reason that parents of struggling learners haven't coalesced is because their common cause, as seen throughout this book, is so misunderstood and concealed. At best, the interventions for struggling learners get lost in the political clamor behind more politically sexy issues, like privatization, testing and attacks on teachers unions.

Even when it comes to fighting for more money, the cause is set back by an unholy alliance of some usually stalwart liberals with conservatives. Some liberals proclaim that until our nation addresses poverty and inequality in jobs, housing, crime, drugs, health and so on, schools will be able to do very little to enable poor children to overcome the odds against them. Unwittingly, these liberals are strange bedfellows of conservatives who for different reasons—they believe family factors are paramount—come to the same conclusion: more money spent on schools would be a waste or not cost-effective.

Nonsense. To be sure, our nation must combat the disadvantages of poor and minority students with government programs outside and inside schools. Such programs would make the task of teachers much easier. Yet, wayward liberals need to more strongly recognize that more school funding and better management of it (see Chapters 6 and 7) can, by themselves, go a long way toward reversing the academic misfortunes of all struggling learners, no matter what their family income and racial or ethnic identity are.

Another fundamental drawback in mobilizing a fighting constituency is the fact that parents who have the most at stake are disproportionately poor and minority. That makes them and their children politically disabled.

However, don't think for one second that lower income parents are less caring and less heartbroken than upper income parents when their children fail in school. Rather, their economic and political powerlessness means they lack the wherewithal to protect their children from educational abuse. Marcus's mother bombarded the school system with pleas for more assistance as early as the first grade, before he was placed in special education. But she lacked the know-how and money to force school officials to take her pleas (and his failure to learn to read) seriously.

Chapter 10 will highlight how parents of struggling learners in general education have virtually no individual legal rights to challenge the system. And it isn't all that much better for parents of students in special education who are supposed to have extensive parental rights under IDEA. These so-called rights exist on paper not in practice.

For example, parents are supposed to participate as partners when school staff meet to decide on the Individual Education Program (IEP) for their child. They are supposed to be given extensive documents including evaluations and be fully informed about instructional options. But much of the process is highly technical, and school members of the IEP team can be resistant, if not hostile, to parents who ask challenging questions. The whole process is lopsided in favor of schools. Parents are also supposed to have numerous avenues of appeal, but these are almost invariably beyond their financial reach. Chapter 10 suggests steps to make parental rights more of a reality.

Ironically, in the political arena, the prospects are more hopeful for parents of students who are Truly Disabled. Unlike the great mass of struggling learners, students with severe disabilities are more visible and amenable to single-focus national and local advocacy groups such as those for Down syndrome, autism, deafness and blindness. Unfortunately, collective action is sometimes missing or weak because of competition over funding. Moreover, sometimes advocacy groups for students with severe disabilities bump heads with advocacy groups for other students in special education, such as those with dyslexia or ADHD.

Mobilizing Teachers Unions and Other Professional Associations

Chapter 10 also poses the challenge of creating solidarity between educators, including teachers unions and other professional associations, and parents. Educators have tended to be absent or tardy, rather than fighting side by side with parents. In part this is a carryover from frequent clashes at IEP meetings. Of course, parents and teachers should be on the same side. When school members of IEP teams are defensive and resentful of my advocacy for better services for students, I tell them "I am advocating for you too!" Better services for students mean more resources and better job satisfaction for teachers.

Most teachers understand this, as many confide to me privately. Still, individual teachers are reluctant to go out on a limb, fearing retribution in assignments or promotions. Individual administrators shy away too for similar reasons. This leaves unions and other professional associations to speak up and act out—unions especially.

Political action is in the unions' DNA. Sometimes it overly protects unsatisfactory teachers, but on balance teachers unions pack the heaviest firepower and do the most to capture the most resources for public school systems. They have not, however, taken up the cause of struggling learners in a way that would greatly benefit students *and teachers*.

While unions have the most political potential, other associations of education professionals must also awake to the challenge. These include pillars of the education establishment including associations of administrators, school superintendents, school boards, and related services providers like psychologists, social workers, speech and language pathologists and occupational therapists. There is an abundance of them. Yet, they tend to be driven, like advocacy groups, by competition for scarce resources and fail to coalesce around collective causes like the plight of struggling learners. If they fail to rise to the challenge, their inaction will be a betrayal of their professional responsibilities and ethics.

A CALL TO ACTION

Ok, this overview of the book has been long on bad news and gigantic obstacles to be overcome if the educational abuse of struggling learners is to end. Still, I have flunked my task if I have not also conveyed the overriding message that reform is possible. RTI is do-able. And parents and teachers, if united, can be a political force to reckon with, especially when the political winds in our country change direction.

Our national politics is cyclical. In K-12 policy, momentum for a renewed national reform movement will build if half of our schoolchildren continue to be unable to proficiently read, write and compute, All of Us will demand the end of this educational abuse.

And the fight can be won, even against the political tide that carried Donald Trump to the presidency. The American people are unified on at least one powerful desire: to improve the education of our children. We are even willing, polls show, to pay more taxes if that's what it takes.

Let's do whatever it takes. Let's build a platform of policy and practice reforms that links more money to evidence-based and well-managed best instructional practices within the framework of RTI. And let's lobby like hell for action. We owe this legally and morally to children whose lives are ruined by educational abuse. And we owe it to ourselves. Our nation cannot prosper economically or survive socially if we do not transform struggling learners into well-prepared citizens.

This book then is more than an indictment of our schools. It is a collective call for action. The pages that follow are meant to empower parents, teachers and policymakers in this do-or-die national struggle.

Chapter 2

....

The Big Lie

*How Struggling Learners Are Illegally
Placed in Special Education*

"*From its inception [the largest disability category, Specific Learning
Disability] has served as a sociological sponge that attempts
to wipe up general education's spills and cleanse its ills.*"
—G. Reid Lyon, Jack M. Fletcher, Sally E. Shaywitz and other reading experts[1]

The Big Lie about students with disabilities is that the great majority of them legally qualify for special education. They don't. Most don't even come close.

For one thing, it is simply not true that most students with disabilities are disabled in any true sense of medical or clinical definitions of disability.

For another, even if struggling learners met some indicators of a true disability, most still would not qualify for special education. That is because IDEA requires that struggling learners should not be found eligible for special education *unless they received adequate prior instruction in general education*. As stated by leading experts, "No person can be defined as learning disabled in the absence of evidence of a lack of adequate response to instruction that is effective with most students. . . ."[2]

The Big Truth is that a large majority of all students in special education would not need special education if they were taught well in general education. But they aren't taught well. They don't receive the extra assistance they need. As a result, general education teachers wind up overwhelmed by too many students in their classes who are too far behind their peers. As a last resort, these students are placed or, more bluntly, "dumped" into special education.

Expediency prevails over the letter and spirit of the Individual with Disabilities Education Act (IDEA), the federal law governing special education. Researchers estimate that between 50 and 75 percent of struggling learners end up unnecessarily (and therefore illegally) in special education.[3]

And that's only the beginning of the educational abuse. In special education, their deficiencies get worse not better. So-called "special" education for these students is false advertising that would make the Federal Trade Commission cringe. Students in special education do not get the "specially designed instruction" and other services that the law mandates. They fall deeper in the academic hole, and are more likely to be worse off than if they remained in general education.[4] The data, summarized in Chapter 3, shows their rock-bottom academic performance.

Moreover, their academic ruin is compounded by the stigma and segregation that they experience in special education. It's bad enough to feel like a "dummy" in general education. But the stigma is much worse when labeled "special education." Sometimes other kids overtly taunt. Most times, other kids convey that they think Kenny and Marcus must be really really dumb to need special education.

The stigma is reinforced by the segregation. Most students in special education are not in classes with only special education students. But even when they are included with general education students, educational apartheid is obvious.

School systems try to hide the stigma and segregation beneath the lofty special education principles of "least restrictive environment (LRE)" and "inclusion." These principles hold that students in special education should be included as much as possible in classroom settings with their non-special education peers. Students in special education are to be placed in separate settings "only when the nature or severity of the disability of a child is such that education in regular classes . . . cannot be achieved satisfactorily."[5]

Who can be against such inclusion or mainstreaming, as it is sometimes called? No one should be—unless it fails to deliver what it promises, which is what usually happens. The high-flying purpose of inclusion often crashes on the rocks of classroom realities. There are many models of inclusion, including co-teaching by general education and special education teachers. But the teachers are simply too overloaded with too many students and lack the specialized training to pull it off effectively. That's why there is so little solid evidence of the effectiveness of inclusion. To the contrary, there is extensive research that inclusion falls far short of its principled goals.[6]

This chapter details how school systems get away with so many untruths, causing so many struggling learners to be mislabeled as disabled, dumped into special education, and educationally abused.

GOOD INTENTIONS GONE BAD

You could say that the Big Lie began with a medium fib. The first federal law that guaranteed the right of students with disabilities to a "free and appropriate" education was the 1975 Education for All Handicapped Children Act (EAHC). Its paramount purpose was unmistakable. At the time of enactment, "more than one million children with disabilities were excluded entirely from the educational system, and more than 50% of all students with disabilities were given only limited access to public schools."[7] These students were predominately students with severe cognitive or physical limitations who, under EAHC, were, for the first time, guaranteed a "free and appropriate education."

EAHC was a whole new ballgame. Prior to its passage, there was no mandate or entitlement that all children who legally qualified as disabled would be served. Since so little funding was available, little attention was paid to who was technically eligible and who wasn't.

That changed under EAHC, and not just for students with severe cognitive or physical conditions. Services were guaranteed for students who met a wide variety of disability classifications. And in one major instance—Specific Learning Disability—the definition was politically compromised, vague, and troublesome from the start. Fears of mission creep and exploding costs were voiced. When President Gerald R. Ford signed the EAHC, he predicted that "Unfortunately, this bill promises more than the Federal Government can deliver."[8]

That prediction proved accurate, and the worst fears were realized. Twenty-five years later, the co-authors of a 2001 article, "Time to Make Special Education 'Special' Again," captured this phenomenon:

> IDEA [the successor to EAHC] has been largely successful in opening up educational opportunities for children with disabilities. Unfortunately, the IDEA also has had some unintended negative consequences. These include the creation of incentives to define an ever-increasing percentage of school-aged children as having disabilities, an enormous redirection of financial resources from regular education to special education, and, perhaps most importantly, the application of an accommodation philosophy to populations better served by prevention or interventions.[9]

The "prevention or interventions" didn't materialize. Rather, as shown in the short history that follows, special education, instead of affording truly specialized services to a small number of severely disabled students, became a dysfunctional repository (a/k/a dumping ground) for struggling learners.

The Political Cat and Mouse Game over Eligibility under IDEA

It wasn't that the framers of EAHC and then IDEA didn't realize what was happening. Over the past 40 years, Congress and school systems nationwide have been locked in a battle over how to limit eligibility for special education. Congress, the cat, has been trying to restrict eligibility to students with severe disabilities that have clear medical and clinical markers. School systems, the mice, have resisted. They are desperate to protect their ability to exploit special education as a lifeline for general education teachers who are drowning because they have too many struggling learners in their classes.

From the 1970s through most of the 1990s, Congress's attempts to curtail mission creep largely flopped. Just as experts had warned, special education rolls and costs grew exponentially. During those years, the number of students in special education grew a little over 30 percent, while the number of students classified as having a Specific Learning

Disability rose over 300 percent.[10] State and local school systems—afraid that general education teachers would lose their lifeline—paid no attention to the requirement that struggling learners should only be referred to special education if they received adequate prior instruction in general education.

In the late 1990s, Congress went back to the drawing board. A starting point was recognition that students in special education were capable of doing much better academically than educators thought. A principal purpose of the 1997 amendments to IDEA was to overcome "low expectations" for student achievement and to change the focus of implementation from procedural compliance to improved instruction and student outcomes.[11]

The No Child Left Behind Act, passed in 2001, was even more explicit in mandating that students in special education be held to the same high academic standards as their peers, and be given full opportunity to meet the standards. Except for students with severe limitations, they were to take the same state tests as their peers; their test scores were to be separately reported; they were supposed to meet the same "annual yearly progress" targets as all other students; and their instruction was supposed to be based on "scientifically based research."[12]

An executive order by President George W. Bush in 2001 summarized the new, higher expectations under NCLB: "It is imperative that special education operate as an integral part of a system that expects high achievement of all children, rather than as a means of avoiding accountability for children who are more challenging to educate or who have fallen behind."[13] (The successor legislation to NCLB, the Every Student Succeeds Act passed in 2016, does not alter this basic intent.)

This Congressional action was headed in the right direction, but didn't go nearly far enough. The changes only focused on research-based instruction for students *after* they were mislabeled as disabled and placed in special education. Neglected altogether was the desperate need for research-based interventions for struggling learners *before* they were placed in special education, as Congress had intended all along.

In 2004 Congress finally confronted the problem head on. Amendments that year to IDEA and subsequent regulations significantly changed the way students suspected of having a Specific Learning Disability, the largest category of students in special education, are identified and found eligible for special education. The regulations provided that eligibility should not be determined unless the student has been "provided with learning experiences and instruction appropriate for the child's age or State-approved grade-level standards" in reading, math and writing. Further, "To ensure that underachievement of a child suspected of having a specific learning disability is not due to lack of appropriate instruction," the IEP Team must consider "Data that demonstrate that prior to, or as part of, the referral process, the child was provided appropriate instruction in regular education settings, delivered by qualified personnel."[14]

Despite this clunky legalese, the meaning was clear: No adequate prior instruction in general education, no Specific Learning Disability eligibility for special education.

The requirement for "appropriate instruction in regular education settings, delivered by qualified personnel" was a prescription for the instructional framework commonly known as "Response to Intervention" (RTI). There was no secret or dispute about what RTI entailed: RTI is the process through which the difficulties of struggling learners should be diagnosed as early as possible, and treated through progressively intense research-based interventions in general education.

Chapter 4 describes RTI in detail and its central role in ending the educational abuse of struggling learners. True, RTI is easier said than done, or else there would be far fewer struggling learners and students mislabeled as disabled. But it can be done, as explained in later chapters. Suffice to say at this point that RTI embodies what Congress intended, and what common sense tells us: if students do not receive adequate instruction in general education, how does anyone know whether they require special education?

Also suffice to say, in the current absence of RTI and other school reforms, the school system mice are still roaring. School systems are about as culpable as ever at mislabeling struggling learners as disabled. This comes into clearest view as we zoom in further on the eligibility of students classified as having a Specific Learning Disability (LD).

The Bogus Eligibility of Students Labeled LD

Approximately 35 percent of all students in special education are classified as LD.[15] LD's dominance of special education is even more powerful because it is often inter-related with other large disability categories such as ADHD, language impairments and emotional disability. LD thus serves as the best lens through which we can examine how and why so many students wind up wrongfully in special education.

As we proceed, keep in mind that virtually without exception, students labeled as LD have the cognitive potential to meet the same academic standards as peers. Their learning problems are not substantially different from those of huge numbers of other struggling learners who are not channeled into special education.

Yet, those who wind up as mislabeled as disabled and educationally abused are caught in the web of three main interconnected strands: (1) teacher desperation; (2) racial and economic class biases that blame the victims; and (3) loopholes in the law. All can be seen in the case of Devon, another child I represented.

WHAT'S WRONG WITH DEVON?
OR SHOULD THE QUESTION BE,
WHAT'S WRONG WITH THE SYSTEM?

Devon is not all that different from Marcus who we met in Chapter 1, except in some ways the facts are even more appalling. Devon, when I met him, was in the fourth grade and living with his siblings and single Mom who was on welfare. The family is African-American, housed (barely) in one of the ravaged inner city neighborhoods in Baltimore.

Starting in pre-kindergarten, Devon fell rapidly behind. Yet, although he received little to no research-based interventions in pre-kindergarten, kindergarten and first grade, he was referred and found eligible for special education in the second grade. At that point, he was reading and writing at kindergarten level. He was classified with LD. Eligibility was based on a "discrepancy gap" (a construct we'll look at in much detail later) between his being in the second grade and his kindergarten performance level.

Though in special education, he still failed to receive research-based "specially designed instruction," as IDEA requires, and he fell further behind. In fourth grade, he was still reading and writing at kindergarten level. And no surprise, his behavior was going downhill along with his literacy deficiencies.

The school's evaluations indicated that Devon had a low-average IQ and some indicators of ADHD. Still, the school got one thing right:

it properly acknowledged that his cognitive capacity was sufficient to enable him to achieve much more progress *if* . . . If what? If who had done what differently? That question was at the center of many contentious meetings with the school-based team charged with developing his special education IEP.

I took the position that Devon would not be in such dire straits if he had received better instruction first in general education and then in special education. In response, school staff on the IEP team were incensed at what they considered an accusation that they hadn't done their jobs as well as they could have. They were professional caring teachers, they said, who had done the best they could. And they offered an alternative explanation for Devon's plight. It boiled down to lack of school effort by Devon and by Mom. It was their own fault.

In the words of members of the IEP team, especially a special education teacher and the school's assistant principal, "what can you expect when Devon won't try in class, doesn't show up for coach class and is always causing trouble?" I countered that his lack of motivation and misconduct was explainable. Can you imagine what it's like for a young child to come to school from pre-kindergarten through fourth grade, all the while falling steadily behind other kids, and increasingly doubting his own ability and self-worth?

Abundant literature ties students lack of motivation and poor behavior to "fear of failure" or "learned helplessness" caused by lack of academic success. As summarized, "Much research has been done over the years on motivating children with LD or ADHD. It tells us that the main reasons these children withdraw mentally from school is fear of failure, frustration with inconsistent performance . . . lack of understanding the schoolwork, emotional problems, anger or desire for attention—even negative attention."[16] Another author observes, "struggling readers may begin to internalize their lack of reading ability and develop learned helplessness . . . They may become unmotivated as learners and fall into what [a preeminent reading expert] calls a 'devastating downward spiral.'"[17]

The IEP team was also insistent that Devon's mother was as much if not more to blame than Devon. Mom, they said, didn't push Devon or back up his teachers. "Without his family helping out more, what can we do?" "What can you expect when Mom doesn't get him to school on time, when he doesn't turn in homework, when she doesn't keep in touch with his teachers?" And so on.

Of course, Devon would have done better in school if his Mom had done all these things and more to provide support at home and at school. Yet, he would have done much, much better—despite the family situation—if he had received timely, quality instruction and other school assistance from kindergarten on up.

Devon is hardly alone. His case illustrates the tragic experience of so many struggling learners who are mislabeled as LD. I noted earlier three main reasons why schools victimized them: teacher desperation, blaming the victims, and loopholes in the law. We examine each of these in more detail, beginning with the predicament of beleaguered general education teachers.

TEACHER DESPERATION

When students fall behind as early as prekindergarten, kindergarten or first grade, and don't receive adequate, evidence-based instructional assistance, the lag can be lethal to them, especially in learning to read, which is the foundation of all learning. It also is very harmful to teachers. Struggling learners—when the class is overloaded with them—bring about struggling teachers.

There are few uncontroversial facts about K-12 public education but "the Matthew effect" on learning to read is one of them. "Rich" readers—those who meet age-appropriate reading standards early—get richer; they grow in reading ability. "Poor" readers—those who don't get off to a good start—almost invariably get poorer. Deficits deepen as the years go by. The psychologist Keith Stanovich explained the impact of "the Matthew effect:"

> Slow reading acquisition has cognitive, behavioral, and motivational consequences that slow the development of other cognitive skills and inhibit performance on many academic tasks. . . . The longer this developmental sequence is allowed to continue, the more generalized the deficits will become, seeping into more and more areas of cognition and behavior.[18]

Or put more simply and sadly, students who fall behind early rarely catch up. More frequently they suffer a kind of academic and behavioral free fall.

When this occurs, when students are stuck in general education class-rooms even though they can't do the work and are holding back the whole class, what are their teachers supposed to do? The teachers are stuck too. Options are few. It's futile for the teacher to ask the school principal for more help. The school doesn't have the funds to reduce class size, or provide supplemental instruction such as tutoring. Nor is the principal likely to be able to beg or finagle more money from the district. Struggling learners, who are disproportionately poor and minority, are concentrated in school districts that are fiscally strapped.

Since the struggling students can't earn legitimate passing grades, they must be either retained in grade or "socially promoted." Social pro-motion means that they pass from grade to grade even though they don't earn valid passing grades, and even though they fall farther behind their peers each time this happens.

However, the alternative of retention (which means holding the stu-dent back in grade) usually doesn't work either. Typically, the retained students are taught the second time around pretty much as they were the first time—without the intense evidence-based interventions that would enable their learning gaps to be narrowed or closed. And, needless to say, such overage students create unmanageable classroom manage-ment problems. A teacher told me that she had a third-grade boy in her class who was 11 years old and needed a shave.

It's at this point that teachers see referrals to special education as their only practical way out. Teachers may or may not be aware that such referrals violate IDEA since the students never received adequate pre-referral instruction. They may even realize that special education in their school may be a disaster area. Still, they think they have no choice. Illegal referrals to special education are the lesser of the evils that con-front them.

RACIAL AND ECONOMIC CLASS BIASES THAT BLAME THE VICTIMS

To further understand why so many struggling learners are mislabeled as disabled, recall how the school team in Devon's case attributed his very poor academic performance and behavior to his and his Mom's lack of effort. In doing so, the school team fell prey, as it was famously phrased by President George W. Bush, to the "soft bigotry of low expectations."[19]

Because our nation as a whole is infected with the poison of discrimination against poor and minority families and children, it's no wonder that discriminatory attitudes and practices seep into our schools. Consequently, too many educators (and policymakers and the public) tend to blame the victims—the child and family—more than school systems for student failure.

The evidence of this is startling. A survey conducted by the National Center on Learning Disabilities found:

- "A majority of the public (55 percent) and parents (55 percent) mistakenly believe learning disabilities are often a product of the home environment in which children are raised. Four in 10 teachers and three in 10 administrators have the same belief.
- "Approximately half (51 percent) think that what people call 'learning disabilities' are the result of laziness."[20]

These findings expose widespread unawareness about the real instructional causes of learning difficulties. Yes, family factors count. But make no mistake: the "home environment" and "laziness" that were cited by the survey respondents are code words for exculpating schools and blaming the victims who are disproportionately poor and minority.

Another study is even more revealing and astonishing. As briefly mentioned in Chapter 1, Galen Alessi, a professor of psychology, surveyed 50 school psychologists who evaluated about 120 students during the year covered by the study to determine whether they qualified for special education. Asked how many times their evaluations concluded that the child's learning problems were mainly due to curriculum, the psychologists' answers were summarized as "usually none." Asked in how many evaluations the student's problems were due primarily to inappropriate teaching practices, "The answer also was none."

So what was causing the students' problems? Alessi asked the school psychologists how many of their evaluations "concluded that child factors were primarily responsible for the referred problem. The answer was 100%." The surveyed psychologists stated "that informal school policy (or 'school culture') dictates that conclusions be limited to child and family factors."[21]

It is hard to imagine evidence that more clearly proves, beyond a reasonable doubt, how school systems internalize economic and racial stereotypes that blame the victims. Alessi satirically summarized: "These 5,000 positive findings uncovered the true weak link in the educational process in these districts: the children themselves. If only these districts had better functioning children with a few more supportive parents, there would be no educational difficulties."[22]

Readers may find this study hard to believe. Its findings are so extreme. It contradicts all that we know about the ability and dedication of school psychologists. Still, there is reason to believe that some psychologists, like teachers and other members of IEP teams, are victims themselves of such institutional attitudes.

School staff are particularly susceptible to prejudicial finger-pointing because they are denied proper training on the instructional causes of learning difficulties. They receive little to no professional supervision or coaching on the job. They are denied the resources that would enable them to experience and appreciate the effectiveness of evidence-based additional instruction. All the while, they live professionally and socially in a society in which prejudicial stereotypes are pervasive.

Here's more proof. I have studied the hidden biases that cause poor and minority children to be systematically ignored in determinations of dyslexia. My study, published in 2003, *The Invisible Dyslexics: How Public School Systems in Baltimore and Elsewhere Discriminate Against Poor Children in the Diagnosis and Treatment of Early Reading Difficulties*, reported that at least 20 percent of the children in Baltimore City public schools and other large urban districts can be called "invisible dyslexics."[23] "Invisible dyslexics" are children whose academic futures are doomed because their problems in learning to read are either diagnosed too late and treated too little, or not diagnosed or treated at all.

And why does this happen with much greater frequency to students who are from poor and minority families? It is because dyslexia is associated in the public mind with children from high-income families who can afford to have dyslexia diagnosed at private expense, often followed by expensive private schooling. Invisible dyslexics are also slighted when their IQs are low-average; yet, IQ scores are considered by many experts to be influenced by cultural biases that disadvantage poor and minority children.

Certainly, economic and educational background and IQ matter. For example, researchers Betty Hart and Todd R. Risley revealed the "thirty million word gap."[24] By the time of school enrollment, children from high-income families were exposed to 30 million more words than children from families on welfare—a developmental chasm that closely predicted later reading difficulties. In innumerable ways, kids in middle and up income families have home field advantages over underprivileged kids.

But all is not doom and gloom for Devon and countless other struggling learners from low-income and minority families. They can achieve much greater academic success notwithstanding their learning difficulties and socio-economic circumstances if they receive timely, adequate additional instruction. Schools, as emphasized throughout this book, should not be let off the hook.

LEGAL LOOPHOLES AND THE "DISCREPANCY CRAP"

The three factors under discussion that underlie why struggling learners are mislabeled as disabled and educationally abused are interdependent. Each—teacher desperation, biases that blame the victim, and now legal loopholes—is cause and effect with the others, and I could have written about legal loopholes first, not third. But if another truth be told, the analyses of statutory and regulatory loopholes in IDEA that follow are technical and heavy going. Still, there is value in understanding them, particularly for professionals who may challenge my indictment of the system. But I hope parents and other general readers will hang in there too.

From the outset, the definition of LD under federal law has been vulnerable to manipulation. It has allowed educators and policymakers to avoid making difficult policy choices. Four decades later, experts still "disagree about the definition and classification of LD; [and] the diagnostic criteria and assessment practices used in the identification process."[25]

As a result, practice nationwide is murky, chaotic and inconsistent. Recall the quip of two leading scholars that the eligibility process is "barely more accurate than a flip of the coin."[26] The only thing that can be said with certainty is that, as practice has evolved, most students found eligible as LD do not legally qualify.

The Source of Confusion and Evasion

The legal standard in the first version of IDEA enacted in 1975 specified that "'children with specific learning disabilities' requires a disorder in one or more of the basic psychological processes involved in understanding or in using language, spoken or written. . . ." It includes but is not limited to certain conditions such as dyslexia.[27]

However, the "disorder" in the definition and the conditions including "dyslexia" were not further defined. Regulations, finalized in 1977, were meant to clarify the criteria and prevent mission creep. They required a finding by the school that "a child has a severe discrepancy between achievement and intellectual ability. . . ."[28]

The criterion of an IQ-achievement discrepancy—commonly known as the "discrepancy gap"—was supposed to diagnose a learning disorder that reflected difficulty in processing information. But from the start, the discrepancy gap was ill-conceived and ill-used. In practice, it opened the floodgates to the mislabeling and mistreatment of millions of struggling learners.

Across the country, it became the almost exclusive eligibility test for LD. The number of LD students skyrocketed, increasing more than 300 percent between 1976 and 2000, though it has since plateaued.[29] All the while, educators either didn't notice or ignored the fact that the evidence base for the discrepancy gap was always "weak to non-existent."[30]

Debunking the Discrepancy Gap

The discrepancy gap has been so discredited that it is derisively called by some the "discrepancy crap." Scientific findings refute the view that a disability can be determined based on a cut-off statistical measure of discrepancy between aptitude (IQ) and achievement.

Rather, as set out in a famous report by the national Committee on Preventing Reading Difficulties in Young Children, there is a "dimensional approach" to the problems of struggling readers. Reading difficulties—which account for 80 to 90 percent of LD eligibility determinations—should be seen as the lower end of a normal distribution of reading ability among all children. The Committee found that "deciding on the precise point on the [distribution] at which to distinguish normal reading from reading disability is quite arbitrary. . . . For instance, children who do not quite meet the arbitrary cutoff score [for the discrepancy gap] have very similar abilities and needs as those of children whose reading levels are just on the other side of the cut-point."[31]

This applies to the diagnosis of dyslexia, the most well-known reading problem. A discrepancy gap is not how to do it. The prominent neuroscientist and best-selling author Sally Shaywitz points out, "there's been a revolution in what we've learned about reading and dyslexia."[32] We've learned, she writes:

- Most reading difficulties including dyslexia are caused by core deficits in phonological awareness.
- Such deficits in phonological awareness are found among children with low as well as high IQs.
- The deficits can usually be identified as early as pre-kindergarten or kindergarten and effectively treated.

Another expert Joseph K. Torgesen cites studies that have "led to the discovery that the early word reading difficulties of children with relatively low general intelligence and verbal ability are associated with the same factors (weaknesses in phonological processing) that interfere with early reading growth in children who have general intelligence in the normal range."[33]

In other words, children with average and low-average IQs generally encounter early reading difficulties for the same basic reasons as children with high IQs. A group of prominent researchers concluded: "the actual comparison of academic achievement scores with IQ scores to derive a discrepancy value is fraught with psychometric, statistical, and conceptual problems that render many comparisons useless."[34]

That doesn't mean that IQ (like the family's educational and economic background) cannot be a factor in why students struggle to learn. Students who are lower in cognitive ability may need more instructional help to master reading skills. But low-income students with low-average IQs can learn to read and succeed in school if they get timely and adequate instructional assistance.

A final point about the discrepancy gap: it usually involves a disastrous "wait to fail" approach. The lower the IQ, the longer it takes for a sufficient discrepancy to accumulate and for students to receive needed extra assistance (chalk up another unfair advantage for children with higher IQs, since their gap shows and grows more quickly).

So why, against all this evidence, is the discrepancy gap still alive and making kids educationally unwell? My prior account of teacher desperation goes a long way in explaining why. The discrepancy gap eligibility test for special education is a survival toolkit for general education teachers. Two authorities put it bluntly: Under the guise of the discrepancy gap, educators "have colluded to relieve regular teachers of responsibilities for teaching children functioning at the bottom of their class . . . there is, in effect, a 'deal' between special and general education."[35]

Is "Psychological Processing" a Viable Alternative to the Discrepancy Gap?

The best that can be said in defense of educators who cling to the otherwise defenseless discrepancy gap is that it is hard to come up with alternatives. The pure statutory definition of LD, as earlier noted, is "a disorder in one or more of the basic psychological processes" involved in learning to read, write and compute. But if the discrepancy gap is the wrong way to determine the existence of the disorder, what is the right way? The search has taken educators and scientists down two main paths, one neuroscience, the other "strengths and weaknesses" in psychological processing.

The Neuroscience of LD

There is wide agreement among scientists that "a true learning disability is neurological and therefore organic to the individual and, presumably, a lifelong disorder."[36] "The field of LD was founded on the assumption that neurobiological factors are the basis of [it]."[37]

Dyslexia is again illuminating. Pure dyslexia, as it is sometimes called, can be located through magnetic and other imaging techniques in the language processing areas of the brain. In Science magazine, MIT professor John Gabrieli summarized, "Functional neuroimaging studies have revealed differences in brain function and connectivity that are characteristic of dyslexia."[38]

The imaging can be prescriptive as well as diagnostic. Gabrieli observes, "There is good evidence that dyslexia can be predicted and prevented in many children."[39] Or if not prevented, it can be treated with instructional interventions aligned with specific processing images. In the future, brain research may also lead to medication to treat dyslexia.

This is all to the good. Yet, teachers and other school personnel, including psychologists, have no present means to put the neuroscience to practical use. Maybe it's not complete science fiction to foresee the day when school teams will be able to readily access brain scans, but that day is not near. In the here and now, schools are still stuck trying to find another way to determine LD based on functional measurements of psychological processes.

Strengths and Weaknesses in Psychological Processing

IDEA regulations say that a learning disorder based on functional impairment in psychological processes can be found if a child "exhibits a pattern of strengths and weaknesses."[40] This means differences that can be revealed "across a battery of cognitive or neuropsychological tests," according to the prominent co-authors of an authoritative book, "Learning Disabilities: From Identification to Intervention." They observe, "The person with LD is one with strengths in many areas but weaknesses in some core cognitive processes that lead to underachievement."[41]

Unfortunately, pinpointing strengths and weaknesses through cognitive or neuropsychological tests is easier said than done. How reliable are they? How well can teachers and school-based psychologists administer the tests and interpret them? Evaluations by school teams, including psychologists, usually rely on basic standardized cognitive and educational measures, without administration of sub-tests that could detect an actual psychological processing disorder. This often includes the failure to detect phonological deficits that are regarded as the most significant and consistent cognitive marker of dyslexia.

As a result, many experts, including the co-authors mentioned above, give a thumbs down to the "strengths and weaknesses" method. Sharon Vaughan and Sylvia Linan-Thompson find, "Although it may be accurate that many students with LD have underlying neurological and/or processing disorders, researchers and educators have been singularly unsuccessful at reliably identifying these difficulties and designing specific treatments to remediate them. . . ."[42] Daniel J. Reschly concludes that "The history of processing constructs and LD over the last 40 years is an excellent example of faith triumphing over reality."[43]

These criticisms may be overstated. It seems likely that state of the art tests and sub-tests, if utilized, can provide school teams with more diagnostic information than they now get. But this information will be more useful in informing adequate instruction in general education than in justifying referral to special education.

So, by process of elimination—by exposing the flaws in the discrepancy gap and "strengths and weaknesses" methods for trying to determine LD—we have arrived at the definitive verdict pronounced by the co-authors of "Learning Disabilities: From Identification to Intervention:" *"No person can be defined as learning disabled in the absence of evidence of a lack of adequate response to instruction that is effective with most students. . . ."* (italics in the original!)[44]

We have thus wound our way back to the all-important necessity for effective, early interventions—that is, RTI. As fully detailed in Chapter 4, it's the only known way to prevent struggling learners from being mislabeled as LD or otherwise mislabeled and educationally abused. And, as we'll see, it's do-able.

THE RTI REQUIREMENT FOR DISABILITIES OTHER THAN LD

There is one more nail to be hammered in the coffin of the Big Lie. It's not just the special education classification of LD that is misleading or downright bogus. Though the legal requirement for other disabilities is not as explicitly worded, the same intent is plain: no prior adequate instruction in general education, no referral to special education.

Federal law specifies that children should not be found eligible for certain other disabilities—including Other Health Impairment (typically Attention Hyperactivity Deficit Disorder), Speech or Language Impairments, Emotional Disability and sometimes Autism—unless the suspected disability "adversely affects the child's educational performance."[45] The phrase "adversely affects the child's educational performance" is not defined, and literature on point is scant.[46] However, it appears to require RTI-like prior instruction before students can be found eligible under these disability classifications, the same as for LD.

This makes perfect sense.[47] How can a school know if a student who is struggling academically really needs special education services unless the student has gotten appropriate RTI-like instruction in general education?

Some states explicitly or implicitly extend the RTI process to a range of other disabilities.[48] For example, the Maryland manual on RTI states that while IDEA only includes the RTI process in the determination of LD, "data from the RTI process can be used to document student performance and the provision of appropriate instruction as part of the identification of other educational disabilities within a comprehensive evaluation."[49]

The equivalency between the pre-referral RTI requirement for LD and the "adverse affect" requirement for other disabilities is particularly persuasive because there is extensive overlap—co-morbidity—between LD and other disabilities. This occurs especially among students suspected of LD, ADHD and language impairments.[50] Researchers conclude that LD is "related to disorders of attention or to social and emotional difficulties—areas of development that are clearly problematic for students with LDs."[51] The National Center on Learning Disabilities reports that "as many as one-third of those with LD also have ADHD."[52]

. . . .

We have come to the end of the exposure of the Big Lie. Unless struggling learners receive timely, adequate RTI instruction, they will be become academic failures whether they are stuck in the purgatory of general education or the hell of special education. Thankfully, this fate can be avoided. Part II of the book tells how, and it will be a relief to turn to some uplifting news.

Still, we have one more essential count in the indictment to unveil in this Part I. The next chapter documents the number of struggling learners (millions) and the depth of their underachievement. It also lays bare the scandalous ways in which school systems try to cover up the abuse.

Chapter 3

....

Underachievement and the Big Cover-Up

"Ain't Nobody Be Learnin' Nothin': The Fraud
and the Fix for High-Poverty Schools"
—Caleb Stewart Rossitor[1]

Chapter 2 exposed how struggling learners—like Kenny, Marcus and millions of others—are illegally mislabeled as disabled and dumped into special education. This chapter highlights data that reveals the extent of the appalling harm that these students suffer. It is far worse than anyone, even parents and those who with general awareness of the problems in our nation's schools, can imagine.

Almost all of the struggling learners, as we have seen, are capable of achieving at or near grade level if they receive adequate instruction in general education. Yet, in the words of a professor of public policy who decided to become a math teacher in public schools, "Ain't Nobody Be Learnin' Nothin.'" Those words are intended to shock, but they're not hyperbole, as the data in this Chapter will show.

We'll see first that in general education, struggling learners learn very little. Around two-thirds of them are below proficiency in reading. Still, it's far worse in special education where they do learn next to "Nothin" (while enduring stigma and often severe segregation from peers). Not only is special education not specially good. It is so bad that most struggling learners would have been better off if they had remained in general education. A scholar writes that some experts "believe that, given the weak effects of special education instructional practices and the social and psychological costs of labeling, the current system of special education is, at best, no more justifiable than simply permitting most students to remain unidentified in regular classrooms. . . ."[2]

In other words, while special education is intended to remedy learning deficits, it does just the opposite. The enormous disparities between the test scores of students in general education (who don't receive special education services) and students who receive special education services, keep getting wider as students in special education move up the grade ladder. If special education were truly special, the disparities would narrow.

Bear in mind too that special education was originally supposed to be short-term services for students who do not have severe cognitive and other limitations. Its purpose was to enable them to catch up and return to general education without special education services. But special education is anything but short-term. According to one account, only about two percent of students with disabilities exit special education.[3] And that minuscule percentage includes students with speech problems (not language problems) who, with the assistance of speech and language pathologists, frequently grow out of the speech disability.

None of this is to suggest that general education is an academic paradise. Struggling learners who remain in general education without special education services also fall farther behind each year. Just not nearly as fast and far are those who are placed in special education. Talk about choosing the lesser of the evils: parents may be forced to choose between what I earlier called the purgatory of general education or the hell of special education.

I wish that were the end of the bad news about underachievement as an indicator of educational abuse. But there's more, much more. The data by themselves don't tell all. This chapter also includes a rap sheet on the criminal ways in which school systems falsify actual student achievement. Test score data are grossly inflated, and school systems cover up the deception. It is near impossible for parents and the public to grasp the depths of the achievement gaps. Public schools, whatever their overall deficiencies, are magna cum laude at cover-up.

THE DATA

The National Assessment of Education Progress (NAEP) tests are recognized as the "gold standard" for measuring the proficiency of U.S. students. Here's what the 2017 NAEP data reveals.[4]

> ***Struggling learners in general education nationwide (who don't receive special education services)***
> In the fourth grade, only 37% of students in general education achieved proficiency in reading and 40% in math. In the eighth grade, the numbers are 37% in reading and 34% in math.

> ***Struggling learners in special education nationwide (most of them mislabeled as disabled)***
> In the fourth grade, only 11% of students in special education achieved proficiency in reading and 14% in math. In the eighth grade, the numbers are 7% in reading and 6% for math.

This big picture is a big national catastrophe. About two-thirds of all struggling learners nationwide are not learning to read or compute well enough to succeed in college or the workforce. And about 90% of students who receive special education services are in the same sinking boat, despite the fact that the overwhelming majority of them have the cognitive ability to meet grade level proficiency. In some large urban school systems, where poor and minority children are clustered, the number of students with disabilities who achieved proficiency was near zero. For example, based on 2015 data, in eighth grade reading, the percentage achieving proficiency was one percent in Philadelphia, two percent in Cleveland, and three percent in Baltimore and several other cities.[5]

If you probe more deeply in the 2017 NAEP data, the abuse is even more obvious. The lowest measure, below proficiency, is "below basic," that is, rock bottom. The percentage of students who scored "below basic" is: for fourth grade reading, 71% for students in special education, 28% for peers in general education; for 8th grade reading, 66% for students in special education, 20% for peers in general education; for fourth grade math, 55% for students in special education, 16% for peers in general education; for eighth grade math, 74% for students in special education, 26% for peers in general education.

And at the risk of incurring a piling-on penalty, we haven't yet hit the absolute bottom. There's another, deeper substratum of proof of the devastating failure of struggling learners. It's found when below proficiency and below basic are converted into the number of grades that students are actually behind their enrolled grade level. For example, Marcus was in the sixth grade and reading at a kindergarten level: the gap was about six years. I have not found any national or state data with this breakdown, and maybe it is not generally collected or published so school systems can avoid further shameful exposure. But in Baltimore, largely unpublished data tell the most appalling story of all. Based on standardized assessment data in reading in 2017:

Achievement grade-level gaps of struggling learners in general education in Baltimore
- Of students in fifth grade, 23% are three or more grade levels behind, including 13% who are still at kindergarten or first grade level.
- Of students in eighth grade, 38% are five or more grade levels behind, including some at kindergarten or first grade level.

Achievement grade-level gaps of students in special education in Baltimore
- By third grade, over 90% are already two or more grade levels behind. By fifth grade, over 60% are three or more grade levels behind, including 16% who are still at kindergarten level and 30% who are at first grade level.
- By eighth grade, 74% are five or more grade levels behind.

It's hard to fully grasp these numbers (and there's no reason to think that comparable large urban school districts are doing better). Even I was amazed. *Among general education students not receiving special education services, 23% of fifth graders are three or more grade levels behind, including 13% who are still at kindergarten or first grade level. Among students who receive special education services, as many as 90 percent of third graders in special education are already two or more grade levels behind.* In other words, during the crucial early years, these students, almost all of them mislabeled as disabled, have learned almost nothing about how to read.

Let's take one more slice at the data, by zeroing in on students in the largest category of disabilities, those identified as having a Specific Learning Disability (LD) such as dyslexia. These students plainly have cognitive abilities that range from low-average to above average. Yet, national data show that in high school at least one fifth of them are reading at five or more grade levels below their enrolled grade level, and close to half are three or more grades below. Students classified as LD are on average 3.4 years behind their enrolled grade level in reading and 3.2 years behind in math.[6]

No wonder that the dropout rates for students in general education and special education are so high. Students in special education drop out at about twice the rate of their non-disabled peers.[7]

In fairness, not all of the data are airtight. The accuracy and analysis of data is limited by the huge number of variables, including the extent to which data on students with severe disabilities, who are usually tested in different ways based on alternate academic standards, may be mixed in. But the breadth and depth of educational abuse is beyond doubt, and so is the cover-up.

THE COVER-UP

By now, in this narrative of underachievement, it may seem that I have run out of horror stories. If only that were true. Believe it or not, even the data just summarized doesn't do complete justice to the complete story of educational abuse. The performance levels are actually much lower and the achievement gaps are actually much higher than they look in the data because of misrepresentations and exaggerations. The cover-up comes in many guises and disguises. The main ones are retentions, "social promotion," and sham high school diplomas.

Retentions

In my experience representing over 200 students in special education, more than half have been retained—that is, at some point along the way not promoted to the next grade. "Flunked," for short. I have not found any data that disaggregates the retention rates of students in general education and special education. But it happens frequently, and it masks how far below grade level a student really is.

Another student I represented, Tyesha, illustrates the problem. She was retained in second grade. Therefore, and thereafter, she was a year older than most of her peers. Not good for her, but good for the school's test scores which measure performance level based on enrolled grade not on chronological age. So when Tyesha was in fifth grade and reading at a second grade level, her gap looked like three years; but in reality she was four years behind her same-age peers.

In theory, retention could be a good thing. It would allow students, particularly in their early school years, to follow a developmentally appropriate course. Students develop socially and academically at difference paces, and most poor and minority children enter school with significant learning deficits. Retention might allow them to catch up, hopefully no later than third grade. But that's not the way it typically works.

Twenty years ago, as a consultant to the Baltimore school system, I wrote a "Study of Promotion/Retention Policies in Urban School Districts," and drafted a groundbreaking set of policies that were later adopted.[8] A common practice then was for some students to be retained more than once, severely harming them and giving general education teachers the unmanageable task of accommodating significantly over-aged students in their already overcrowded classes. The reform policies eliminated double retentions and required structured interventions for struggling learners in danger of retention. Today, double retentions are gone, but, no surprise, structured interventions never arrived.

By one fairly recent count, about 16 states have policies calling for third grade students to be retained unless they pass a reading assessment.[9] Being able to read by third grade is generally considered the crucial gateway to success throughout K-12 schooling. And some states purport to require RTI-like interventions before or after retention.[10] Yet, teachers around the country say that such policies "are another example of lofty educational goals paired with insufficient resources."[11] The interventions are too little, or not available at all, and the policies fall flat. According to Johns Hopkins University researcher Robert Slavin, retention looks good for a while because the retained children are a year older than their classmates, but it "is rarely an effective or necessary policy."[12]

In fact, neither retention nor promotion works without RTI. If you learned the lessons in Chapter 2, you know what often happens next. General education teachers, weighed down by so many students who are so far below grade level, mislabel some of them as disabled and unload them into special education. And virtually all of them are subjected to the permanent injury of "social promotion."

Social Promotion

"Social promotion" occurs when students in either general education or special education are promoted from one grade to the next despite their inability to meet state standards or otherwise legitimately earn passing grades. It happens almost all the time with struggling learners. Otherwise, how—when they are so far behind grade level in reading and/or math—are they promoted from one grade to the next?

The answer is that they are given passing grades no matter how badly they are performing. Report cards telling parents that Marcus or Tyesha has passed are typically pure fiction. Parents are, of course, deceived. They look at their child's report card and think the passing grades are genuine. The report card may also claim that the student has made good improvement. But there is usually no truth to any of these labels of progress. Struggling learners like Marcus and Tyesha are usually far behind peers, and "good improvement" may be more indicative of good behavior and effort than actual academic growth.

Thus, social promotion conceals huge gaps between students' actual ability and regular passing standards for the grades they are in. And the public, like parents, are fooled by the deception, the same as with bogus high school diplomas.

The Hoax of Graduation Diplomas

Once upon a time, a high school diploma was worth the paper it was written on. No more, to an astounding extent. In early 2018, an article in Education Week reported on "revelations" of "bogus graduation-rate practices."[13]

Caleb Steward Rossiter is a college professor who descended from the ivory tower to teach math in the Washington, D.C. public schools. He taught pre-calculus to high school seniors. But he wasn't able to teach them much: half of them, he found, could not figure correctly second grade math problems. Yet, while he wasn't able to teach them a lot, they taught him a lot.

His book *Ain't Nobody Be Learnin' Nothin': The Fraud and the Fix for High-Poverty Schools* tells of malpractice on a grand scale. One teacher told him about a particular student in pre-calculus: "That boy can't add two plus two . . . [but] of course I passed him . . . Everybody knows that a D for a special education student means nothing but that he came in once in a while."[14]

Rossiter's experience is part of a nationwide epidemic of scandalously inflated graduation rates.[15] While grade inflation is rampant beginning in early elementary school, the practice peaks in high school. Although huge numbers of general education students and almost all special education students are near hopelessly behind, schools are under the gun to pass them, keeping graduation rates high and dropout rates low.

Several decades ago, there was a movement across the states to require demanding high school exit exams. To colleges and potential employers, high school diplomas had lost their credibility. The exit exams were allied to the accountability reforms that led to passage of the No Child Left Behind Act. Over half the states imposed them. But now that number is dwindling rapidly.[16] Why? Because too many students simply can't pass them.

The retreat includes states abolishing the tests as a graduation requirement, states watering down the tests, and states allowing students to bypass the tests altogether. In Prince George's County in Maryland, a populous bedroom suburb for Washington, D.C, a media disclosure of grade-tampering led to a state audit that showed that in the 2016 graduating class, grades for nearly 5,500 students were changed right before graduation over a two-year period.[17]

And just over the county line, the D.C. schools were also guilty of widespread fraud. A study disclosed, "One of every three graduates from the District's public schools last year missed too many classes or improperly took make-up classes, undermining the validity of hundreds of diplomas."[18]

Further manipulation occurs in states like Maryland that allow students who can't pass the exit exams to substitute an alternate route: "bridge projects." Maryland's 39-page manual spells out so-called safeguards for what are called a "Bridge Plan for Academic Validation."[19] But the numbers of students who take them, and their easy nature, have grown to shameful proportions.

In Baltimore, as many as one-third of all students earning a regular diploma have done so via such bridge projects.[20] I have represented several students who were in the 10th or 11th grade though reading at first, second or third grade levels. They had lost all motivation, did little work, intermittently caused trouble, and attended school sporadically. Yet, they passed courses and bridge projects as long as they professed interest in graduating, made some effort, and didn't act out badly enough to warrant expulsion. As one teacher said to me, the bridge projects make jock courses for college athletes look rigorous.

Since fake grades and diplomas have been exposed nationwide, investigations will follow, followed by vows by school systems to stiffen requirements. But, as Robert Slavin points out, you would be better off buying the Brooklyn Bridge than believing much will change, as long as so many struggling learners are socially promoted through elementary, middle and high schools and lack the preparation to legitimately pass high school coursework.[21]

But there's still much more of the cover-up to be uncovered

Improper "Accommodations" and "Modifications" in Special Education

Fake grades and diplomas conceal the failure of struggling learners in general education and special education. Moreover in special education, the cover-up goes even deeper, where student achievement can be further inflated through "accommodations" and "modifications" on Individual Education Programs (IEPs).

"Accommodations" are intended to level the playing field, enabling students labeled as disabled to have "access" to the same curriculum as nondisabled peers, and to make progress in that curriculum.[22] Accommodations are also necessary to enable students to demonstrate their true ability on tests despite their disabilities. But accommodations are not supposed to lower standards.

"Modifications" are supposed to be different. The Accommodations Manual published by The Council of Chief State School Officers puts it this way. "Accommodations do not reduce learning expectations. They provide access. However, modifications or alterations refer to practices that change, lower, or reduce learning expectations."[23]

Clearly, modifications should be limited to students with significant cognitive or other disabilities who cannot be expected to meet regular academic standards. They should not be given to other students in special education—like students mislabeled as disabled—who, as we learned in Chapter 2, are able to meet regular standards if they receive adequate instruction and related services.

The difference shouldn't be hard for school staff who develop IEPs to keep straight. But schools pay little heed. They do this because improper accommodations and modifications inflate grades. Schools look better though students are worse off. And the wrongdoing is rampant. Here's how the system is rigged.

Accommodating Failure

Proper accommodations vary for students. The most obvious example would be Braille or recorded text for students who are blind. But other accommodations, particularly for students who are not severely disabled, are not so straightforward. Chief among them is "read-aloud," also known as "verbatim reading," in which all or selected portions of lessons or tests are read to a student in special education who qualifies for the accommodation Another accommodation, almost always included on IEPs, is "extended time." Other common accommodations are a calculator if a student's disability affects basic mathematics, and a "scribe" if a student's learning disability impedes written expression.

Accommodations enable students to overcome their big deficits in foundational skills of reading, math and writing. Assume Tyesha is now in the ninth grade with a Specific Learning Disability and reading skills at a third grade level. She couldn't at that point read and comprehend on her own ninth grade textbooks and other materials in her literature, science, math and social studies courses. Unless found eligible for the read-aloud accommodation, she would not be able, as IDEA requires, to have "access to the general curriculum." With the accommodation, she can listen to a recorded text or have someone read to her, and thus have a chance to keep up in class and earn passing grades.

However, most accommodations, particularly read-aloud, lose their legitimacy when used to cover up early deficits in foundational skills that should have been addressed through timely interventions. I have represented many students who were mislabeled as disabled and received the read-aloud accommodation *as early as the first or second grades.* One of them was Kenny who we met in the Preface and actually had materials read to him in the first grade. That is far too soon to put a struggling young reader on crutches that will almost surely impede development of independent skills. A writer on special education observes, "What is 'special' about reading to a youngster who should learn to read? Or providing a calculator, instead of teaching her 'number facts'?"[24]

Yet, school systems do this all the time, while necessary intervention services are delayed or denied altogether. Almost invariably, students in special education don't receive the "specially designed instruction" required by IDEA that would enable them to *independently* meet state standards in reading, mathematics and writing. Rather than being curbed, read-aloud accommodations are increasing nationally.

Modifying (a/k/a Dumbing Down) Standards

Improper modifications are also rampant though harder to spot. For example, the Baltimore school system provides school IEP teams with long checklists of what are known as "supplementary aids and services." Most are classroom pieties such as "Check for understanding," "Paraphrase questions and instruction," and "Encourage student to ask for assistance when needed." Such supplementary aids and services are obviously not special; rather they are instructional techniques that good teachers might employ with any student in general education as well as special education.

Yet, the checklists serve as open invitations for IEP teams to illegally lower standards for students who are not severely disabled. They contain an open-ended place for "Modified curriculum." Further, the template for IEPs has a place for "Program Modification."

Under these headings, it is not always easy to prove how teachers lower the standards. "Modification" can be a relative term, and it can be subtly embedded in daily instruction. Still, many students receive modified, dumbed-down assignments, content, and tests in ways that overstep proper boundaries.

There are simply too many reasons for teachers to do otherwise (same as with improper accommodations). They know many of their students are very far below grade level. They realize they are unable, despite their best efforts—because of huge teacher-student ratios, insufficient training and other constraints—to provide adequate instruction. They care deeply about their students (their "babies" as they often call them, whether in first grade or high school) and want to enable them in any way possible to achieve passing grades. And they are under intense explicit or implicit pressure from administrators to overuse accommodations and modifications to inflate the student's, the school's, and the school district's test scores.

School administrators bury their heads in the sand. Teachers get little guidance or training on improper modifications and accommodations. Nor is there any monitoring to discover and correct wrongdoing. Out-and-out cheating creeps in too.

Cheating on Standardized Tests

Honesty is not the best policy followed by some school systems when confronted with evidence of underachievement and cover-ups. There may be a fine line between misuse of accommodations and modifications and outright cheating on standardized tests that measure student proficiency. Outsiders have no real way of knowing how often the line is crossed. But we can be sure that dishonesty happens a lot.

Cheating in testing has been a national scourge for at least a decade.[25] Usually it is rogue teachers and principals, occasionally reaching to central office. The urge to cheat is tempting since educators at all levels increasingly live or die professionally based on test scores. It is also easier than it should be because some top administrators adopt a "don't ask, don't tell" attitude toward testing practices.

It is also easiest to pull off in special education. There are more opportunities to cheat because many students in special education are tested separately, individually or in small groups where they receive accommodations like read-aloud. Such a secluded setting is fertile ground for dishonesty. Baltimore school personnel sometimes whisper to me that it sometimes takes place.

That said, there is no doubt that only a tiny fraction of educators engages in outright cheating. Still, cheating—along with retentions, social promotion, diploma hoaxes, and improper accommodations and modifications—add up to a massive cover-up of student failure and educational abuse.

What will it take to improve instruction and close down the cover-ups? The next part of the book tells how it can be done.

PART II

························

THE RIGHT INSTRUCTION AT THE RIGHT TIME

This part of the book is the most uplifting part. It tells the story of how the framework of Response to Intervention (RTI) can enable almost all struggling learners to meet academic standards. The story, however, doesn't have a completely happy ending. While it tells how RTI could work, it also tells how RTI, for many reasons, is not working as it should.

In telling the story, I am drawn to the children's fable of *The Little Engine That Could* as a metaphor for RTI. I read it often to my children and grandchildren and I hope readers of this book will get its message as well. We've been conditioned to believe that success for struggling learners is as big and forbidding a mountain as the one that the Little Engine was up against. But the Little Engine could, and we as a nation can. We can enable struggling learners to succeed if we are smart and determined, and RTI is the engine to get us there.

Of course, many readers—policymakers and educators among them—will say, dream on. The Little Engine is make-believe. The real-world path up the mountain for struggling learners is blocked by ridge after ridge of educational and political obstacles. Isn't RTI just another sounds-good grand reform that will fall off the cliffs? Isn't the massive weight of struggling readers, with deep learning deficits caused by impoverished family circumstances, simply too much for the Little Engine to carry to the top?

For sure, the obstacles in the way of RTI are formidable. But effective RTI is no instructional pipedream. If set as a national goal, if supported by evidence-based and cost-effective resources, and if school systems can get their management act together, RTI can bring almost all struggling learners up to grade-level proficiency. We have the know-how. At the very least, we can ascend much higher than we ever have, or even thought we could.

Chapter 4 first looks at the basic design and operating principles of RTI. How is it supposed to work? What are the best practices in classroom instruction that fuel its power? And, since it's so good and do-able, why hasn't it been done on a large scale?

Chapter 5 moves from RTI in general education to RTI-like "specially designed instruction" in special education. Even if RTI were effectively implemented in general education, a small percentage of struggling learners would still require special education. In addition, no matter how hard we try, RTI will not get to its destination overnight. Therefore, RTI-like instruction for students in special education is a dire necessity now. A nationally acclaimed model to make this happen—to raise the bar and improve outcomes in special education—is underway in the Baltimore City public schools and is described in Chapter 5.

··

Chapter 4

RTI to the Rescue of Struggling Learners

"Being against RTI [Response to Intervention]
is like being against motherhood."[1]

RTI is a rarity in K-12 school policy. There is no dispute over its worthiness. It is supported by voluminous literature setting forth its principles and potential effectiveness.[2] And its principles are not new either. Long before the concept of RTI made its way into federal laws (including IDEA, the No Child Left Behind Act and the Every Student Succeeds Act), many state laws called for early identification and intervention processes identical or similar to RTI.

The principal features of RTI are:

- Data analysis as early as possible to identify learning problems.
- Continuous monitoring of student progress.
- Three tiers of increasingly intense research-based interventions to enable struggling learners to meet age appropriate benchmarks.

Simply put: If done right, struggling learners who do not have severe disabilities can meet grade level standards.

RTI can also be understood as a call to action. As a group of researchers and practitioners put it, "RTI is designed to remove the oh-so-human temptation to speculate and slowly mull over learning problems, and instead spur teachers into action to improve learning, see if the actions worked, and make adjustments in a continuous loop."[3] It imposes the clear expectations and structure that are usually lacking in the management of classroom instruction. It prevents the "wait to fail" syndrome that typically delays timely extra help for struggling learners.

BEHAVIOR AS A FACTOR

One preliminary issue is how much RTI should focus on behavior as well as academics. In principle, RTI should address the full range of students' academic and behavior problems. Nonetheless, RTI in this book focuses almost entirely on instructional services, especially in reading. The predominant reason why learners struggle is because of their failure to learn to read: this is true of 80 to 90 percent of students found eligible for special education under the classification of a Specific Learning Disability (LD).[4]

At the same time, it is often hard to determine which is the chicken and which is the egg between the academic and behavioral causes of learning difficulties. Do students struggle and fall behind academically because of social and emotional problems? Or do students develop social and emotional conditions because of frustration and embarrassment when they can't keep up academically with their peers?

In my own advocacy for students, I have seen many students for whom it's the academic failure that comes first. Remember Devon from Chapter 2? (I hope you can't forget Devon and how he suffered so much, so unnecessarily.) He is one of many students I've represented who fell behind early and was classified as LD. Then, as they got older and didn't receive adequate instruction in special education, they fell farther and farther behind. They were seen by peers and they saw themselves as "dummies." They acted out, becoming more unmanageable in the classroom and on the school grounds. Sometimes, their disability classification was changed, almost always wrongly, to Emotional Disability (ED). It's not much of a stretch to say that frequently general education and special education are so bad that they drive struggling learners to seem crazy.

Still, bonafide behavior problems endanger academic success. They, like reading problems, should be nipped in the bud, and can be. There is extensive literature and research on the relative effectiveness of a variety of positive behavior support systems.[5] Some practitioners, particularly those in the behavioral support field, prefer to align their work to a framework called Multi-tier System of Support (MTSS), rather than RTI. By and large, MTSS encompasses RTI with more emphases on behavioral issues and, ideally, on all learners, not just struggling ones.[6] That's a lot of acronyms but the plain point is that behavioral issues should not be neglected.

RTI ADDS UP FOR MATH TOO

This Chapter's focus on reading is also not intended to slight the applicability of RTI principles to math, and there are promising math RTI practices.[7] Still, reading is the gateway for children and adults to the worlds of math, science, history, arts and other vistas of knowledge and culture. An article published by the Brookings Institute was titled "A counterintuitive approach to improving math education: Focus on English language arts."[8]

THE ENGINE PARTS OF RTI

There are two basic dimensions to RTI. One is the framework of the three Tiers. The other is the key operational elements in each of the Tiers.

The Framework of RTI Tiers 1, 2 and 3

RTI isn't as simple as 1, 2, 3, but it isn't all that complicated either. Tier 1 consists of instruction for the whole class in general education. The core curriculum for everyone should be research-based, and struggling learners should receive both "differentiated" (individualized) and some small group instruction.

Struggling learners and their skill gaps are identified through regular screening of all students, usually a minimum of three times per year. Parent alert: Contrary to some public accounts, these screenings are not cumbersome for the child, the teacher, or the class. That is, they are short, individual assessments, often built right into the whole class curricula. They are not a separate statewide test. They don't require prep, stress or teaching-to-the-test.

Based on the screening data, students who are not meeting appropriate benchmarks should be placed in Tier 2. Tier 2 provides tutoring or small group instruction to supplement not supplant Tier 1. Though models differ, the extra dose of instruction is usually prescribed in the range of 20–30 minutes per day, four or five days per week. Some guidelines set the Tier 2 group size at 4–8 students who have relatively similar skill levels and needs.

Depending on the student's individualized needs, the Tier 2 intervention instruction can be more intensive instruction in the core (Tier 1) program and/or an additional research-based intervention program targeted at particular skill deficits. Either way, the teacher should be well-qualified to provide the Tier 2 intervention.

The amount of time spent in Tier 2 varies, but is generally around eight weeks. The progress monitoring data determines (along with teacher judgment) whether a student is adequately responding and catching up. Non-responders, those who are still behind where they should be, can stay longer in Tier 2 or move on Tier 3.

Tier 3 instruction is even more intensive and specialized, and it too should supplement not supplant Tier 1. It does, however, replace Tier 2—the student would not receive Tier 2 and Tier 3 instruction. The range of time is about 20–30 minutes per day, four or five days per week, but with lower, including one-to-one, teacher-student ratios. The supplemental instruction is usually a research-based intervention program that should be taught by a teacher who is trained and experienced in that particular program.

A student who still does not respond sufficiently in Tier 3 should then be referred for evaluation to determine eligibility for special education. In effect, special education should be "Tier 4" with special education delivering even more intense and specialized instruction. Unfortunately, the system almost never functions that way. Almost invariably, students referred for special education did not receive appropriate Tier 2 and Tier 3 instruction in general education (as they should have). In theory, special education services would fill in for the missing Tier 2 and Tier 3 instruction. But that doesn't happen either. Special education instruction also falls far short of providing appropriate Tier 2 and Tier 3 interventions. As a result, as I've described already, special education services almost invariably turn out to be too little, too late to enable struggling learners to narrow their achievement deficits and avoid educational abuse.

What does it take for the three Tiers to operate the way they are supposed to? There are three cardinal elements: the quality of the data collection and analysis; reliance on interventions that are strongly research-based; and early (very early!) identification and intervention.

Data, Data, Data

If what really matters in real estate is location, location, location, what really matters in RTI is data, data, data. Data must be gathered through an array of reliable instruments, from relatively short screening tools to curriculum-based assessments to standardized tests. The data must drive every chug of the RTI engine, from initial identification of learning problems, to data-driven instruction, to placement in tiers, to selection of interventions, and to progress monitoring.

By and large, state of the art screening and assessment instruments are up to the task, and the supply of data is up to the demand. With reasonably good diagnostic data in the hands of teachers, the obstacles to effective RTI lie elsewhere, including, as discussed in a later chapter, better training of teachers in how to understand and apply the data.

Research-Based Instruction

The terms research-based, evidence-based, and scientifically-based are used fairly interchangeably in K-12 education. By any name, the requirement that research-based best practices be used at every step of the way in RTI should be a no-brainer. The No Child Left Behind Act, by one count, employed the term "scientifically based research" about 110 times in an effort to force federal funds to be effectively spent.[9] Its successor, the Every Student Succeeds Act (ESSA), goes to great lengths to clarify and strengthen the research that qualifies as "evidence based."[10]

There is a strong link between these requirements for all students in general education and for students in special education under IDEA. Under IDEA, as spelled out in Chapter 2, federal regulations state that before a child is found eligible as student with LD, the school should determine whether the child has made "sufficient progress to meet age or State-approved grade-level standards . . . when using a process based on the child's response to scientific, research-based intervention. . . ."[11]

Needless to say, that's easier said than done. One of the stumbling blocks is the complexity and confusion over what qualifies as research-based. There have been some hits and many misses as to what qualifies. Random trials peer-reviewed research is the "gold standard" but also the most difficult to meet. ESSA tries to address this. According to a Brookings Institute report: "ESSA is the first federal education law to define the term 'evidence-based' and to distinguish between activities with 'strong,' 'moderate,' and 'promising' support . . . the law also treats as evidence-based a fourth category comprising activities that have a research-based rationale but lack direct empirical support."[12]

Yet for the present, the practical supply of such research—no matter how defined—is less than the demand. The supply is limited by the maze of school variables that complicate the research, by the dearth of educational research in general (and in education departments in universities in particular), and by school systems' weak research and development (R&D) management practices detailed later.

Still, as we will see, there is a substantial body of research that supports the effectiveness of instructional best practices within an RTI framework, particularly tutoring in the early grades.

Early (Very Early!) Identification and Intervention
There is proof that timely research-based interventions can enable struggling learners to regain lost ground. But how much ground they can regain depends on how much ground there is to make up.

The downward spiral in learning to read starts very early. As discussed in Chapter 2, students who fall behind rarely catch up. Without early identification and intervention, the "Matthew effect"—"rich" readers get richer, "poor" readers get poorer—dooms struggling learners. Still, as preeminent reading researcher Joseph K. Torgesen has concluded:

> The good news is we now have tools to reliably identify the children who are likely destined for this early reading failure. . . . Most importantly, given the results of a number of intervention studies, we can say with confidence that if we intervene early, intensively, and appropriately, we can provide these children with the early reading

skills that can prevent almost all of them from the nasty downward spiral. . . .[13]

Torgesen added that "while the exact effects of the interventions [in the studies described in the article] varied, they were all successful in bringing most students (56 to 92 percent) to well within the average range of reading ability."[14] What's more, "strategic early interventions" can decrease the number of students found eligible for special education by between 50 and 75 percent.[15]

Still, in the maddening education wars, one important element of early identification and intervention is not without controversy. That's the battle over what is developmentally appropriate literacy instruction in prekindergarten and kindergarten.

Over the past decade or so, instruction in foundational skills like reading has increased in prekindergarten and kindergarten programs. This movement is in step with growing research showing that reading difficulties, including dyslexia, can be identified at those early ages, and treated with developmentally appropriate interventions. Prekindergarten programs for three-year olds as well as four-year olds are gaining traction too.[16]

However, there has been resistance by some early childhood educators and parents. They team up with education progressives out of fear that children are being over-tested and prematurely drilled-and-killed, while missing out on social and emotional development. The Head Start program for a long time has been caught in the crossfire.

Some of the controversy can be traced to economic class differences. Children from non-poor families do not need the same kind of very early interventions as children from low-income families. Children from disadvantaged backgrounds enter school, even at age 4, with profound deficits in language and other readiness skills. As revealed in a famous early childhood study, children from non-poor families enter school having been exposed to 30 million more spoken words than children from families on welfare.[17]

Thus, low-income children, unlike peers from non-disadvantaged homes, require academic preparation (it might even be called academic remediation) from the earliest possible moment. Not to the exclusion of growth in social and emotional attributes, but in a healthy balance across all domains. That is happening in many places, and early identification of learning difficulties is becoming more the norm.

While the importance of early identification and intervention cannot be overstated, a few words need to be said about RTI for older students. Even if RTI doesn't kick in early enough and with sufficient intensity, it is not completely three strikes and you're out. All need not be lost. Even far-behind older students can be assisted through tutoring, as seen later in this chapter, particularly if the interventions occur in general education rather than in special education.[18]

BEST RESEARCH-BASED PRACTICES IN CLASSROOM INSTRUCTION

RTI's reliance on data, research and very early intervention does not mean that we can be certain that it will work as advertised. In fact, there is no evidence that it has been effectively implemented on a large scale in any large school system. The reasons are plainly revealed in this Chapter and elsewhere in the book: mainly lack of money for interventions, poor teacher training, and failure to use evidence-based programs and practices.

Still, there is a whole lot of evidence that we know how to do it, if it's done right.[19] RTI, bear in mind, is less a discrete program and more a process with innumerable moving components. This section scrutinizes the most crucial components, in particular evidence-based tutoring, and shows how they can provide ample fuel for the engine of RTI to carry struggling learners to academic success.

Tier 1: "the First Teach"

The inventory of best practices in the classroom that enable struggling readers to meet state standards begins with RTI Tier 1: that is, "core" instruction in general education for all students beginning in prekindergarten and up the school ladder. Sometimes called "the first teach," it's an indispensable foundation for academic success. Done well, it can prevent or mitigate the necessity of interventions in Tiers 2 and 3.

That said, this book does not attempt to catalogue, much less examine closely, best practices in it. The subject is simply too open-ended. Because Tier 1 is universal for all students whether they are struggling learners or not, it involves virtually every aspect of schooling. It is near impossible to name an education reform that does not impact mightily on Tier 1 instruction. To name a few major reforms du jour—teacher quality, class size, school choice including privatization, and technology in the classroom.

Teacher quality is the most vivid example. Suppose the U.S. adopted reforms that would elevate teaching to the ranks of high-performing nations around the world. The reforms could strengthen the applicant pool by raising admission standards for teacher education programs in colleges and universities and improving the relevance and depth of the coursework; provide incentives for teaching in low-performing schools; increase professional development including classroom coaching and mentoring; and raise salaries.

The potential power of such a radical overhaul of teacher quality has been authoritatively documented in the National Center on Education and the Economy's comparison of the U.S. with "high performing" school systems around the world.[20] It is difficult to imagine any movement that would be more transformational. Yet, that is unlikely to happen in the near term; the political obstacles are simply too overwhelming. More-over, a certain percentage of students, no matter how skilled the teach-ers, will require extra help. Nor is any other mega-reform—including the privatization crusade of the Trump education department headed by sec-retary Betty DeVos—likely to happen in the foreseeable future in a way that would substantially alter Tier 1 (or Tiers 2 and 3).

Curriculum Matters

On the other hand, though not conventionally recognized as a mega-reform like "teacher quality," stronger curricula have under-appreciated potential to strengthen Tier 1. The curriculum refers to both standards for what students should know and be able to do (think of the famous or infamous Common Core standards) and the textbooks and learning materials that are aligned to the standards, which teachers should be expected to use. Yet, the selection of textbooks and materials, including lesson plans, has been habitually neglected.

My 2010 book, *It's the Classroom, Stupid*, lamented the absence of educational reform strategies that focused directly on how to improve teaching and learning in the classroom. Classroom teachers are denied well-designed, teacher-friendly curricula that would greatly boost teacher effectiveness, especially in Tier 1.

A 2017 report of the Johns Hopkins School of Education brought welcome attention to this. A summary by David Steiner, executive director of the Johns Hopkins Institute for Education Policy, highlights both the underestimated importance of curricular choices and how state and local districts fall down on the job of assuring high quality textbooks and materials. In this too, the U.S. lags behind high-performing school systems in other countries.[21]

Chester E. Finn, Jr., for decades one of the nation's leading K-12 policy intellectuals, has sought to explain why curriculum reform, regrettably, has been missing from policy reform debates.

> Many shun curriculum because content choices are often culture-war battles . . . Talk of a "national curriculum" is taboo and when states venture into these waters, it's almost as controversial. . . . Curriculum, therefore, is generally left to districts, which frequently leave it to individual schools and often to individual teachers or departments within them.[22]

This neglected subject is further discussed in a later chapter on how school systems mismanage what I call the instructional infrastructure, including curricula.

The Delusion of "Differentiation"

Educators, in part, underestimate the consequences of poor curricula by overestimating the power of "differentiated" instruction. It has long been an act of faith in the education establishment that many problems of struggling learners can be overcome if teachers would only give more individual attention to the multiple learning styles and difficulties of individual students. The mantra of "one size doesn't fit all" is invoked. Who can be against such "differentiation"?

Well, I'm happy to say that some experts, in my view for good reason, are deeply skeptical if not altogether dismissive. No one can be against it in theory, but in practice, theory collides with the reality of the classroom life of teachers.

To see why, let's start with a fairly typical description of differentiated instruction. It recognizes that learners differ in factors such as culture, learning style, and gender. In order to address those differences, teachers need to approach each student by their unique readiness, interests and learning profile. Sounds good. Yet, the other side of it is portrayed by a seasoned educator in an article titled "Differentiation Doesn't Work:" "Although fine in theory, differentiation in practice is harder to implement in a heterogeneous classroom than it is to juggle with one arm tied behind your back . . . the only educators who assert differentiation is doable are those who have never tried to implement it themselves: university professors, curriculum coordinators, and school principals."[23]

Of course teachers must individualize instruction as much as they can. But there are simply too many kids with too many differences to expect overloaded teachers to pull it off well. An ex-teacher recalls being "Differentiated to death."[24] No doubt many teachers in the trenches feel the same way, though they keep their opinions to themselves to keep from getting in trouble with administrators.

Two newer versions of differentiated instruction making the rounds these days are Universal Design for Learning, and "personalized learning." As set forth by a national program that ardently advocates for UDL: "UDL provides students of all abilities equal chances to learn. With UDL, educators design flexible and motivating lessons that draw on students' strengths to learn and show what they have learned. Students are offered many ways to access the same information."[25] Yet, UDL's lofty principles encounter facts on the ground that make it extremely hard, if not impossible, for everyday teachers to implement the principles.

Still, UDL has many theorists who have gained it favorable footing in both federal and state laws.[26] And no wonder. Like differentiated instruction, UDL appeals to the best instincts of idealistic educators and cost-conscious policymakers and politicians. Both differentiated instruction and UDL are low-cost, compared to tutoring and other reforms.

The drumbeat for differentiation is being amplified by growing attention to "personalized learning." It too "tailors educational approaches to an individual student's needs, strength, interests, and aspirations."[27] But it bumps into the same challenges, mainly the overburden on teachers and the large and varying skill deficits of students.

As a result, evidence of effective implementation of differentiation and its alter egos is scant if not absent altogether. And worse, by setting unrealistic expectations for the degree of individualization that overloaded and under-supported teachers are supposed to deliver, teachers are scapegoated and demoralized (and the need for RTI interventions is downplayed).

Too Much of a Good Thing?

My experience in Baltimore over the past decade leads me to one final note of caution about best practices in Tier 1. As a member of the Baltimore school board and an advocate for system-wide reform, I have struggled for many years to get top school officials to develop a stronger RTI framework for Tiers 2 and 3. For the most part they have put me off, but not because they don't understand the necessity of RTI and how it should be done.

Rather, their mantra is, we have got to get the Tier 1 "first teach" down pat first. In principle, they have a point. The better Tier 1 is, the lesser the number of struggling learners. But they take the point too far by their almost exclusive focus on it to the neglect of Tiers 2 and 3. In Baltimore, for example, Tier 1 teaching has been a recognized, relative strength of the system. It is also easier to get stuck on Tier 1 because instruction in Tiers 2 and 3 costs more money up front (though it will save money down the line).

Other school systems may have fallen into the same trap. The best Tier 1 in the world will not eliminate the need for additional Tier 2 and Tier 3 assistance for a significant number of struggling learners, predominately poor and minority students.

Interventions in Tiers 2 and 3, Especially Tutoring

With Tier 1 a vast work in progress, Tiers 2 and 3 will be required in large doses for a long time. But what exactly does that mean? What are the Tier 2 and Tier 3 interventions, and what are their prospects for success? How will I back up my claim that there is a convincing body of research on Tier 2 and Tier 3 instructional best practices?

The definitive piece in this puzzle is tutoring. Its proven benefits surpass other intervention best practices. However, before showcasing tutoring as the star of the RTI show, we should take notice of some vital supporting players.

There is a vast range of them. One helpful approach is found in the 2016 study by consultants to the Maryland Commission on Innovation and Excellence on Education (of which I am a member). The Commission's principal charge is to make recommendations to the Maryland governor and state legislature on the cost of an adequate education in the public schools (and how the big bill should be divvied up by state and local governments). Adequate is defined as the resources necessary so that all students can meet state standards. But putting a price tag on it has been elusive.

All states—often prodded by lawsuits and judicial decisions—have grappled with the issue, and the study for the Maryland Commission is a state-of-the art approach. Its recommendations are based on evidence-based research and educators' professional judgment.[28] They confront head-on the central challenge of this book and RTI: What resources are necessary to enable struggling learners to receive adequate instruction in general education so they avoid being mislabeled as disabled, and educationally abused?

The Commission study does this by first identifying the resources that should be part of the "base" per pupil costs. These are the "Core Programs"—in essence, Tier 1—that should be available for all students in general education. They run the gamut from teacher-student ratios in general education classrooms to central and school-based administrators to supportive services like technology, guidance counselors, nurses and librarians.

Second, the study identifies the additional resources that are necessary to enable students "at-risk of academic failure" to meet state standards. These are essentially the costs of Tier 2 and Tier 3 interventions. Included are tutors within an RTI framework, additional pupil support positions like counselors, extended day and summer school programs, and additional teachers and related services for Limited English Proficiency (LEP) and special education students. The per pupil costs for these resources are added to the base.

"At-risk" students in the Commission study are not exactly the same as this book's struggling learners, but they're close. At-risk in the study is defined only in terms of poverty (using eligibility for Free and Reduced Price Meals as a proxy) and LEP students. By contrast, struggling learners in this book—though disproportionately poor and minority—include all students who fall behind in general education. To illustrate, in Maryland about 50 percent of students are poor and minority, but about 60 percent of all students are below proficiency in reading and math.

There is another significant difference between the study and the conventional RTI framework. While the study calls for an RTI approach, it only calls for Tier 2 prior to referral to special education; in the study, Tier 3 is special education. This is a clear departure from the national consensus that three tiers of instruction should precede referral to special education.

The study appeared to justify the omission of Tier 3 based on its belief that a financially ample base and Tier 2 interventions would eliminate the need for further interventions in general education. This is a worthy premise, but there are substantial risks and doubts. If there is only one tier between the Tier 1 core and special education, and if the Tier 1 and Tier 2 costs are not adequately estimated, or are not fully funded, or don't work as well as hoped, it becomes much more likely that many struggling learners will be referred to special education before they have received enough progressively intense interventions in general education. Many more struggling learners will be mislabeled as disabled and exposed to future educational abuse.

Despite this mis-step, the study still has the right idea about the need to specify, largely through the RTI process, the programs that will bring struggling learners up to meeting grade level standards. And it shines the spotlight, first and foremost, on the most powerful intervention—tutoring.

COULD TUTORING REALLY BE A SILVER BULLET?

The evidence of the effectiveness of tutoring towers above the evidence of any other intervention strategy.[29] For example, a review of research on interventions for struggling readers was in effect a catalogue of proven and promising tutoring interventions.[30]

An insightful perspective comes from R. Barker Bausell, a retired medical bio-statistician and professor at the University of Maryland, Baltimore. Though not a K-12 educator, he has long pursued a passion for research on how to teach children to read and write. He distilled his findings in a 2011 book *Too Simple to Fail*. The "simple" way to reform public education, he wrote, involves replacing a lot of ineffective whole class instruction with "the most effective instructional paradigm ever developed"—tutoring. Tutoring delivers the "massive doses"[31] of intensive instructional time that struggling learners require. He outlines scenarios with various tutor-to-student ratios and time allocations.

On a less professorial note, a Bloomberg View journalist's column was titled "Want to fix education? Give a kid a tutor."[32] That seems an apt summary of the research, but what are the devilish details?

Tutoring, of course, can mean many different things. The consultants to the Maryland Commission thought that the "most powerful and effective approach . . . is individual one-to-one or small group (one-to-three or one-to-five) tutoring provided by licensed teachers."[33] But there are countless models with a variety of features.

- Pupil-teacher ratios that vary from one-on-one to small groups.
- Tutors who are highly trained teachers or para-professionals or volunteers who may or may not receive stipends.[34]
- Tutoring programs that have a prescriptive design compared to those that allow tutors more leeway.
- Focus of the tutoring from random homework help to seamless integration with classroom instruction.
- Funding via "hard money" that is reliable and sustained over several years to constant annual scrounging to pay the bills.
- Goals that range from remedial interventions for struggling learners to private tutoring to give upper-income students a further leg up in competition for grades and selective school admissions.

These models cover a huge amount of ground. But the very good news is that a thousand flowers are blooming, and many varieties, including those for struggling learners, have the sweet smell of success.[35]

Tutoring within the Framework of RTI

In the framework of RTI, Tier 2 and Tier 3 tutoring generally fall within well-recognized design boundaries. For example, here are guidelines drawn from the Maryland RTI Guidance Manual:[36]

Tier 2
- *Size of instructional group*: Small needs-based groups with 2–4 students (the number recommended in much research) and/or other customized groupings.
- *Amount of time*: Additional time that exceeds the core program block of time. Often a minimum of 30–60 minutes, 2–5 times per week.
- *Duration*: Approximately 6–12 weeks as determined by the response of the student to an intervention program implemented with fidelity.
- *Instructor qualifications*: Tier 2 should be provided by school personnel who have been trained in the core curriculum and/or intervention program.

Tier 3
- *Size of instructional group*: Small group or more usually individual instruction based on the use of individual diagnostic-prescriptive data that targets the student's skill deficits.
- *Amount of time*: Additional time that exceeds the core instructional block of time. Usually a minimum of 30–60 minutes, 4–5 times per week.
- *Duration*: Approximately 6–12 weeks.
- *Instructor qualifications*: This tier focuses on delivering the most intense interventions and thus the instructor must be highly trained and skilled.

RTI models across the country are rarely if ever identical, but the Maryland manual is mainstream. Among the many variables, the tutor-pupil ratio has drawn the most research attention because of its cost impacts.[37] Tutor-pupil ratios should undoubtedly vary depending on circumstances. But a red flag needs to be raised about the frequent prescription of "small group" tutoring. No term has been more misused in RTI and in Individual Education Programs (IEPs) for special education students. I have witnessed many instances in which a group of 10–15 students has been defended as being "small." To say that a group that size qualifies as tutoring is nothing less than a scam on parents and students. The research telling us that 1:5 should be the maximum tutor to student ratio reflects common sense. Not only are larger groups unwieldy for one teacher in a 30 to 45 minutes tutoring session, but a larger group of students will almost certainly vary widely in their skill levels and needs, making individualized assistance even more problematical.

Another common issue is whether the tutoring instruction should be more or less prescribed for the tutor. How much latitude should the tutor have? The issue is frequently overlooked but has been framed as whether a "problem-solving" approach or a "standard treatment protocol" should be the best way to deliver the Tier 2 and Tier 3 tutoring.[38] Problem-solving involves giving IEP teams and tutors a lot of flexibility to prescribe what they think best for each student. A standard treatment protocol is more evidence-based and off the shelf, and more closely ties the teacher's hands.

The easy answer to the question of which approach is preferable is: it depends. From there it gets more complicated. What are the student's individualized needs? How strong is the evidence behind the particular standard treatment protocol? Are we talking about tutoring in Tier 2 and/ or Tier 3? What are the teacher's qualifications?

Still, there are some basic pros and cons to each approach. Problem-solving is ideal in principle, but in practice it may add to the overload on already overburdened teachers. Does the average teacher tutor, much less volunteer tutor, have the knowledge and time to cook up individualized and research-based instructional recipes?

Some experts in tutoring would raise the ante even higher for the requisite tutoring skills. The developers of a promising tutoring model (in math) concluded "that tutoring is a task that is fundamentally different from regular classroom teaching."[39] In a fascinating article that examines the tradeoffs of problem-solving and standard treatment protocols, three scholars go even farther, calling for "expert instructors" able to fashion individualized "experimental teaching" for students who struggle the most.[40] But such "expert instructors" and "experimental teaching" seem to be beyond practical reach. We can accomplish the aims of RTI with tutoring that is a pragmatic combination of standard treatment protocols and problem-solving approaches.

With all its permutations and combinations, tutoring still has as good a Good Schoolkeeping Seal of Approval as any reform strategy in K-12 research and practice. Moreover, it is largely immune from the great plague of almost all instructional reforms: the difficulty in replicating proven or promising programs on a large scale. Tutoring, even allow-ing for all its variables, is relatively easy to put into practice. The pool of tutors—professional teachers, para-professionals and volunteers who are part-time and full-time, inside and outside of public schools, includ-ing retired teachers—seems bottomless. There is already a flourishing industry in tutors for private school students.

So, parents must be wondering, if RTI with tutoring is so great, why isn't there more of it?

WHY IS THE ENGINE OF RTI SO STUCK IN THE STATION?

Why hasn't RTI been effectively implemented on a large scale any-where? Chapter 6 on money (not enough of it to pay for the Tier 2 and Tier 3 interventions) and Chapter 7 on management (how educators don't spend cost-effectively the money they have) are primers on the two most fundamental reasons. The management shortcomings include poor teacher training and failure to employ best reading programs and practices.[41]

But there are others that are not so clear-cut. First, states, with one notable exception, are in denial about the absence of RTI. Second, there is the tendency of educators to bungle and shoot themselves in the foot in their approach to RTI.

Denial

States falsely claim to be doing RTI. Ask any state or local administrator and they say "we're doing that." To try to prove the point, they usually allude to some document or manual that spells out RTI guidance and maybe best practices. But they don't say how much of it they are doing, or how well. They don't document at what scale they are doing it, what models they are using, and any data on its effectiveness. They're bluffing.

Tennessee Is at the Top of the Class in RTI

Tennessee is an exception. It has put in more effort than any state. And best of all, it is remarkably candid about its shortcomings.

A 2018 report, "Assessing Progress, Four Years of Learnings from RTI2 Implementation in Tennessee"[42] and the manual that laid the foundation[43] should be required reading. The Tennessee Department of Education launched a statewide initiative in 2014, and made sure it was more than fanfare. It followed implementation closely, and the 2018 progress report bared the good and not-so good news.

The RTI initiative demonstrated promising results. It widely influenced practice and particularly reduced the number of students who were inappropriately referred to special education and mislabeled as disabled. Most administrators and teachers were supportive.

Yet, it fell short in many central ways. There were shortages of staff and school time to carry out the intervention process and instruction. To some teachers, the procedures in the state manual were too prescriptive and burdensome. And implementation in high schools, because of huge learning deficits and scheduling challenges, was especially questionable.

In other words, exemplary effort in Tennessee to implement RTI has so far turned out just as you might expect from the nation's first's large scale initiative. Full of holes in funding and implementation, but full of promise. It's not proof of what RTI could accomplish if done right. But the premise and promise are unmistakable. If it is begun earlier rather than later; if it is supported by more resources and better managed; and if it is part of a sustained process of ongoing improvement—it's on the right track. And other states should follow suit.

Maryland and Other States Are Flunking

Maryland is typical of states that try to fake it. I testified and lobbied for legislation in the Maryland state legislature in 2017 that sought to require local school systems to report on students who received early intervention services. In their comments on the legislation, local departments of education hemmed, hawed and hid. They alleged that they were providing a lot of such services, but statutory reporting would be too burdensome. In truth, their opposition wasn't as much that they would be overburdened if they had to report the data; it was that, having very little to no meaningful RTI, they had very little to no data to report.

The bill, as enacted, required the Maryland State Department of Education (MSDE) to issue guidelines for the local reports.[44] But the state department was no more enthusiastic than the local departments, fearing that its own negligent lack of action to support (or mandate) RTI would be exposed. MSDE's lengthy 2008 manual, "A Tiered Instructional

Approach to Support Achievement for All Students: Maryland's Response to Intervention Framework," says all the right things about how RTI should be done.[45] But it is simply exhortatory. There have been no meaningful follow-up steps like directives, professional development, dissemination of best practices and monitoring to spur implementation. The state has virtually nothing to show for it, and as of this writing, is still trying to evade its responsibilities under the legislation.

No state, except Tennessee, or local school system is doing much more than Maryland. According to a survey by the Education Commission of the States in 2014, over 30 states "require or recommend that that school districts offer some type of intervention or remediation for struggling readers for a P-3 grade. Some states require specific interventions while others let districts choose from a list of suggested interventions."[46] But the absence of data or other reports on implementation indicate that these efforts are mainly window dressing.

So don't believe the local and state school systems across the country that boast, when asked about RTI, "we're doing that." They're not. If they were, we would have heard about it. Parents would not have so many children—estimated in Chapter 3 at more than half of all students—struggling and not meeting basic standards.

Bungling

Perhaps a section on "bungling" is redundant and overkill. It may also be too much inside baseball for parents. But educators should understand and heed its lessons.

We have already established that school systems across the country are in denial about their failure to get aboard the engine of RTI. But we should also recognize that the failure sometimes goes beyond just inaction, and educators create additional obstacles for themselves. Several examples follow.

Is RTI a "Billion-Dollar Boondoggle"?

Among the bunglers are educational researchers. In early 2017, four of them co-authored a paper titled "The Concept of RTI: Billion-Dollar Boondoggle."[47] It ignited a firestorm. A counterattack by a group of 24 at least equally expert researchers, calling themselves the Consortium for Evidence-based Early Intervention, condemned the Boondoggle paper as "pages of disconnected, incoherent topics that are characterized by distortions, half-truths, and just plain falsehoods."[48]

This scholarly rumble—which smacks of a schoolyard fight among adolescents—highlights how something as seemingly straightforward as RTI can become ensnarled in education politics and false dichotomies. I come down strongly on the side of the counterattackers but that isn't the main point, as we'll see.

The Boondoggle uproar began with a November 2015 report, "Evaluation of Response to Intervention Practices for Elementary School Reading."[49] Its co-authors represented several well-known organizations, backed by a large Technical Working Group, under contract to the federal Institute of Education Sciences National Center for Education Evaluation and Regional Assistance. This academic pedigree would hardly signal a report likely to cause a big fight among researchers.

Nor did the overall findings of the study (308 pages long and methodologically dense) augur fierce controversy. The study reported that for some students, the reading interventions did not improve reading outcomes; rather they produced "negative impacts."[50] Yet, even with the reference to "negative impacts," the study overall had more caveats than clear conclusions. And it criticized its own limitations—the report "does *not* assess whether the [RTI] framework as a whole is effective in improving student outcomes."[51] (Italics in the original.)

Nonetheless, the Boondoggle authors attacked all RTI as a rip-off. They were especially outraged that RTI was "not better than other methods of identifying LD."[52] The "boondoggle" was the waste of money on RTI, including "commercially produced" intervention programs.[53]

The Consortium counterattack unleashed its own heavy rhetorical artillery. It expressed surprise at the "sensationalized title . . . and unclear, rambling, disjointed, factually incorrect, and misguided piece."[54] The Boondoggle-ists were especially off the mark, said the Consortium, in their "implicit endorsement of the use of ability achievement discrepancy models" for identification of LD, rather than RTI.[55] (I strongly agree with them. Reminder: the discrepancy model is a cardinal sin according to the teachings in Chapter 2 of this book.)

The lesson to be learned from the Boondoggle brouhaha is captured by leading RTI researcher Douglas Fuchs (who was not one of the Boondoggle authors or a member of the Consortium). He offered a wise and calming perspective as reported in Education Week: "Researchers need to know more about the differences in the quality of instruction, the types of interventions, and the progress-monitoring used in each of the schools studied. . . . More detail about RTI practices are needed . . . for school leaders to draw lessons from the study."[56]

He's right and the Boondoggle-ists are not just wrong: They squandered precious time and attention from constructive approaches to scaling up effective RTI, like those offered by Fuchs. They even bungled legitimate concerns about how school systems may misuse RTI to delay eligibility for special education.

RTI and the LD Connection

Recall that the 2004 amendments to IDEA tried to substitute RTI for the discrepancy gap as the appropriate gateway to eligibility under the classification of Specific Learning Disability (LD).[57] Though RTI is acknowledged to be far superior to the discrepancy gap, some parents fear that school systems will use RTI more to delay referrals for special education than to prevent them, thereby saving money. These savvy parents are on to a real danger.

An article by famed researcher on dyslexia Sally E. Shaywitz and a co-author is titled "Response to Intervention: Ready or Not? Or, From Wait-to-Fail to Watch-Them-Fail."[58] The Council of Parent Attorneys and Advocates expressed similar concerns.[59] In response to protests, the federal Office of Special Education Programs admitted that it has come to our attention "that, in some instances, local educational agencies (LEAs) may be using Response to Intervention (RTI) strategies to delay or deny a timely initial evaluation for children suspected of having a disability."[60] The federal Office stated that this should not be allowed to happen.

But can state and local school systems be trusted to make sure it doesn't happen? Two professors of special education published a thorough and insightful study of RTI as a pre-condition for LD eligibility. The picture they portray is not pretty. At its best "each state has developed its own set of RTI regulations . . . resulting in considerable variability in policy and practices."[61] In a separate article, the same experts elaborated on the failure of states to provide guidance, collect data and monitor fidelity and effectiveness.[62]

And so, in the hands of many school system mis-managers, the dangers of misuse of the process of RTI are real. Parents must be on guard and prepared to take action to prevent abuses. Chapter 10 spells out steps that can empower parents in such situations. The first one is for parents to get true knowledge of school system abuses. Hopefully this chapter has given parents knowledge of the dangers that school systems will in fact bungle the letter and spirit of RTI. They may not only not provide RTI but delay *proper* referrals to special education.

HOW MANY STUDENTS ARE ON THE PASSENGER WAITING LIST FOR RTI?

The scale of the number of struggling learners who need RTI interventions is an obstacle all its own. The scale is so immense that educators (and policymakers) are in danger of being paralyzed.

The children waiting in line for RTI include struggling learners in general education who have not been referred to special education, and students who have been referred and typically mislabeled as disabled. But the exact number in each category is hard to pinpoint.

For starters, it is difficult to estimate precisely the number of struggling learners who wind up in special education. Still, as mentioned in Chapter 1, it could be as many as about 85 percent of the 6.5 million students who receive special education services, about 5.5 million children in all.[63]

If that isn't astonishing and depressing enough, there are far more in general education. Let's call them stranded struggling learners: those who are not referred to special education but remain in general education, waiting for adequate RTI to fire on all cylinders.

Exact estimates of these stranded struggling learners don't exist. But a back-of-the-envelope calculation starts with a count of all students who do not meet rigorous academic standards. Using the "gold standard" National Assessment of Educational Progress (NAEP) scores for fourth and eighth grade reading and math, about two-thirds of all students in grades K to 12 are below proficiency, totaling roughly 28 million students.[64] Then subtract the approximately 6.5 million students in special education (those with and without severe disabilities). This leaves about 22 million stranded struggling learners who are being academically shortchanged, if not educationally abused, in general education. And no surprise, poor and minority students are disproportionately found in the back of the line.[65]

Still, despite the staggering numbers, the humongous queue of struggling learners is no excuse for reformers to throw up their hands in surrender. The problem is manageable—not only educationally but fiscally and politically, as we will see in later parts of the book.

But before that, the next chapter explores RTI-like "specially designed instruction" for students in special education. Yes, most of these students, almost all of them mislabeled as disabled, wouldn't need special education if they received RTI-like interventions in general education. Still, these students who are now stuck in special education and the relatively small number of students in special education who legally belong there are entitled to and can benefit greatly from RTI-like instructional and related services in special education.

....

Chapter 5

Special Education Is Not Special Enough

*Special education is not special
and it's barely education.*[1]

The system of special education nationwide is in desperate straits. It deserves all the abuse I heap on it in retaliation for all the educational abuse it heaps on so many struggling learners. And yet, as prior chapters have explained, special education is not itself the prime offender. It's overloaded with students who are mislabeled as disabled and dumped into special education because RTI is not done right in general education. Our first priority then is to keep these mislabeled students out of special education.

Still, as long as any children–wrongfully or rightly–are in special education, parents have a right to expect teaching and learning that is truly "special" education. But special education is far from that. As we now know, virtually all students in special education make little to no academic progress. They are stigmatized and segregated. They would almost always be better off if they remained in general education.

Why? Why is special education not nearly special enough? A look at what happened to Kimberly shines light on how and why special education goes astray.

KIMBERLY'S CASE

Kimberly, when I first met her and her Mom over a decade ago, was shy and really didn't want to talk about school. And no wonder. She was in the fourth grade but reading at a first grade level. She had been retained in the first grade and so was already three to four years behind where she should have been. She had been found eligible for special education in the third grade under the classification of Other Health Impediment, which for her was ADHD. But as a practical matter, the real basis for eligibility was the big discrepancy gap between her reading level and her enrolled grade level.

On her Individual Education Program (IEP) at the time, "Goals" and "Objectives" for reading phonics, fluency and comprehension stated that she "will make progress" over the one year period of the IEP. But how much progress? There was no specific indication of how much progress she would make. Six months? Nine months? Twelve months? I asked how that could be. Didn't the law require "measurable Goals"—for example, that she progress over the next school year from her first grade current performance level to say the second grade level? Without numerical Goals, how could parents hold the school accountable for any amount of progress?

Members of the school IEP team responded first that the Goals were not measurable because the central administration said they didn't have to be. About a year before, the routine practice of setting Goals calling for one year's progress over a school year had been stopped. Why? Administrators said that each student was different and Goals had to be set individually for each student. Well then, how did IEP teams go about deciding on individualized Goals? And why weren't the individualized Goals written on the IEP?

The team's answer to these questions was, trust us, we'll do the best we can. But the team also said, don't expect even one year's progress. After all, she has a disability, and look at how little progress she's made so far.

In the course of an IEP meeting that lasted five hours (and still had to be continued to another day), I particularly zeroed in on the team's reliance on her lack of prior progress. Well, I asked: couldn't Kimberly have made more progress if she had received more and better services? The team was indignant. The team chairperson said, we "love our baby,

Kimberly's a wonderful child who gives us no problem in class, and don't you think we're doing all that we can to help her? We don't appreciate that you think we're not . . . And even if we had more services to give to Kimberly, we'd have to do the same for many other children who are as far behind as she is, and that's impossible."

The message was (a) the school didn't have the staff or money to give her and other students more services; and (b) the staff were not going to bend over backward to give Kimberly special treatment just because she had an aggressive advocate. Those considerations overrode the fact that Kimberly was clearly denied her legal rights under IDEA and suffering irreparable injury.

Kimberly's meeting was par for the course then in the Baltimore public schools. There was enough illegality and absurd illogic in the Team's actions and inactions to fill a textbook on educational abuse. But that was more than a decade ago. How much has changed since then? Would Kimberly be better off today? Not much as we'll sadly see. Parents pay heed.

WHAT WOULD SPECIAL EDUCATION BE LIKE IF IT WERE TRULY SPECIAL?

Is it realistic to think that even the world's best special education services can enable Kimberly to overcome the four-year gap between her age and class grade levels and her first grade reading level?

No doubt, closing such a gap is very difficult if near-impossible. In the absence of early (very early!) RTI, the students who wind up in special education are too far behind. Remember the "Matthew effect": students who fall behind early keep falling farther and farther behind. Kimberly's achievement gap is not unusual. The deficit for struggling learners in special education is often five years or more by the time they get to middle school and high school. Many, because of their frustration at being so far below their peers, have lost their motivation and engage in problematic behaviors. As a result, special education services are usually too little, too late. So, the best thing we can do for Kimberly is to implement RTI in general education.

Nonetheless, special education need not be a total lost cause. Special education can be a whole lot more "special" than it is. Learning deficits can be closed or narrowed if specially designed instruction and related services are substantially upgraded. This means generally the Tier 2 and Tier 3 interventions, notably tutoring, that Kimberly and other struggling learners should have gotten in general education but didn't get.

This Chapter describes steps to bring about such realistic and dramatic improvements in special education. To start with, deeply engrained habits of mind and practice must be overcome. Most of all, the misbelief that students in special education are doomed to failure—the bigotry of low expectations—must be rooted out. It must be replaced by an understanding that the overwhelming majority of struggling learners in special education are capable of attaining much higher heights of academic success than they do.

How High Is Up for Students in Special Education?

Each student's IEP is supposed to contain measurable "Goals" that specify the amount of expected progress.[2] For example, let's return to Kimberly. Given that she was in the fourth grade (including having been retained once) and reading at a first grade level, where should her reading Goals for the next school year have been set? How much growth should have been expected?

Those are the questions I've posed not just to Kimberly's IEP team but to innumerable local administrators and teachers and national experts over two decades. Yet, almost without exception, they cannot or will not give parents a straight answer. They dodge and evade as Kimberly's IEP team did. Either they don't know the law or they deliberately ignore it. Answers have been all over the map but there are common threads. They say things like:

- It depends. No one can say. Each child has different abilities and disabilities. It's about the individual "I" in IEP.
- It really doesn't matter. We want the best for "our babies" and we'll do all we can to make sure they move ahead as quickly as we can, regardless of what the Goals might be.
- The student made about six months progress last year and that seems reasonable for someone with her disability.

If you didn't know from Chapter 2 that so many students were mislabeled as disabled and that their learning ability had been underestimated, these answers would seem to make common sense. But what seems intuitively right turns out to be almost wholly wrong. It ignores the fact that, if the students receive proper instruction in special education (which they should have received in general education), they have the cognitive ability to narrow or close achievement gaps.

That's what the federal Individual with Disabilities Education Act (IDEA) recognizes. The basic legal mandate goes like this: *Students in special education (who are not significantly cognitively disabled or otherwise severely disabled) are entitled to services that are reasonably calculated to enable them to meet regular state academic standards.*

Whoa. Did I really just write that students in special education should be enabled to meet the same academic standards as their non-disabled peers who aren't in special education? Yes, I did, and yes, they can.

That's not to say that the legal standard has been bright and clear from the start. Recall the history introduced in Chapter 2. The law has evolved since the first version of IDEA passed in 1975. It guaranteed students with disabilities a "free and appropriate" education. But Congress never defined how much student progress was "appropriate." And over the past forty years or so, that definitional void has led to confusion, controversy and educational abuse.

From time to time Congress tried to clarify its intent, usually with the explicit purpose of raising the bar for the meaning of "appropriate" instruction and progress. Amendments to IDEA in 2004 stated that students with disabilities must receive "specially designed instruction . . . to ensure access of the child to the general education curriculum, *so that the child can meet the education standards . . . that apply to all children.*" (italics added)[3] In other words, "appropriate" meant that students should be enabled to meet the same state academic standards as other students.

The No Child Left Behind Act of 2001 had paved the way. NCLB explicitly mandated that students with disabilities be held to the same academic standards as their non-disabled peers and be given full opportunity to meet those standards. All students in special education, except for a small number of students with the most severe disabilities, were to take the same state tests as their peers, their test scores were to be separately reported, and states and local districts were equally accountable for the performance of students with and without disabilities.[4] A manual on testing of students with disabilities under NCLB published by the Council of Chief State School Officers states that "Step 1" is "Expect Students with Disabilities to Achieve Grade-Level Academic Content Standards."[5] The relevant provisions in NCLB are essentially preserved in the successor Every Student Succeeds Act of 2015.

The federal legal standard also went hand-in-hand with the growing movement in the states beginning in the 1980s for "standards-based IEPs." As specified by the National Association of State Directors of Special Education, standards-based IEPs "contain goals aligned with, and chosen to facilitate the student's achievement of state grade-level academic standards." States vary in their approaches but standards-based IEPs point towards "goals that designate the necessary learning—the specially designed instruction—that will lead to the student's attaining the [state] standards. . . ."[6]

Surveying the legal landscape, two experts in special education and civil rights law summarized that special education instruction and other services must *"be reasonably calculated to enable the child to achieve passing marks, achieve passing scores on high-stakes exams, and advance from grade to grade, eventually meeting state and district graduation requirements."* (italics in the original)[7]

But educators didn't follow the law then and they don't follow it now. The intent of federal laws has been in lost in practice. Practice varies among states, school districts, schools, and even classrooms within the same school. Still, school systems across the country almost universally apply a low, minimalist standard for how much progress students in special education should be expected and enabled to achieve. In particular, as will be explained later in this chapter, they fail to expect and enable students to achieve basic proficiency in the foundational skills of reading, math and writing. For all practical purposes, the de facto standard has been that almost any progress is enough.

A Supreme Legal Disappointment

Parents should be scratching their heads: How do school systems get away with violating the law? In part the Supreme Court has given them cover, beginning with the landmark Supreme Court decision, *Board of Education v. Rowley*, decided in 1982.[8] That decision was the first to try to interpret the basic provisions of federal special education law and has been cited endlessly. But the Court's ruling was a source of massive uncertainty that allowed millions of students in special education to be greatly harmed.

The pivotal language in the Rowley decision was that "some benefit" was the standard for whether students received appropriate services. But "some" was expressly left undefined. The Court declined "to establish any one test for determining the adequacy of educational benefits conferred upon all children covered by [IDEA]."[9] As a result, confusion bordering on educational chaos ensued.

It would take a legal treatise to convey the multitude of hazy and conflicting post-Rowley court interpretations. Courts attempted to clarify the meaning of "some benefit" through a wide variety of would-be explanatory phrases. Among them, "equal opportunity," "significant," "meaningful" and "more than *de minimis*." But even these phrases were themselves susceptible to different interpretations. The net effect of the uncertainty was that school systems had wide leeway to set low expectations, dumb down Goals and minimize their responsibilities, which they did.

In an eagerly anticipated ruling, *Endrew F. v. Douglas County School District*, decided March 22, 2017, the Supreme Court was called upon to dispel the confusion. However, the Court, as in the Rowley decision, wasted the opportunity and missed the mark.

Chief Justice John G. Roberts Jr., writing for a unanimous Court, stated that the standard is whether the services are "reasonably calculated to enable a child to make progress appropriate in light of the child's circumstances." That, the Court reasoned, means more than *de minimis,* but how much more? The Court chose not to say. The vague language was deliberate to allow, Chief Justice Roberts explained, "deference" to the expertise and judgment of school authorities.

Some observers hailed the decision as a victory for students with disabilities. But don't believe it. Under the prior *de minimis* standard, there was almost nowhere to go but up, and the Court went up only a very little. An 8–0 vote by a Court that is usually sharply divided is a sign that the decision may lack clarity or bite.

The Endrew F. decision lacks both. The Court displayed a superficial understanding of special education in three crucial ways. One, it did not recognize that IDEA, ESSA and the standards-based movement in the states called for the great majority of students with disabilities—those without severe disabilities—to receive services that would enable them to meet regular state academic standards.

Two, it failed to take into account research showing that students without severe cognitive limitations were capable of meeting the standards if they received adequate instruction. As found by the National Center on Educational Outcomes, the leading research organization on accountability for the achievement of students with disabilities, "The vast majority of special education students (80–85 percent) can meet the same achievement standards as other students if they are given specially designed instruction, appropriate access, supports and accommodations as required [by federal law]."[10]

Three, the Court failed to comprehend the critical distinction between IEP Goals that enable students to pass their content courses like literature, science and social studies, and Goals that enable them to meet standards for *independent proficiency in the foundational skills of reading, writing and math*. This distinction befuddled the Court justices, as it has educators, and will be further discussed shortly.

Notwithstanding these errors, some advocates applauded the decision. But they viewed it almost exclusively through the lens of how it might raise the bar for services for students with the most severe disabilities. That is a welcome possibility but it is too soon to tell.

It is not too soon, however, to foresee that the decision will be of little help to the four times as many students in special education who are not severely disabled—most of whom are mislabeled as disabled. The Court decision did not preclude schools from providing services reasonably calculated to enable them to meet grade-level standards in foundational skills like reading. But it simply left them with too much room to keep doing what they are doing, which is to harbor low expectations and set low Goals for student progress.

As this book goes to press, there have been few consequential court decisions that try to interpret Endrew F. However, a leading legal expert on special education law observed in early 2018 that the decision's "net effect appears to have been close to negligible."[11]

Students deserve better, school systems could do better, and Baltimore, of all places, is attempting to show the way.

BALTIMORE'S BIG PLUS FOR STUDENTS IN SPECIAL EDUCATION

Brooks Robinson and John Unitas have pretty much faded from memory. The city of Baltimore, my hometown, has become—in the wake of the television shows Homicide and The Wire, the killing of Freddie Gray and other sad stories—a poster child for the tragedy of urban America.

The disrepute includes our schools. We are in many respects worse than urban public school systems elsewhere. The data cited in Chapter 3 shows, for example, that in Baltimore over 90% of third graders in special education are already two or more grade levels behind in reading. By fifth grade, over 60% are three or more grade levels behind, including 16% who are still at kindergarten level and 30% who are at first grade level. Still, there is one point of pride: our school system's trailblazing initiative to raise the bar for student achievement in special education.

It got underway when, as a member of the Baltimore school board in 2005, I approached our new CEO Andres Alonso about my distressing experiences as an advocate for students in IEP team meetings. At the time, an informal memorandum by Baltimore school officials tied Goals to the student's disability and IQ. For a student with a Specific Learning Disability (LD) and low average cognitive ability, the memorandum said, "The IEP team may determine that the student will be able to make 6 months' growth in a year."[12] In a discussion of the memorandum, administrators added that as few as four months progress could be a realistic expectation. In other words, *it was expected that students with LD (including students with dyslexia) would fall six to eight months further behind grade level each year.*

What was especially astounding at that time was that no one in the school system ever mentioned the possibility, much less probability, that students could achieve much better progress if they received much better instruction. No one ever factored in the inter-relationship between Goals and services. Wouldn't the amount of expected progress depend on the quality of the research-based "specially designed instruction" and related services that the student received?

It boggles the mind that educators could disregard what is so obvious. Yet, they did, for reasons that include some we've already uncovered and others discussed in the next two chapters. No matter. To Dr. Alonso and me, no excuses were acceptable. The Baltimore school system was, in violation of IDEA, either writing Goals for one year's progress but not taking them seriously, or not writing measurable Goals at all. Low expectations reigned.

Dr. Alonso, a former special education teacher and bold reformer, was the first educator I encountered, locally or nationally, who understood how the system abused children. Together he and I developed what became known as the "One Year Plus" policy.[13] It stated:

- IEPs for students who are on a diploma track (that is, who are not severely disabled) should contain Goals for at least twelve months (*one year*) academic progress in foundational skills over the twelve months covered by the IEP; and
- When there is a significant gap between the student's enrolled grade level and actual level of performance (for example, a student like Kimberly who is in 4th grade and reading at a 1st grade level, a gap of at least three years), the Goals should ordinarily express the expectation of twelve months progress *plus* a reasonable reduction in the gap (for example, 15-18 months progress); and
- Exceptions to the One Year Plus policy must be based on compelling individualized circumstances that are documented by the IEP team; and
- IEP services must be research-based and reasonably calculated to enable the student to achieve the Goals. IEPs are not a guarantee that the Goals will be met. Students differ and IEPs must be individualized. But the IEP services should reflect the professional judgment of the IEP Team that the Goals will be achieved if services are delivered as promised, and the student's circumstances—including the nature of the disability and attendance—do not change significantly.
- Parents were to receive at IEP meetings a brochure, in family-friendly language, that explained the One Year Plus policy.

Dr. Alonso and I acknowledged that even if the policy were well implemented, it would hardly be a surefire educational lifesaver. For Kimberly, it would be difficult to close the performance gap between her first grade reading level and her enrolled fourth grade level. She had fewer than two years left in elementary school, so even if the gap were narrowed by three to six months per year, she would still be at least three years behind when she entered middle school. And once any student gets to middle and high schools, narrowing the gap, much less closing it, is even more problematic because secondary schools have far less teaching capacity and teaching time for remedial instruction in foundational skills.

Still, better late than never. 15 or 18 months progress in reading over one or more school years would reverse the student's steady decline, increase the ability to understand demanding coursework in upper grades, and probably boost the student's motivation to try harder to succeed. Of course, all of this is *if* the One Year Plus policy is implemented effectively. A big *if* as we shall see. Yet there is widespread agreement that the policy has transformative potential.

The National Potential of One Year Plus

Shout-outs across the country greeted the adoption of the One Year Plus policy. Baltimore's special education plight, as bad as it is, is not substantially different than school systems across the country. And so One Year Plus was seen as a model for nationwide reform. Here's a sample of the high hopes of renowned special education experts:[14]

- "One Year Plus is right on target! Our research shows that the students under the policy CAN meet the 1 + year expectation."

  Donald Deshler, then Professor of Special Education, Director of Center for Research on Learning, University of Kansas.
- "The Baltimore City schools have an important story to tell. The One Year Plus policy should be highlighted nationally as a promising path to raising expectations and academic achievement for all students with disabilities."

  Rachel Quenemoen, then National Center and State Collaborative Project Director at the National Center on Educational Outcomes.
- "Baltimore's One Year Plus policy is a step ahead of the nation in raising and meeting expectations for students with disabilities. School systems nationwide should consider similar policy steps. Now the burden is on schools, school boards and educators of all ranks to operationalize such a policy using rigorous evidence-based instruction that will enable all students (including those who have

been identified with severe cognitive disabilities, if appropriate) to achieve One Year Plus goals and meet state standards."

Edward Kame'enui, first commissioner of the National Center for Special Education Research in the Institute of Education Sciences and then professor and director of the Center on Teaching and Learning, University of Oregon.

This acclaim helped to lay the foundation for a national stamp of approval by the U.S. Department of Education near the end of President Barack Obama's second term. A federal guidance letter dated November 15, 2015, though not explicitly mentioning the One Year Plus policy by name, adhered closely to it.[15] Then secretary of education Arne Duncan had long been on record as seeking to shift the federal role in special education from enforcement of procedural compliance to lifting student achievement. "No belief," he declared, "is more damaging in education than the misperception that children with disabilities cannot really and shouldn't be challenged to reach the same high standards as all children."[16]

The guidance letter says, "Research has demonstrated that children with disabilities who struggle in reading and mathematics can successfully learn grade-level content and make significant academic progress when appropriate instruction, services, and supports are provided."[17] To that end, "[G]oals should be sufficiently ambitious to help close the gap" between performance levels and grade levels. In the example in the guidance, a student in the sixth grade and reading at a second grade level might—dependent on individualized needs and circumstances—have a Goal of "an increase of at least 1.5 grade levels in reading fluency."[18] That is, the student should be expected to progress from say early second grade in reading fluency to mid-third grade, narrowing the gap. The guidance letter conforms closely to the letter and spirit of the One Year Plus policy.

That's the good news. The not-so-good news is that there is no reason to believe that the U.S. Department of Education under President Donald Trump and Secretary Betsy DeVos will pursue the cause. Still, some day, parents and other reformers can take advantage of the federal foothold in the guidance, as detailed in Chapter 9.

In the meantime, no state or local school district has adopted Baltimore's pioneering approach. That includes the state of Maryland which is generally reputed to be near the top of state rankings for K-12 public school systems. So far, to its credit, the Maryland State Department of Education has acknowledged the need to have a "narrowing the gap" policy, and has recently developed policy and practice guidance for local school systems.[19] But it remains to be seen whether it will take concrete actions—like dissemination of best practices and especially rigorous monitoring—to assure statewide implementation.

The situation is worse nationwide. The spark of the One Year Plus model has not caught fire. It has been snuffed out by all the forces—chiefly lack of funds to provide the additional instruction, low expectations and poorly trained teachers—that cause struggling learners to be mislabeled as disabled and dispatched to special education in the first place. Moreover, another painful truth is that Baltimore has botched the chance to be a beacon for the nation.

Baltimore's Failure to Follow Through

The Baltimore school system has done a feeble job of implementing the One Year Plus policy. The first question any parent should rightfully ask about its implementation is: Is my child really improving and narrowing the gap? What does the data on student performance show? When the answer is, Baltimore doesn't have any specific data tracking implementation of One Year Plus, the first question tends to be the last question. Interest quickly dries up.

For a while, after system-wide adoption of the One Year Plus policy in 2013, there was a modest effort to collect data. But it collapsed after initial monitoring exposed the lack of effective implementation and improvement in student achievement.

In fact, Baltimore's experience with One Year Plus has been full of disappointments. That's hard for its architects and supporters, me included, to swallow. But it's best to own up, and take stock of how Baltimore has fallen short. There have been two particularly vexing trials and tribulations that, as an alert to parents, are briefly summarized.

Misuse of "Accommodations"

The great majority of students in special education receive "accommodations" under their IEPs. As discussed in Chapter 3, accommodations are intended to fulfill the IDEA requirement that students in special education have "access" to the general education curriculum and are enabled to meet state standards. In other words, accommodations are supposed to level the playing field so students can pass courses and demonstrate their true ability on tests despite their disabilities.

Accommodations can thus be necessary and proper. But they can also be misused to inflate the student's actual progress in meeting Goals. This almost invariably occurs with the read-aloud accommodation that allows texts to be read to the student during classroom instruction and on tests.

For example, suppose Kimberly made it (without dropping out) to the 10th grade, and suppose, generously, she is by then reading at a third or fourth grade level. The read-aloud accommodation would enable her to have "access" to the materials in the general curriculum and earn passing grades in her high school literature, science, advanced mathematics and social studies courses. Without this accommodation, she would be unable to understand the textbooks and other materials and have no chance of passing.

So far, so good. But in other ways the accommodation can do serious harm. When students have materials read to them, especially in the early grades, they don't learn to read on their own. The read-aloud accommodation conceals deep deficits in their ability to read independently. Proper IEP services are delayed, shortchanged or denied altogether.

As earlier noted, I have represented many students who received the read-aloud accommodations *as early as the first or second grades.* That stunts their independent growth. When Kimberly is on her own in the world of work, she won't have someone to read to her.

Legal restrictions exist to prevent this misuse. But IEP teams are tempted to cross the line in order to pump up student achievement and overall test scores. Baltimore is no exception. The One Year Plus policy sought to get schools to strike the right balance between proper accommodations that provide access to the general curriculum and improper accommodations that mask students' lack of independent foundational skills, especially in reading. But it hasn't happened yet.

Separating Legitimate Exemptions from Illegitimate Excuses
The One Year Plus policy permits exemptions. Goals can be less than One Year Plus based on compelling individualized circumstances that are documented by the IEP Team. For example, Kimberly may be much

farther behind in reading than math so her Goals for math might be for just one year's progress. There is only so much time in the school schedule and only so much intense instruction that a student can absorb. Or Kimberly may be subject to absences for sickness beyond her control, or in the midst of what appears to be a short-term emotional problem involving her family and/or relationships with other students.

Yet, many IEP Teams persist in finding unwarranted exemptions. They think, as in Kimberly's case, that the student cannot be expected to make one year's progress, much less One Year Plus, because the student progressed far less than one year in the prior year(s). They do not take into consideration the interdependency of Goals and services: student could grow more if given more nutritious instruction.

They also claim bogus exemptions based on the student's "lack of effort" or "lack of motivation." They say, what can we do when Kimberly won't try? Of course, they overlook the likely fact that, as much research shows, what they think is Kimberly's indifference is actually fear of further failure, as explored in Chapter 2. Students are discouraged when they are so far behind peers and stigmatized as "dummies." These students figure, why not play it cool and pretend not to care, while diverting attention with disruptive behaviors?

In some instances, the off-putting motivation or behavior may be intrinsic to a valid disability. For example, brain research has shown a link between lack of motivation and attention deficit disorders.[20] Still, the fundamental purpose of IDEA is to require services that enable students to overcome common learning problems. When these services aren't provided, schools shouldn't be allowed to get away with unjustified exemptions that give schools a "Get Out of Jail" card.

To correct the illegitimate exemptions and misuse of accommodations, Baltimore has conducted frequent staff trainings, issued guidances, and for a long while convened an advisory panel of advocates and school officials to discuss ongoing concerns. Nonetheless, implementation in general and crucial monitoring in particular are still lagging badly.

THE STANDARD FOR PROGRESS AND APPLICATION OF ONE YEAR PLUS TO STUDENTS WITH THE MOST SEVERE DISABILITIES

There is one more dimension to the Baltimore experience that demands attention. Does One Year Plus apply to students with severe disabilities? The short answer is, it doesn't apply explicitly but its basic principles should.

As earlier shown, only about 15 to 20 per cent of students in special education have severe disabilities, mainly involving significant cognitive limitations like Intellectual Disability, Autism, and Multiple Disabilities. It is painfully true that sometimes the cognitive capacity of these students is underestimated. Yet as a general rule, even assuming they receive excellent instruction and other services, they cannot be expected to meet the same state standards as other students. They do not earn regular graduation diplomas but far less rigorous "certificates of completion."

Therefore, these low-incidence students do not fit exactly into the One Year Plus policy which is based on the legal premise that students who are not severely disabled should be enabled to close performance gaps and achieve regular state standards. Baltimore applied the policy only to "students who are on a diploma track (that is, who are not severely cognitively disabled)."

In retrospect, this policy choice was shortsighted. There is no reason why its underlying principles should not be adapted to raise the bar for growth of students with severe disabilities. They too can achieve at higher levels of academic achievement and other functional life skills than they do. Yet, let me as an architect of the Baltimore policy explain (not justify) why they were left out of the policy.

One reason was the fear of biting off more than the school system could chew. The One Year Policy was a giant leap. It was clear that the school system could barely manage to try to implement the policy for students who are not severely disabled, much less take on both populations at the same time. While the underlying principles for both are similar, they involve fairly distinct educational nuts and bolts.

Until lately, the process for developing Goals for students with severe disabilities has been uncharted and neglected. School systems have ignored guidance from the U.S. Department of Education that alternate assessments and standards for them must "Reflect professional judgment of the highest achievement possible."[21] That should and could change.

Vital technical assistance is available to guide schools and to hold them accountable for offering appropriate Goals and services. The National Center and State Collaborative (NCSC) has developed common alternate assessments and standards for about 25 partnering states, including Maryland. The NCSC model is described as a comprehensive system of curriculum, instruction, and assessment. Part of the process is to strengthen the body of research-based best practices for students with severe disabilities. To date, there has been meager alignment of alternative standards with growing research on how to raise performance levels, notably for students with autism and intellectual disabilities.

Another factor that went into the judgment to exclude students with severe disabilities from the One Year Plus initiative is the fact that, as noted in Chapter 1, these students—compared to students in special education who are mislabeled as disabled—are relatively well served. Which of course is not good enough.

In Baltimore the NCSC model has not yet taken hold. IEP teams are not trained in the research on best practices and cling to outdated low expectations. And as always, they are handcuffed by pressure to keep down costs. Reform is overdue.

. . . .

Up to now, we have seen how—through RTI and the principles of One Year Plus–struggling learners can be enabled to succeed in general education and benefit more in special education. We can end educational abuse. We desperately want to do it and know how to do it, but we're not doing it. Why not? The next part of the book answers that question. We look at the causes of inaction and who's to blame.

PART III

....

WHO'S TO BLAME?

We know what to do to end the educational abuse of struggling learners. It has more to do with general education than special education. And it ain't rocket science. Topping the list of essential reforms is early identification and intervention for struggling learners through the RTI framework.

Yes, this will cost more money. But just more money isn't enough either. The money must be spent on evidence-based best practices and must be more efficiently managed.

Yet, our nation does none of this. Which is surprising since, even in the super-politicized era of Donald Trump, the American people express a common desire to see public schools dramatically improved. Most of us are even willing to pay more taxes if necessary.[1] Nonetheless, reform of general education and reform of special education are at best treading water, while millions of children, particularly poor children of color, are drowning academically.

Where do we turn for reform? One place to start is to identify those who dug the deep hole in which K-12 public schools are mired. Who's to blame?

This part of the book lines up the usual and some unusual suspects in two large groupings: "Us" and "Educators." Us includes policymakers and the general public who don't do enough to support Educators and therefore aid and abet the abuse.

But Us/we aren't the only culprits. Educators are complicit too. Do I mean to wrap all educators in a blanket accusation? No. Am I talking about the able, caring, hardworking and underpaid teachers in our schools? Absolutely not. The wrongdoers, let me underscore emphatically, are not frontline teachers and other school-based staff.

Rather, as I have tried to make clear throughout the book, the Educators who stand charged are, first and foremost, those I term the "education establishment." They are officials in the upper ranks of federal, state and local departments of education, teachers colleges, national associations of education professionals, and, though less culpable in my view, teachers unions. They, directly and indirectly, set the tone and call the shots for K-12 school policy. They are primarily responsible for how schools are managed and mismanaged. In sum, education establishment major-domos betray the rank and file. And the profession as a whole is victimized.

To be sure, the realities of public school policy and politics make it hard to isolate the wrongs that Us do to Educators and what Educators do to themselves. That's apparent when we line up the usual and unusual suspects under the sub-groupings of Money and Management. Money is mainly the fault of Us. We don't provide Educators with enough of it, while Management—rampant mismanagement really—is the fault of Educators. Educators don't convince Us that they spend the money at hand as wisely and efficiently as they should. Would Us put up more money if we had more confidence that Educators would better spend it? Would Educators spend it better if they had more money up front for state-of-the-art management capacity?

The next two chapters try to unscramble this chicken-and-egg who's-to-blame omelet. Chapter 6 focuses on Us and our collective failure to provide educators with adequate resources and support. Chapter 7 focuses on Educators and particularly their management failures.

Chapter 6

....

Show Teachers the Money

What if the Defense Department had to hold
a bake sale to make ends meet?[1]

Is there any public school parent anywhere in the U.S. who hasn't been called on repeatedly to raise or put up money for their child's school? PTAs (parent-teacher associations) in all communities sell Girl Scout cookies and have bake sales, raffles, car washes and auctions. The money isn't for frills but for classroom supplies and other everyday essentials that are lacking, even after teachers have famously dug into their own pockets. According to a recent study, 94 percent of public school teachers spend an average of nearly $500 per year of their own money for such regular school items.[2]

And that's not all. In wealthier communities, parents have been known to contribute lots of money for big-ticket items like after-school programs and school security. I don't blame them. But as a practical matter, the ability of upper income parents to add a significant amount of private money to a school budget creates further disparities between poorer and wealthier school communities. Also, these better-off parents are less likely to politically crusade for more funding for all schools.

These local begathons are the tip of the iceberg of the underfunding of K-12 public schools across our country. You may remember Cuba Gooding, Jr., the pro football character in the movie Jerry Maguire, bellowing to his agent played by Tom Cruise, "Show me the money." That's what teachers should be screaming at Us. More than anything else, we as a nation can do our part to end the educational abuse of struggling learners by providing adequate funding. Money isn't all that matters, but by the great weight of evidence and common sense, it matters a lot. It matters particularly if focused on early interventions for struggling learners through the framework of RTI.

This chapter also addresses what Us can do to hold Educators more accountable for spending the money wisely. Educators need to do a whole lot on their own to improve management (see Chapter 7), but we can make their job easier and more efficient if we streamline K-12 governance. Educators have a right to clearer policy guidance and oversight than our fragmented governance of public schools—a mix and muddle of federal, state and local authority—allows. We also need a truce in the ideological education wars that divert attention from classroom instruction and over-politicize the process of reform.

HOW MUCH MONEY IS ENOUGH?

Parents don't mince words. Lack of funding is their biggest complaint about public schools. Yet, no subject in the annals of school reform and education warfare has produced as much bitter controversy. How much does money really matter in affording all students equal opportunity to be prepared for college and careers, including students who struggle to learn how to read, compute and write? Do school systems, if they were more efficiently managed, have enough money already to pay for RTI and other essentials, such as higher teacher salaries?

There is no dispute that wide disparities exist between funding for schools in low-wealth districts in big cities, rural areas and some declining suburbs, and high-wealth districts in still-affluent suburbs.[3] In these schools, it's not just the absence of enough money for RTI in general education and IEP services in special education. Across the board in poor districts, class sizes are too large, teachers are less experienced and trained, facilities are decrepit, student support services are missing, school safety is compromised, and so on. Liberals claim that these "savage inequalities" (in Jonathan Kozol's famous words[4]), rooted in economic and racial class inequality, are the main reason for achievement gaps.

Conservatives respond that other factors are more important. Since the 1960s, they say, education spending has more than doubled after adjusting for inflation, but student performance is still dismal. They cite the argument, going back to the famous Coleman Report in 1966,[5] that school resources don't matter nearly as much as the socio-economic status of parents. They trumpet research that purports to show that dollars spent on specific school initiatives from smaller class sizes to higher teacher salaries don't pay off in improved academic achievement. In any event, they argue, there's plenty of money to go around if bureaucratic waste were reduced, if teachers unions stopped hogging all the revenues for excessive salaries and benefits, and if privatization ruled the policy roost.

Liberals counter with their own research that they say shows significant student gains from budget investments in such areas as class size, teacher incentives, early childhood education, tutoring and summer school. And for nearly 50 years, they have instigated a flood of lawsuits to try to force states to provide "equal opportunity" funding for such programs.

In 1973 the U.S. Supreme Court in a 5–4 decision held that the U.S. Constitution did not require states to remedy huge disparities in funding between high- and low-wealth school districts.[6] Since then, there has been similar litigation in almost every state alleging violations of state constitutions. Initially the suits sought "equity" or equal spending, but the concept of "adequacy" soon took hold. Adequacy asserts that low-income and other at-risk students, because of their learning deficits and other family and neighborhood disadvantages, require more-than-equal spending if they are to meet academic standards.

The principle of adequacy has become well established law.[7] In a majority of the cases, challenges to existing state funding systems have prevailed. Nevertheless, judicial and legislative remedies have been slow to materialize. In some cases, the litigation has dragged on for decades. The disparities in funding persist, from $18,165 per pupil in New York to $5,838 in Utah, when adjusted for regional cost differences.[8] About half the states provide more state and local funding to students *not* in poverty. Twenty-one states provide less funding to school districts with higher concentrations of low-income students.[9] As a result, according to an incisive recent analysis, the movement may be evolving in new directions,[10] including the constitutional "right to literacy" legal actions discussed in Chapter 9.

All the while, conclusive evidence on how much money matters remains a contentious work in progress. Emerging research tends to show that money matters under some circumstances. A New York Times article in 2016 was headlined, "It Turns Out Spending More Probably Does Improve Education."[11] Hardly a ringing endorsement. But there is probably more agreement than popularly realized. Here's how it is framed by Eric A. Hanushak, who for several decades has been the go-to scholar and spokesperson for conservative views on school funding.

> Of course, it is always important to recognize that none of this dis-cussion suggests that money never matters. Or that money cannot matter. It just says that the outcomes observed over the past half century—no matter how massaged—do not suggest that just throw-ing money at schools is likely to be a policy that solves the significant U.S. schooling problems seen in the levels and distribution of out-comes. We really cannot get around the necessity of focusing on how money is spent on schools.[12]

Fair enough. Liberals like me should admit that our efforts to increase school funding have paid too little attention to how the money is spent. Which brings us to Maryland's current attempts to chart a fairly unique course to both define adequacy and assure that the money is well spent, including expenditures that can end the educational abuse of struggling learners.

WHAT IS MARYLAND TRYING TO TEACH THE NATION ABOUT TRUE "ADEQUACY" FOR RTI?

By happy coincidence, my immersion in this book came at about the same time as I was appointed to the Maryland commission charged with recommending major reforms in K-12 policy and funding. The commis-sion, formally known as the Commission on Innovation and Excellence in Education (widely referred to as the Kirwan Commission, after its chair Brit Kirwan, former chancellor of the University System of Maryland), was created by legislation enacted by the Maryland legislature and signed by the governor in 2016.

Its charge was to update the work of an earlier commission whose report in 2002 led to legislation that vaulted Maryland to at or near the top of the national class in school funding. That legislation called for its funding formulas to be reviewed in about 10 years (which would have been 2012). But state officials didn't get around to it until 2016. Although the adequacy of school funding had dropped precipitously, elected officials were anxious to avoid as long as possible any consideration of raising taxes or otherwise coming up with revenues to restore or increase the 2002 formulas.

When the Kirwan Commission was established, the Maryland legislature was heavily Democratic, the governor was Republican, and the membership of the Commission was bi-partisan. The 25 members would also generally qualify as "blue ribbon." They included four ranking members from each of the Maryland House and Senate, the State Superintendent of Schools, one member of the State Board of Education, the governor's budget secretary, the current chancellor of the University System of Maryland, and representatives of various constituencies including teachers unions, local school boards, and parent advocates.

I was the member of the public appointed by the House Speaker. My reputation as a school reform practitioner and advocate paved the way (but it didn't hurt that my daughter-in-law is an elected House delegate). And my special mission, no surprise, was to focus on special education and other policies that would end the educational abuse of struggling learners and prevent students from being mislabeled as disabled.

The Course of the Kirwan Commission:
RTI Adequacy and Accountability

There have been as many studies in the various states to define and cost out adequacy as there have been lawsuits. A blizzard of them in fact, though the studies, whether under the auspices of elected officials, commissions, or judges, have employed relatively similar processes. Mainly they have relied upon a small band of consultants who specialize in adequacy studies and use similar methodologies.

The Kirwan Commission, however, departed in several respects. Initially, the state legislature hired a principal consultant whose study was essentially completed before the Commission was underway. That was a mistake. Over the two years before the Commission convened, the consultant wrote numerous reports and accompanying documents that numbered well over 1000 pages. The Commission members had no chance to interact or influence the study, and that delayed the Commission's work. But, fortunately, that was a small misstep.

Of far more importance, the Commission has sought to take a great leap forward in the field of adequacy policymaking. As this book goes to press in October 2018, the Commission has been striving for nearly two years to break fresh ground. First, to raise the bar for what constitutes "adequacy." Second, to erect a twin edifice of "accountability." Our chairperson Brit Kirwan has repeatedly exhorted us to make Maryland a beacon for the U.S. and among the best school systems in the world.[13]

In its Preliminary Report in January 2018, the Commission made breath-taking recommendations: for early childhood programs including pre-kindergarten for four and three year olds and other family supports; greatly elevated requirements for teacher preparation while expanding career ladders and substantially raising salaries; world-class college and career readiness standards and innovative and comprehensive students pathways, including career and technical education; and more resources for students at risk, including all struggling learners.

The latter is where RTI and a whole new ballgame for special education come in.

Adequacy for RTI

The consultants to the Kirwan Commission recognized the importance of RTI with tutoring as its essential element. It recited some of the research to this effect. Yet, its specific recommendations fell far short of any reasonable estimate of the *adequate* tutoring that would enable struggling learners to achieve proficiency in foundational literacy and math. The consultants were simply doing business as usual; no state had ever attempted a full and fine-grained estimate of adequate RTI costs.

At my suggestion, Robert Slavin—arguably the nation's pre-eminent expert on RTI and tutoring as we learned in Chapter 4—was invited to take a stab at it. His presentation to the Commission approximated in persuasive detail the tutoring variables and their costs: the number of students below proficiency in literacy; how far below proficiency they were; and the intensity of the tutoring that would be needed, including tutor/student ratios, years of tutoring anticipated, and days per week and minutes per day of the tutoring in RTI Tiers 2 and 3. These estimates were gleaned from specifically identified evidence-based tutoring programs.[14]

Dr. Slavin's rationale for the tutoring that would be required went unchallenged. But with 60 percent of all Maryland students performing below proficiency and therefore in need of some dose of tutoring, the cost estimates—how should I say this?—freaked out the Commission. Still, Dr. Slavin and I pointed out that the enormous immediate need and costs would be greatly reduced over the years as the tutoring took hold. The tutoring would be less intense as deficits closed, some students would no longer need any tutoring, and best of all, special education referrals and services would significantly decrease over time. The Commission's final recommendations are yet to be determined, but it can be safely said that there is now a new national model for costing out adequate RTI and tutoring services for struggling learners.

It is also likely that the Commission will raise the national bar for accountability for effective spending of funds for RTI-related programs. For all my liberal desire to spend more money for K-12 education in general and RTI in particular, no one on the Commission spoke out more insistently than I did for more accountability for how the money is spent. As explored in the next chapter on management of classroom instruction for struggling learners, there must be unprecedented capacity for evaluation of implementation within an ongoing system of robust R & D (Research and Development).

As I write this, the fate of my proposals and all the Commission's ambitious recommendations are up in the air. Our final report is not due until the end of December 2018 (after this book had gone to press), and even then, the Commission's recommendations are purely advisory. The legislature and governor must act on the report, and that is likely to involve a tsunami of politically charged factors: the sweeping program recommendations; the huge price tag; how to raise the revenue and allocate shares of the cost to state and local governments; and, perhaps the stealthiest issue of all, division of authority between state and local educators over policy and practice (i.e., "local control").

It's impossible to predict how it will all end. But the implications for RTI and special education in Maryland and the nation could be monumental. Hopefully, Us—in this instance parents, advocacy groups and the general public in Maryland—will mobilize to persuade and pressure our elected officials to seize the moment. No state is more poised to lead a national campaign for school reform that ends the educational abuse of struggling learners than Maryland. We are at or near the top in state wealth. And we are one of the bluest of politically liberal states. So we should be headed in the right (ok, the left) direction.

Still, suppose Maryland fulfills its potential and does its duty. Suppose Maryland raises its per pupil spending by a whopping amount. Where does that leave the children in the 40 or so states that are already spending less than Maryland? How and when will they have the money to pay for RTI for their educationally abused schoolchildren?

A Federal Guarantee of Adequate School Funding

Even apart from rock-bottom states like Texas and Mississippi, states like California and Colorado spend about $4000 per child (roughly $100,000 per classroom) less than Maryland.[15] These disparities are far more than differences in regional costs of living.

Are the kids in the lesser-spending states just out of luck? Should each child's ability to learn to read depend on which state or school district she/he lives in? It takes someone pretty hardheaded and hardhearted to say, well tough luck. That's just the way public schools are run (and run down) in our country.

That the system works this way is another count in the national indictment of educational abuse. There is no rational reason why states should vary so dramatically in the educational opportunity afforded their schoolchildren. This book's Chapter 8 describes the folly of state and local control of some basic elements of K-12 schooling. For example, how does it make sense that most of the 50 states and about 15,000 school districts have different standards for English, math, science, and social studies and different tests that measure proficiency in those subjects? And with specific reference to the educational abuse of struggling learners, why should there be vast differences in the amounts spent per child on RTI and special education based solely on where a child lives, bearing in mind that where a child lives and attends school is closely correlated with economic and racial class?

The answers to these questions are self-evident. And so is the fact that there is no rational reason why adequate school funding should not be realized nationwide for all struggling learners. As a condition of federal aid, Congress could require states to fund adequate education on a wealth-equalized basis. That is, the amount of federal aid would be based on equal tax effort by the states, taking into account their relative taxable wealth.

With so many of our students ill-prepared for higher education, the workforce and civic participation, we are, in the title of the famous 1983 report on the state of our public schools, "A Nation at Risk."[16] We're more at risk now than ever. As a *nation*! And so there must be national action to address the failure of state and local governments and school systems.

A federal guarantee of adequacy is not as far-fetched as you may think. Polls, time after time, year after year, show that taxpayers will pay for higher school spending if they think the money will be well spent. And it can be accomplished without forcing state and local school systems to relinquish major control, as shortly discussed. Sooner rather than later—aided by the political strategies outlined in Part IV of this book—we may as a nation come to our senses and truly guarantee equal educational opportunity for all our children.

Still, more money is not all that Us/we owe our schools. There are two other insufficiently understood ways in which we impede school reforms including RTI. One is micro-management, the other is the "disability of ideology."

MICRO-MANAGEMENT BY US

The next chapter of this book zeroes in on how Educators are a major cause of their own problems. The overarching charge is, as the chapter is titled, "Mismanagement of classroom instruction." So how do I reconcile Educators' responsibility for mismanagement with micro-management by Us?

Not easily in the mad, mad world of K-12 politics and practice. But, in essence, we make it harder for them to be better managers and harder for Us to hold them accountable. First of all, we subject school systems to a maze of incoherent and constantly changing federal, state and local regulations. I wrote a few years ago:

One underlying reason education reform isn't cooking is because there are too many cooks in the school cafeteria. Who is in charge of K-12 public schooling anyway? The local school board or mayor? The 50 governors and state departments of education? The president, the Congress and the U.S. Department of Education? It's all the above, which means no one. The buck is passed among educators and elected officials at all levels, and the public doesn't know who, if anyone, to hold accountable.[17]

We must clarify and simplify this balkanization of educational governance. High-performing school systems around the world do it a lot differently than the U.S. All have, in effect, national ministries of education that have overall authority.[18]

Let's strike a proper balance. To that end, I have proposed what I call a "New Education Federalism" in which the federal government sets standards for *what* educational opportunity every child is entitled to, while state and local governments retain wide autonomy in *how* the standards are met. State and local officials can decide—based on the spectrum of evidence-based best practices like RTI—how students are taught, teachers are selected and trained, and how school dollars are spent.[19]

Within the framework of this New Education Federalism, I would abolish school boards. This would be another step toward reducing the micro-management of Educators though the proposal steps on the toes of diehard localists. I proposed this even when I was a member of the Baltimore school board. For sure, school boards are a hot-button topic, and only a little time can be devoted to them it in these pages. But let me recount briefly two of my personal encounters with the issue.

One was when I applied to be a member of the Baltimore board in the early 2000s. At that time, members were jointly appointed by the governor and Baltimore mayor. The governor, an ardent Republican, wanted me to shake things up while the mayor, an ardent and liberal Democrat, didn't. That seemed strange since I was unmistakably on the progressive-left. But the mayor opposed me because the city schools CEO (superintendent), who was well respected and liked, threatened to resign, fearing that, as an outspoken advocate for school reform, I would micro-manage school administration.

On my third application for appointment, the mayor relented and I was appointed. And you know what? The then CEO's fear was well-founded.

I was a leader in the board's decision to conduct a national search for someone who would be bold and outside the mainstream of superintendents. We were lucky to find such a person (recall how he and I later teamed up to develop the Baltimore One Year Plus policy).

And that led to my second personal encounter with micro-management by school boards. The CEO we hired was so smart and assertive that in the contract he negotiated, he insisted on what became known as "the Buzzy clause." Buzzy is my nickname. And the clause explicitly prohibited micro-management by board members.

In fact, both the old CEO and new CEO were right in that respect. Board members should hire and fire superintendents, set basic policy, and conduct oversight. They should not second guess and interfere with policy operations. But they almost universally do.

Fiery debate over school boards is usually over whether members should be elected or appointed. To which I say, the only thing worse than an appointed board is an elected one. Both kinds should be abolished. True, giving sole power to mayors or county executives to hire and fire superintendents involves "politics." But aren't board appointees politically chosen, with elected boards raising the political heat to an even greater boil?

Many localists—liberals and conservatives alike—are horrified over the potential diminution of "community control." But there is no evidence that even John and Jane Q Citizen parents, as passionate board members, add enough value to offset the disadvantages. The business of K-12 schooling is simply too complicated for very part-time volunteer policy-makers. The problem is even more acute in school districts with large poor and minority populations, where community involvement is weak despite the best engagement efforts. Not only do school boards do little good; they do actual damage by decreasing the accountability of mayors and county executives, and frequently inserting excess politics into school decision-making. No governance method way is foolproof, but we would do educators and schoolchildren a favor, on balance, by residing authority and accountability in one elected official.

To double down on my heresy, I have come around to the conclusion that for similar reasons, state boards of education should also be abolished. The Kirwan Commission's quest to hold the state department of education more accountable for how money is spent would be enhanced if a state board did not stand in the way of clear executive authority and accountability. Let the governor appoint the state superintendent with legislative advice and consent and directly take the heat for the educational abuse of struggling learners.

THE "DISABILITY OF IDEOLOGY," AND COLLATERAL DAMAGE FROM THE EDUCATION WARS

One more way in which Us/we overstep boundaries and make school life more difficult for Educators is the ideological and political polarization of education policy-making. Those words—the ideological and political polarization of education policymaking—are a mouthful. But their meaning is plain. The "education wars" that have plagued school reform forever have been waged mostly by ideological combatants.

That's as obvious today as it has ever been. At present liberals favor more money, support teachers unions, waffle on charter schools, and tend to oppose strong accountability measures. Shame on us: liberals fought and gained some (though not enough) federal funding for low-income students and students with disabilities in the 1960s and 1970s; yet, we never followed up to see whether the funds were being well spent. Conservatives had a field day, with some justification, complaining that the money was not being well spent and achieving the intended results.

Conservatives, now a political majority in the federal and most state governments, argue even more fervently that more money isn't needed. They are hellbent on busting teachers unions and privatizing public schools through charter schools, vouchers, tax credits and other aid to private schools.

Add to this, believe it or not, the "reading wars" that are still being waged despite research that should have led to a peace treaty many years ago. Whole language partisans—predominantly education "progressives"—are still fighting rearguard actions against the science of reading instruction.

Lost in the fog of these wars is middle ground. Most of all, we must pay strict attention to and support improvements in classroom instruction. My previous book was called *It's the Classroom, Stupid,* and in it I echoed the sentiment of Charles M. Payne, a distinguished professor at the University of Chicago. "A Curse on Both Their Houses" is the title of his superb analysis of the failure of school reform. Reform suffers, he writes, from the "disability of ideology and the way it distorts" policy discussion.[20] Preeminent education historian David Tyack observes that the education wars have long "resembled the battles of the old Chinese warlords, who assembled their armies, hurled insults at each other, and then departed, leaving the landscape as it was."[21]

The "disability of ideology" should be trashed along with the bogus disabilities of students who are mislabeled as disabled and educationally abused. Us/we will be doing Educators and parents a great favor if we do.

· · · · · · · · · ·

From this self-censure of Us for our failing report card on money, micromanagement, and ideological interference, we turn to Educators and how they are sometimes their own worst enemies.

Chapter 7

....

Mismanagement of Classroom Instruction

Everyone has a plan for education reform, except educators.[1]

When I was a member of the Baltimore school board, the then new Baltimore schools CEO recruited a highly sought person to head the central office on "curriculum and instruction." That person encountered bureaucratic obstacles from day one. She was stymied trying to hire central staff though funding was in the budget. Regional superintendents ignored or evaded her efforts to require instructional best practices. Communication up and down the chain of command was hit or miss. Bear in mind, she was the instructional commander; you can imagine how the instructional rank and file are left to fend for themselves (whether they want assistance or not).

Chapter 6 laid out how we have failed to get behind our K-12 educators. They don't get the supports that could make RTI a reality and end the nightmare of students mislabeled as disabled. But if we have let down them, they have let down "Us." This chapter exposes the self-inflicted damage done by their own mismanagement. It should compel school systems to own up to their share of culpability for the educational abuse of struggling learners.

Unfortunately, this mismanagement is misunderstood, though parents are aware of how school system bureaucracies bungle everyday operations. Hardly a day goes by without media accounts of budget errors and overspending, data systems that run amuck, school buses that run late, personnel papers that are lost, heating and air-conditioning systems that malfunction, textbooks that are misplaced, and you name it. But as bad as all that is, there is another kind of mismanagement that is a more potent and insidious cause of the learning failures of schoolchildren.

That cause is mismanagement of classroom instruction itself. RTI programs, in their infancy, are smothered in the crib. School officials fail to provide teachers with sound curricula, training, classroom coaching, lesson plans, and supervisory feedback and assistance. Teachers who quit teaching cite inadequate support in the classroom more than pay or hard work as their main reason for leaving.

This mismanagement has complex, tangled roots. This chapter looks first at the absence of and resistance to management norms. Educators embody a culture of professional autonomy that resists accountability. This sounds clunky and abstract. But it seeps insidiously into every-day classroom teaching. As a result, educators are slow to identify and acknowledge their own shortcomings. Many educators complain bit-terly that accountability laws like the No Child Left Behind Act and its watered-down successor the Every Student Succeeds Act interfere with their professional expertise. Yet, they fail to realize that such "external" regulation has been imposed on them because they have been so lax in holding themselves accountable, particularly for the low performance of struggling learners who are disproportionately poor and minority.

The resistance to management norms is compounded by the feeble training and support received by classroom teachers. The missing sup-port includes lack of on-the-job coaching and research-based teaching tools. Teacher toolboxes do not contain anywhere near the research-based materials that would enable more student achievement and more teacher satisfaction. Teachers are often saddled with unrealistic expec-tations of the curricula they are supposed to cover, and the differenti-ated instruction they are supposed to give. They are overloaded with paperwork, most notoriously in special education. And while it is cus-tomary to blame the paperwork overload on federal requirements, it is far more self-imposed, unnecessary and time-wasting than it need be. All the while, teachers receive few supervisory supports, such as knowl-edgeable classroom coaching and observations. Moreover, personnel evaluations are tainted by tolerance for unsatisfactory performance. Collegial lenience is as much a factor in the survival of unsatisfactory teachers and administrators as union contracts are.

Before further detailing these management deficiencies, let's note the possibility that this mismanagement is so little known and understood because, in the big scheme of things, it's no big deal. Doesn't its impact pale in comparison to other more familiar causes of the failure of public schools? Like money and family poverty for which, as explored in Chapter 6, Us/we bear the blame.

Yes, they are major factors but so are the self-imposed management failures of the education establishment. The mismanagement alone adds up to a powerful indictment of the profession. Leon Botstein, a university president and acute critic of public schools, beat me to the punch in characterizing the system's failures as criminal. In an interview several years ago, after lamenting that our public schools are "broken," and after chastising elected officials, he stated that "the education establishment is routinely committing a kind of crime."[2]

Botstein also put his finger on a crucial distinction in identifying the main perpetrators. It is the same point I have tried to emphasize throughout this book: The main wrongdoers aren't frontline teachers and school administrators. They, along with students, are also victims of the "system." Rather, it is the "education establishment" that is primarily responsible for the "system." The guilty establishmentarians, as defined earlier, include officials in the upper ranks of federal, state and local school systems, teachers colleges, national associations of education professionals, foundations and think tanks.

Against this backdrop, we turn now to the particulars of the mismanagement of classroom instruction, and how it does so much harm to struggling learners, especially students who are mislabeled as disabled.

ABSENCE OF AND RESISTANCE TO MANAGEMENT NORMS

The education establishment is not inclined by professional training, disposition or culture to adhere to management practices that are the norm in business and other professional spheres. Ok, there's Dilbert and bureaucratic inanities in corporate workplaces. But when it comes to mismanagement follies, public school systems may be in a class by themselves. For one thing, educators fail to set accountability standards for their own performance.

Failure to Hold Themselves Accountable

The education profession is quick to complain that political officials interfere and second-guess their professional expertise. The backlash against the late No Child Left Behind Act of 2001 (NCLB), with its requirements for holding schools accountable for the failure of struggling learners, is a prime example. Opponents of NCLB raged: Who were the feds to tell local schools and classroom teachers what to teach and how to teach it and impose sanctions if students didn't make substantial annual gains in performance?

In fact, NCLB didn't do most of what it was condemned for doing. It actually allowed states to set their own academic standards, tests and sanctions. Nonetheless, states were fearful of *any* strict accountability, no matter who imposed it. And so they threw up a cloud of smoke. They set up federal officials as the bad guys. And they responded with a "race to the bottom" in which their own accountability measures were deflated and students test scores were inflated.

Lost in the din of battle was the bipartisan justification for NCLB, enacted under Republican president George W. Bush. Before then, parents and policymakers were in the dark about how well (not well at all, actually) students were learning. Left to their own devices, states and local school districts had done little to hold themselves accountable for the dismal academic performance of students. Congressional legislators on both sides of the aisle saw that our nation's economic competitiveness was endangered, and our children, especially poor and minority children, were fated to bleak futures. NCLB sought to overturn this state and local inaction and injustice. NCLB would not have been enacted if the education establishment had been proactive in taking strong reform steps on its own.

For sure, NCLB had some inept provisions. Still, the law could have been mended not ended. Instead, bowing to fierce pressure from educators, who also stoked up parental opposition, the Congress and President Obama capitulated. The successor law, the Every Student Succeeds Act (ESSA) passed in 2015, grants states virtual autonomy over accountability.

A Wall Street Journal editorial heralded ESSA as "the greatest devolution of power back to the states in education in 25 years."[3]

The education establishment's victory, in the wake of the downfall of NCLB, is a loss for struggling learners including students mislabeled as disabled. Lower academic standards and weaker tests are probable in many, if not most, states. There will be much less pressure on schools to invigorate RTI and other reforms. In mid-2017, an education reporter for the Washington Post concluded, "Two years after Congress scrapped federal formulas for fixing troubled schools, states for the most part are producing only the vaguest of plans to address persistent education failure."[4] A recent study claimed that states, "by and large" were making their accountability systems "clearer and fairer," but don't bet that states will in fact carry out meaningful action to significantly improve achievement.[5]

My skepticism about counting on the states is a good transition into a discussion of the general spinelessness of state departments of education.

The Spinelessness of State Departments of Education

State departments of education should and could be forcing evidence-based RTI programs and practices on local school districts. But that isn't the way the "system" works. In 2007 the liberal think tank Center for American Progress and the conservative U.S. Chamber of Commerce found common cause in a state-by-state report card on the role of state education agencies. The report's "unambiguous" bottom line was that "states need to do a far better job of monitoring and delivering quality schools;" states tended to "systematically paint a much rosier picture of how their schools are doing than is actually the case."[6]

That's still the pattern though there are exceptions. Some states try harder and do better than others. Yet, as a whole, the track record of state departments of education is dismal. So much so that they deserve to be singled out for their part in the education establishment's lax self-regulation and resistance to accountability. In our federal system of government, states have primary authority over public schooling.

Their institutional spinelessness starts with abject surrender to the professional culture, described in detail below that rejects management norms. That's their fault, though in fairness, there is a mitigating factor that is the fault of Us. We tend to put state departments of education between a rock (the feds) and a hard place (local school systems) when they try to impose accountability. Our nation has a fixation on "local control" of public schools. State educators, even if they have the management will to act tough, are under intense political pressure to allow local education agencies to do their own thing. This resistance even impedes efforts to require local school districts to use evidence-based instructional best practices within a framework of RTI, or to monitor whether instructional practices, best or otherwise, are being effectively implemented.

To bring this close to home, the Maryland department of education is not one of the worst offenders, but it has been virtually missing in action on management accountability for RTI and tutoring for struggling learners. As alluded to in Chapter 6, in the discussion of the work of the Kirwan Commission on which I serve, it must dramatically step up its management game. Otherwise, as history teaches us, funding for RTI and tutoring will not be spent as effectively and efficiently as it should. Maryland education officials must disseminate standards and best program models for evidence-based tutoring, monitor implementation, and assure robust ongoing R & D.

That doesn't mean that the state departments of education have to carry out all these functions internally. Given the inherent limits of politically-charged and management-challenged bureaucracies like education departments, I have proposed that much of the accountability work be contracted out to outside entities that are likely to have greater expertise, capacity and independence. It won't, however, be easy to bring this about since state officials are disposed to want to cover their flanks and protect their turf.

The Culture of Professional Antipathy toward Management Norms

Not so long ago, I was a member of a task force mainly composed of a local school district's high-level managers. Its assignment was to develop a priority plan for comprehensive RTI, and certain planning tasks were laid out. At which point, the task force chairperson asked which school system staff wanted to volunteer for which of the tasks. Was the chairperson kidding, or did he really believe that asking for volunteers was the most efficient way to get the job done? Were key tasks to be assigned to those who felt like doing them, as opposed to those who were deemed most able to do them? Can you imagine such a catch-as-catch-can scenario unfolding in the corporate world?

This is a small but not atypical example of how educators resist management norms. It illustrates the tendency of educators to form collegial rather than hierarchical relationships. And there are many other examples of how basic elements of management 101—such as structured planning, decision-making and accountability—are at odds with the temperament of many who enter the teaching profession. Even allowing for the risk of overgeneralization, it is safe to say that affinity for management norms is not part of the profession's DNA. As one scholar on how teachers think and work put it, "the motives, values, and aspirations of those entering the teaching occupation differ dramatically from those entering many other occupations."[7]

Altruism—the desire to help children—is educators' main motivation, not personal power or financial profit. Nor do they like to be put in positions where they have to make decisions for which they are individually accountable. As noted above, collegial not hierarchical staff work is vastly preferred. To be sure, broad staff participation in and ownership of decision-making can be invaluable, but not if carried to the extreme in which an endless procession of committees, work groups and task forces avoid hard choices and gravitate toward the least common denominator. In a book *Inside Teaching: How Classroom Life Undermines Reform*, the expert author wrote about the "The Mysterious Gap Between Reform Ideals and Everyday Teaching."[8] The gap is attributable in part to the predisposition of teachers to avoid management practices that are commonplace in other professions.

There are exceptions of course. Good teachers sometimes make good school managers. But some of the best teachers and principals shy away from opportunities to move up the administrative ladder intro central positions, even though the mission of those positions is to support teachers in the classroom. If the best teachers don't step up, who will? I have often urged outstanding teachers or principals to move up to central management; I argue that there they can do more good for more students.

Yet, many resist for a variety of motives. They may realize they are temperamentally unfit or just can't bear the idea of sitting in a bureaucratic cubicle all day without direct contact with students. They may also think that central positions are a waste of time, based on their own experience with so-called central support that they regarded as useless paperwork or vague guidance. Or they may be wary of the Peter Principle that in large organizations, people rise to the level of their own incompetence.

Naturally, if the best teachers and principals don't seek promotions to higher administrative offices, the inept output and bad reputation of central managers become self-perpetuating. The Public Education Leadership Project at Stanford University found that "[central] offices are often dumping grounds for administrators and teachers who performed poorly in the schools."[9] And the tendency to mismanagement is compounded by the fact the teachers colleges not only don't teach teachers how to teach (more on that below); they are even worse at preparing educators to be good managers.

The Culture of Professional Autonomy in Classroom Teaching

Another fundamental factor in the mismanagement of classroom instruction is the enshrined principle of professional autonomy. It wasn't very long ago that the National Council on Teacher Quality reported that teachers colleges cast the decision about how best to teach reading "as a personal one, to be decided by the aspiring teachers."[10] In a recent book *The Teacher Wars*, journalist Dana Goldstein writes that "At teacher colleges, 'autonomy' in the individual classroom has been promoted as a key ethos of the profession."[11] When this chapter turns to how teachers are unsupported by enough research-based instructional tools, keep in mind that some teachers employ professional autonomy to resist using the tools they are given. A leading researcher has noted that in RTI practice, "some teachers regard [standard research-based intervention requirements] as presumptive if not insulting of their professionalism."[12]

And here's the most telling quote of all: Richard Elmore, a leading authority on school management at Harvard University, observes: "[Educators] subscribe to an extremely peculiar view of professionalism: that professionalism equals autonomy in practice. So when I come to your classroom and say, 'Why are you teaching in this way?' it is viewed as a violation of your autonomy and professionalism."[13] Elmore refers to educators as "solo practitioners," which prompts a further analogy. In medicine, if doctors don't use evidence-based treatments, it's called malpractice. In education, if teachers don't use evidence-based instructional practices, it's called professional autonomy.

Parents: linger with this point a little longer. If a doctor prescribed medicine for your child that had been long discredited by medical research, you'd be outraged. Yet, this happens all the time in public school classrooms when instruction is based less on educational research and more on the materials and methods teachers have been using for the past 25 years or so.

In part, teachers get away with this because the ethos of professional autonomy is interwoven with obsession over local control of schools. The principle of local control sets off a chain reaction. Federal and state education agencies, as already noted, defer to local districts. Local districts then delegate a lot of instructional decision-making to individual schools. But that's not the end. Principals in turn give individual teachers great leeway. A familiar quip is that education policy is what happens when a teacher closes her or his classroom door. Another quip describes a school as a series of autonomous classrooms connected by a common parking lot.

This autonomy is not found in high-performing school systems across the world, according to the National Center on Education and the Economy (NCEE). The culture of central standards for classroom practice in these countries is in fact "foreign" to us. The president of NCEE observed that in U.S. schools there are significant differences in instructional practices and outcomes even within a particular school. He refers to the typical U.S. "egg crate school" with "each teacher in her own classroom and the door shut."[14]

It's not that extreme. Instructional materials and methods may be more or less prescribed in some school districts or individual schools. And less experienced teachers are looking for all the help they can get. They are much more prone to latch on to mandates or guidance from above than veteran teachers. "Expecting teachers to be expert pedagogues and instructional designers," says education policy analyst Robert Pondiscio, "is one of the ways in which we push the job far beyond the abilities of mere mortals."[15]

In fairness, the balance of central versus school-based authority is far from simple. By whatever name it's called—school-based management, school autonomy, decentralization, community control, or so on—it has been a battleground in the education wars for decades. Lost then and still lacking today is sensible common ground between school-based decision-making that balances teacher and principal professionalism with central evidence-based management dictates. Yet, finding such an equilibrium has itself been mismanaged. Rather than seeking a course that recognizes the trade-offs, the education establishment has taken the easier road of educational laissez faire. Professional autonomy continues to overshadow professional accountability. Frontline teachers are often left in the lurch without proper management support.

Lack of Management Training

Educators lack the management know-how that would overcome their discomfort with management norms. To begin with, teachers colleges are a total bust at management training. The most astute and outspoken critic of teacher-education programs in recent decades has been Arthur Levine, at one time president of the prestigious Teachers College at Columbia University. Levine has written that preparation of school system administrators is "the weakest of all programs at the nation's education schools."[16] Such programs, he writes, lack coherent and rigorous curricula, admit nearly everyone who applies, and employ faculty who have little to no administrative experience themselves.

On-the-job training is equally anemic. School system chains of command have too many weak links. School administrators learn little from their own supervisors and colleagues who are themselves ill-prepared. Organization charts of central offices tend to have mazes of dotted lines that diffuse authority and accountability. At the school level, supervision of teachers is at best lenient, at worst nonexistent. Supervision ideally is a mixture of being a good coach/mentor and evaluator. But the principal is usually too busy or too rusty on classroom instruction to fulfill the role of coach/mentor; and rarely is there an instructional specialist or lead teacher who can fulfill it.

Then there is the infamous "dance of the lemons"—the familiar practice whereby staff who don't measure up are transferred or even promoted, rather than fired, disciplined or required to undergo further training. Educators are famously protective of each other. Administrators are extraordinarily reluctant to give bad evaluations that can jeopardize a colleague's future. They fear that if they zealously evaluate others, they may be subject to closer scrutiny themselves. Also, informal personal and social connections, like sororities and fraternities, stand in the way of objective evaluations.

As a reform-minded member of the Baltimore school board, nothing I did was more resented by the school establishment than my public objections to top-level appointments. Too many appeared to be based more on chummy personal relationships than merit. Of some consolation was the fact that some administrators thanked me privately for telling it like it was. But I was pretty powerless to stop the golden-parachuting of weak managers into other positions for which they were unqualified.

Having taken school administrators to task for failing to be tough enough in evaluating teachers, I want to anticipate the objection that blame should really be laid on teachers unions. Certainly, teachers unions are far from perfect. They are prominent players in the education establishment and generally oppose accountability measures. Yet, they are the strongest fighters in the political arena on behalf of adequate school funding, especially for low-wealth school districts with predominantly poor and minority students. And though conservatives claim that teachers unions are guilty of allowing the "dance of the lemons" and other safe havens for unsatisfactory teachers, these conservatives ignore the significant roles that others play in these problems.

It takes two to tango: collective bargaining contracts must be agreed to by school boards. And while contract provisions impose burdens on the discipline and removal process, they are nowhere near as restrictive as commonly portrayed. Principals have much more authority than they exercise. Two experts drive the point home: "The problem is not that the teachers unions enjoy too much power or leverage, it is that other constituencies [including principals and superintendents] exercise too little."[17] No less revealing, the conservative Thomas B. Fordham Institute, which is generally critical of teachers unions, did a fair-minded study of union contracts in 50 large school districts. The study reported "the most surprising finding is that labor agreements in a majority of large districts are neither blessedly flexible nor crazily restrictive; they are simply ambiguous, silent on many key areas of management flexibility. . . . it means that, for a majority of big districts, the depiction of [collective bargaining agreements] as an all-powerful, insurmountable barrier to reform may be overstated."[18]

TEACHERS LACK TRAINING IN HOW TO TEACH

The absence of management norms and skills carries over into the lack of training and support for classroom teachers. Perhaps it's understandable that educators are not by nature or nurture good managers. Still, you would think that they would be good at teaching teachers how to teach all students, including struggling learners. Think again.

Acclaimed reading scientist Mark Seidenberg wrote in 2017 that "the culture of education . . . didn't develop because teachers lack integrity, commitment, motivation, sincerity, and intelligence. It developed because they were poorly trained and advised."[19] Primal screams for day-to-day help from inexperienced teachers, who make up a large percentage of the staff in urban school systems, are suppressed. These teachers are afraid of being labeled whiners or troublemakers. Still, it is clear that most teachers crave more training on how to teach the curricula and handle classroom misbehavior. They want realistic expectations of what they—handcuffed by limits on classroom time and large pupil-teacher ratios—can be expected to teach effectively. They yearn for curricula, materials and lesson plans that are aligned with academic standards and guidance on evidence-based best instructional practices.

Yet, they get very little of any of the above. In a book *Learning to Improve: How America's Schools Can Get Better at Getting Better*, the co-authors question "how our nation could possibly improve our schools without a transformation in the ways it develops and supports school professionals and the materials, ideas, and evidence with which they work."[20] "School districts are not especially proactive," they add, "in developing and improving instructional materials, practices, and programs based on careful design and testing."[21]

Of all the roots of educational abuse of struggling learners, this seems the most puzzling. Why do educators flunk management of classroom instruction since classroom teaching is the heart and soul of their profession and what they should know best?

Woeful Teacher Training in Teachers Colleges and on the Job

Teachers and administrators aren't taught the knowledge of research-based best practices that should guide proper RTI-like instruction. They aren't taught that they are breaking the law when struggling learners are referred for special education without receiving adequate instruction in general education. They aren't taught the fallacy and bias behind stereotypical low expectations of poor and minority children. They aren't taught that almost all struggling learners, including those who are mislabeled as disabled, have the capacity to meet academic standards if they receive timely research-based instructional interventions.

I have participated in hundreds of school meetings, most for students in special education, in which instructional services for struggling learners were determined. I have never heard any school staff cite specific research in support of their determinations—and "never" is not an exaggeration. Yes, there are bald statements that their instruction is research-based, but there is no reference or discussion of specific literature on point. On more than one occasion, I've been bluntly told, "we don't need to know the research . . . we know what we're doing."

These gaps in teacher knowledge are first caused by teachers colleges. Their preparation of teachers, although widely discredited, has withstood decades of reform attempts. The only surprise may be that some of the harshest critics have been deans of graduate schools of education, led by Arthur Levine, who was quoted earlier. Teacher-education programs have been indicted as "third-tier backwaters" with low admission standards, shallow and irrelevant course content, rock-bottom research capacity, and ill-prepared faculty.[22]

In particular, struggling learners never catch up (and many become mislabeled as disabled) because general education teachers are not properly trained to teach foundational reading in the early grades. The National Council on Teacher Quality reported in 2014: "We are disheartened that the teacher education field continues to disregard scientifically based methods of reading instruction: coursework in just 17 percent of programs equips their elementary and special education teachers to use all five fundamental components of reading instruction. . . ."[23]

What's more, you may be shocked to hear that these same unprepared general education teachers teach reading to students in special education.

Students in special education are taught by general education teachers in a variety of instructional settings: namely, "inclusion" in the general education classroom, with or without co-teaching, and some pull-out groups.

The Under-Preparation of Special Education Teachers

The under-preparation of special education teachers is even more miserable than the poor training of general education teachers. It begins with dismal programs in teachers colleges. The National Council on Teacher Quality reported in 2011: "States' requirements for the preparation of special education teachers continue to be abysmal. Most states set an exceedingly low bar for the content knowledge special education teachers must have to work with students with special needs. Only 17 states require elementary special education candidates to demonstrate content knowledge on a subject-matter test—just like what would be expected of any other elementary school teacher."[24]

Special education teachers must also shoulder the near-impossible burden of being prepared to teach students with a wide range of disabilities. As astounding as it should be, state certification as a special education teacher is mostly unspecialized beyond courses in the broad theory and practice of special education. Parents should shudder at the thought. Suppose your child has a rare disease but is being treated only by a general internist, not a specialist. That's what, by analogy, occurs in special education.

35 states allow special education teachers to earn a completely generic special education license to teach any special education students in any grade, K-12. The so-called training is the same whether the teacher is teaching students without cognitive limitations to learn to read in the first grade or teaching students with severe cognitive limitations to learn science in the twelfth grade. The generic license is the only license offered in 19 of those states.[25] And yet, it is hard to imagine any argument against requiring teacher specialization based on the markedly different students being taught.

The plot thickens. Once upon a time, "special educators" were truly special. As recounted by leading authorities in the field, they "were regarded as expert instructors—'go-to' professionals at the building level to whom general educators would take their most difficult-to-teach children."[26] Most of these children were on the severe end of the continuum of students with disabilities. In those days there were relatively few of the struggling learners who over the decades were mislabeled as disabled and overwhelmed special education and "special educators."

But those days are long gone. Now, students who are mislabeled as disabled comprise the great majority of students in special education, and therefore the job description of special educators is blurred.[27] For practical purposes, teaching those in special education who I've called the Mainly Mislabeled does not require expertise different than what general education teachers should be expected to possess.

The sorting out of the training of general and special educators would be most easily accomplished by the overall "reinvention" of special education that is recommended in Chapter 9. Special education, as we know it, would exist only for students with the most severe disabilities, and special educators would be true specialists in those disabilities.

A full consideration of proposals to improve preparation of general and special education teachers in teachers colleges is beyond the scope of this book. But action across the board is all the more urgent because on-the-job training for teachers once they enter the classroom fills in little of the holes dug by teacher colleges.

"Professional Development Sucks"

On-the-job training for teachers, known typically as "professional development (PD)," isn't very professional or developmental. It does next to nothing to improve teaching skills. An astute education policy analyst has observed:

> Teachers don't agree on much. Ask about curriculum pedagogy, school culture or discipline and you're likely to encounter deeply held and conflicting opinions. But if there's one belief that unites nearly all of the nation's three million teachers, it's this: Professional development sucks. . . .
>
> Despite an estimated $18 billion spent on PD per year, little evidence exists linking any of it consistently to effective improvement in teacher practices or student outcomes.[28]

Why is it so bad? Because it consists primarily of episodic and shallow workshops that don't relate to teachers' real practice needs. And what would it take to make it so much better? Most of all, classroom-embedded coaches in subject matter, classroom management, and mentoring of new teachers. Teachers would also benefit from more time in the school day to plan lessons and consult with other teachers. These PD essentials are costly, and chalk up the missing money to Us, not educators themselves. Still, the education establishment has not blown the whistle on itself and owned up to the inadequacy in current PD.

Teacher Toolboxes Lack Sufficient Materials and Instructions

Not only don't teachers get proper preparation in teachers college and on-the-job training. They also aren't given the tools to deliver all facets of RTI instruction in the classroom.

Take, for example, the mismanagement of curricula. As mentioned in Chapter 4 in the discussion of Tier 1 instruction in the RTI framework, the quality of the curricula that teachers are supposed to teach matters a lot. Curricula mean the standards for what students should be expected to know and the textbooks and learning materials that are aligned to the standards. You would suppose that research-based curricula would be readily available. But not so.

A prominent authority Chester E. Finn Jr. explains this phenomenon.

> Educators shun curriculum because content choices are often culture-war battles. . . . Talk of a "national curriculum" is taboo and when states venture into these waters, it's almost as controversial. . . . Curriculum, therefore, is generally left to districts, which frequently leave it to individual schools and often to individual teachers or departments within them.[29]

The national fight over the Common Core standards is an obvious example. The genesis of the Common Core standards was the absurdity of 50 states (much less 15,000 local school districts) having their own versions of what students should learn about reading, math, history and science. (More on this in Chapter 8.) Yet, the standards became a battleground in the education wars. Both liberals and conservatives have their own reasons for irrational adoration of local control of academic standards. As a result, "common" (de facto national) standards and tests remain in dispute, defying logic, impeding instruction, and taking up much too much time and space in the national debates over school reform.

Still, the battle over Common Core is only about *what* teachers should teach. There is an even larger problem: teachers are not given sufficient evidence-based tools on *how* to teach students, within RTI and otherwise, to meet the standards. This fault line is caused, foremost, by the absence of R & D as an essential management component in K-12 policy and practice. R & D is taken for granted in business, medicine, science, technology and other fields. But it is a backwater in public education.

It starts with poor research, especially in teachers colleges and universities. Graduate students receive inferior training in how to do excellent research. And research faculty are constrained by cozy relationships with state and local school districts because higher education departments of education depend on school districts for enrollments, intern placements and research sites. According to two well-known critics, these departments "have relatively little incentive to want to critically study issues of productivity and costs [in public school systems]."[30]

Some of the research void is filled by federal dollars channeled through the Institute for Educational Sciences under the U. S. Department of Education. Its funding, along with foundation grants, flows to non-university affiliated nonprofit organizations and think tanks that produce evaluations and policy research. To name a few: the American Institutes of Research, the Manpower Demonstration Research Corporation, the Thomas B. Fordham Institute, and the Education Trust.

In addition, reviews of research and dissemination of best practices are the mission of several organizations. One is the What Works Clearinghouse. Under the auspices of the federal Institute of Education Sciences, it publishes reviews of research across a wide range of K-12 policies and practices. Two others research clearinghouses are located at the Johns Hopkins University: the Best Evidence Encyclopedia; and a newer website Evidence for ESSA that is geared to provide information on programs that meet evidence standards under ESSA. Both of the Hopkins sites are orchestrated by Robert Slavin, the nation's top expert on the use and misuse of claims that programs are evidence-based.

For certain, there aren't enough R & D dollars to go around. Federal funds are scant. And R & D on K-12 public schooling probably has more confounding variables and impediments than other fields. Consequently, evidence-based best instructional practices tend, out of practical necessity, to fall short of "gold standard" research. ESSA allows, in effect, a sliding scale of proof of effectiveness.

Reluctance to Use the Tools at Hand

Even when there is a reliable pool of research-based instructional practices within RTI, many teachers resist diving in. We have encountered the resistance earlier in the book. They hold back in part because of professional autonomy. But there are other reasons, chief among them being the perennial educational Hatfields and McCoys who refuse to end the reading wars. The National Research Council Committee on the Prevention of Reading Difficulties in Young Children pointed out 20 years ago that scientific findings about the causes and cures of early reading difficulties have "been embraced by most researchers, although not yet by a majority of educators."[31] That's still the case. Despite the vast research in support of the "phonics" approach to early literacy, "whole language" still holds sway among many teachers colleges and teachers, especially veteran teachers.

Another example is found in disputes over what is "developmentally appropriate" reading instruction in the critical pre-kindergarten to first grades. Some early childhood practitioners want to delay what others regard as developmentally appropriate identification and intervention practices. They believe that slow learners in the earliest grades are developing at their own pace and most will grow out of it. They're usually wrong.

Many parents of students of students I've represented have told me that, as soon as their child entered pre-kindergarten, they could sense "something was wrong." Their other children hadn't experienced the same frustrations. Yet, even when the parent first asked and then pleaded with the school to diagnose and treat the child's learning difficulty, the school would say something like, "Be patient . . . your child will get over it." That's simply not true. As we have seen, most lose precious early learning time and never catch up.

Beyond professional autonomy and pedagogical warfare, teachers are further dissuaded from embracing research by another customary feature of the educational R & D landscape—"institutional attention deficit disorder." Federal, state and local educators are forever jumping from one reform to another. When this happens and happens and happens, as it does, teachers, especially veterans, choose to ignore the latest reform du jour and wait out what they see as another quick fix which won't be around for long.

There's got to be a better way to effect change, and there is: what I call revolution by evolution.

REVOLUTION BY EVOLUTION

The obstacles that prevent teachers from sufficiently employing research-based tools of the trade must be overcome through sustained R & D. R & D to sustain RTI sounds wonky but it goes to the heart of our goal of ending educational abuse of struggling learners. Another way to capture the idea is a term I borrowed from another context: "revolution by evolution."[32] Revolution by evolution is basically ongoing, reiterative R & D: determining and disseminating evidence-based best RTI practices, professional development, faithful implementation, monitoring, evaluation, feedback loops and incremental improvements. In other words, keep plugging 'till you get it right.

Take the example of tutoring. Few if any components of public schools in general and classroom instruction in particular are as well researched. Yet, as the discussion in Chapter 4 illustrated, there are endless variables and uncertainties. RTI and tutoring will not succeed unless tutoring, in words I heard someone say, "gets better all the time."

Improvement of classroom instruction takes time. That's true in medicine, science, technology and other professions. Yet, educators show little patience or long-term thinking. Rather, they suffer, as noted earlier, from institutional attention deficit disorder. But in fairness, the disorder is more our fault, than theirs. We tend to demand that education leaders pull off short-term solutions. For example, in the hiring process for state and local school superintendents, there is a public clamor by parents and public officials for assurance of a fast turnaround.

However, no such thing in the realm of K-12 public education is possible. Yet, superintendent candidates feel under the gun to over-promise and then once at the helm, to make decisions "that are politically expedient rather than managerially sound."[33] They also feel compelled to make a fast imprint by discarding the reform strategies of predecessors, though those strategies have not sufficient time to take hold. As an old saying goes, when it comes to school reform, "we keep pulling up the roots to see if the grass is growing."

Sustained R & D also runs afoul of the obsession with "innovation" as the watchword for how to rescue public schools. These days, not unlike many past eras in the fickle world of K-12 reform, innovation is in. Not so long ago President Obama called for "a new vision for a 21st-century education—one where we aren't just supporting existing schools, but spurring innovation." A leading consulting firm has pushed a "U.S. Education Innovation Index." The full name of the Maryland Kirwan Commission—charged with recommending how Maryland should prepare students for the global economy—is the Commission on Innovation and Excellence in Education.

Innovation sounds irresistible. (Silicon Valley goes even further and preaches disruption.) And who can be against finding new ways to do old things in public schools when things are going as badly as they are? Still, revolution by evolution requires that we innovate less and execute more. Robert Slavin has said it best: "The problem of education reform is not a lack of good ideas, but a lack of good ideas sensibly implemented."[34] We don't know everything that could be done to implement RTI at large scale. Online education, for example, could be instrumental in the future. But we know far more than innovation gurus and other reformers, left and right, would lead us to believe.

The result of all this attention deficit disorder is unrealistic expectations for classroom instruction and all-too-real disappointments. When reality kicks in, school leaders are kicked out. The average tenure of urban school superintendents is longer than customarily thought.[35] Yet, the revolving door of people and programs and the constant churn of educational reforms, often fads, continue to set back instructional improvement. We have been forever "Tinkering Toward Utopia," the title of a classic history of American public schools, with erratic false stops and starts that derail reform. Its authors concluded, "Change where it counts the most—in the daily interactions of teachers and students—is the hardest to achieve [though] the most important."[36]

That's a succinct summary of the chief lesson that this chapter intends to impart. Mismanagement of classroom instruction must be better recognized as the Achilles heel of reforms like RTI. Still, the endgame of RTI that ends the educational abuse of struggling learners can be won. It calls on Us and Educators to get our collective act together. The next part of the book tells how an allied force for reform can be mobilized.

PART IV

....

THE POSSIBILITIES AND POLITICS OF REFORM

If given the chance, educators can end the educational abuse of struggling learners in general education and special education. It can happen in rich and poor, and urban, suburban and rural school districts. The tools to get it done—the evidence-based best instructional practices under the framework of Response to Intervention (RTI)—exist. But they're not in the hands of teachers.

As seen in the preceding chapters, that's because of both Us and Educators. Money and management are in short supply. And the overriding cause is the stalemated politics of school reform. How do we change that? How do we muster the political will to reform the system? This part of the book sets out the steps it will take.

The starting point is to confront the reality that federal action is unavoidable. Chapter 8 exposes the folly of expecting otherwise. The long-cherished American love affair with "local control" of public schools has been and always will be a disaster for disadvantaged children, especially struggling learners who are disproportionately poor and minority.

To overcome resistance to a prominent federal presence, we the people must face squarely the full extent of unequal educational opportunity throughout our land. We must recognize once and for all that learning to read, write and compute is a basic civil right. Chapter 9 lays out various ways to fulfill that right. Amendments to IDEA and the Every Student Succeeds Act could provide federal guarantees that assure RTI in general education. These laws could also reinvent special education as we know it by making IDEA apply only to students with severe cognitive and other disabilities.

What's more, the realization of equal educational opportunity could be accelerated by civil rights lawsuits like those now pending in Detroit and Berkeley that seek to establish a constitutional right to literacy. It's worth underscoring that any such federal guarantees do not negate the vital roles that state and local school systems can and should play in carrying them out.

Chapter 10 tackles how to mobilize political power behind reform. What's the starting lineup of political players and what's the playbook? Parents should be in the lead; the one saving grace for parents of struggling learners is that there are lots of them. Yet, developing a strong, cohesive constituency is harder than you would think. A major impediment is that a disproportionate percentage of the parents of struggling learners are poor and minority, and therefore lack political muscle. Then too, some tensions exist among parents and advocacy organizations representing different groups of struggling learners, caused by competition for scarce funding.

To surmount these hurdles, political liberals and especially teachers unions must be pressured by parents and other wannabe reformers to lend more support than they have in the past. Parents and teachers should be allies not adversaries in the struggle. This concluding part of the book calls for urgent, collective political action.

....

Chapter 8

The Folly of Reliance on State and Local Reform

David Driscoll, the celebrated former commissioner of education in Massachusetts, writes that relinquishment of the federal role in K-12 school reform in favor of more state and local control is like "giving the keys back to the drivers who caused the accident in the first place."[1]

Is it realistic to expect the 50 states and 15,000 local districts to mend their ways? Chapter 6 pointed out that states and local districts couldn't be counted on to equalize funding for schools nationwide. There's also no realistic chance that they will, left to their own devices, pay attention to the letter and spirit of IDEA and not mislabel struggling learners as students with disabilities. Or that they will finally pay more than lip service to the legal justification and evidence-based necessity for RTI.

According to the old saying generally attributed to Einstein, insanity is doing the same thing over and over again and expecting different results. By that definition, our nation is insane if after generations of unequal educational opportunity and educationally abused children, we are still willing to trust state and local school systems to reform themselves. Here's a brief history lesson that proves it.

Local control was a mainstay—if not a secular religion—throughout the evolution of free public schooling in the U.S. As Chief Justice Warren Burger wrote in a 1974 decision of the Supreme Court: "No single tradition in public education is more deeply rooted than local control over the operation of schools."[2]

But that faith in local control has proven unequal to the task of equal educational opportunity. Few parents (but many grandparents) have experienced what public schools were like in the U.S. prior to the 1950's. But you have a good historical perspective. You know that separate-but-equal schooling was educationally and morally shameful. Still, it persisted until the U.S. Supreme Court unmasked and invalidated it. The *Brown v. Board of Education* desegregation ruling in 1954 marked a turning point. Soon thereafter, the civil rights movement and President Lyndon B. Johnson's Great Society crusade led to Congressional passage of the Elementary and Secondary Education Act of 1965, which eventually morphed into the No Child Left Behind Act and then the Every Student Succeeds Act. These acts asserted a strong federal role, linked to sizable federal aid to poor schoolchildren in poor communities.

The same quest for equal educational opportunity fueled the enactment by Congress in 1974 of the Education for All Handicapped Children Act, the original predecessor of IDEA. Its federal mandates sought to guarantee children with disabilities a "free and appropriate education," and tied federal dollars to compliance with the law.

But there was little payoff on these federal investments. Public schools faltered nationwide. Their failure made us, as cited earlier, "A Nation at Risk," the famous title of the 1983 landmark report of President Ronald Reagan's National Commission on Excellence in Education.

The nation's risk cried out for national action. Policymakers began to realize that state and local school systems were circumventing federal mandates and inefficiently spending the federal funds. (Political liberals like me bear a heavy share of the fault for this; we were asleep at the switch or afraid to blow the whistle, fearing that the federal aid would be reduced or repealed altogether.) Moreover, state and local officials continued to do too little on their own to confront the decline in student achievement and prepare American children to compete in a global economy. State and local school districts were still going their separate ways, but headed nowhere.

And so, over the 1980s, bipartisan support grew for federal steps to raise academic standards and student performance. That movement culminated in the passage in 2001 of the No Child Left Behind Act.

NCLB's enactment was a political miracle. From the start, the bill was widely regarded as the most radical federal assault ever on state and local control. Yet, in a Nixon-goes-to-China moment, President George W. Bush fought for it with the aid of Democrats like Sen. Edward Kennedy. Confronting Republicans' abhorrence of a federal role in public schools, President Bush declared educational excellence to be a national issue, and "change will not come by disdaining or dismantling the federal role."[3]

The federal role under NCLB was to hold states accountable for student performance. It required states to impose high academic standards and tests, and to break down the results by poverty, race, and students with disabilities. It also sought to compel states to close or turnaround failing schools.

But the backlash came fast and furious. The education establishment feared high standards and rigorous tests would expose how little students were actually learning. Individual states feared that they would look bad compared to other states. Moreover, egged on by educators, parents—particularly those in the upper income ranks—protested that their children were being over-tested and over-pressured. There was some truth to those charges. However, no one in the education establishment pointed out that the feds were not mainly to blame. Under NCLB, states and local school systems had great flexibility to set their own the testing regimens; it was their own poor choices and mismanagement of testing that provoked the furor.

No wonder there was a bipartisan political cave-in. NCLB had weaknesses, like unrealistic goals for student progress. But its fatal flaw was counterintuitive and much deeper: NCLB didn't give too much power to federal education officials, but too little. It left states and local districts with the discretion to set their own standards and tests, leading to the infamous "race to the bottom" in which states lowered standards and dumbed down tests. To thwart this, U.S. education secretary Arne Duncan cajoled and coerced states to adopt rigorous national (Common Core) standards and tests.

It seemed like a good idea to those of us who support the aims of NCLB. But in retrospect, Duncan's aggressiveness only added fuel to the political fire. The ferocious counterattack was led, predictably, by conservatives who oppose any federal role. But they were aided and abetted by education progressives and liberal teachers unions who resist accountability in general and testing in particular. The rallying cry was to emasculate NCLB, and even before presidential candidate Donald Trump bashed Common Core and testing, the political die had been cast.

The Every Student Succeeds Act (ESSA), enacted at the end of President Obama's tenure with bipartisan backing, embodies this educational realpolitik. It severely reduces the authority of the U.S. education secretary, virtually guaranteeing state and local autonomy over standards, testing and sanctions. Gary Orfield, a preeminent expert on the intersection of civil rights and public school policy, observes that NCLB was "very assertive and interventionist," while ESSA strips federal funding of its "leverage for any national purpose."[4]

William J. Bennett, a conservative bigwig and former U.S. secretary of education under President Ronald Reagan, crowed that "for years, states, districts, superintendents and teachers have had their focus distracted and hands tied by burdensome federal regulation. For years they have been asking for relief. Now they have it."[5]

But how much good will they do with it? In all likelihood, it will be "deja vu all over again." History is not on the side of those who put their faith in state and local control. Just as the states' "race to the bottom" undermined the lofty intent of NCLB, and just as states and local districts did not desegregate or educate students with disabilities prior to national mandates, so they are unlikely to end the educational abuse of struggling learners unless forced to by national law.

Let's face it: the cherished principle of state and local control over public education still exerts a powerful influence on public sentiment. No matter that it defies logic and common sense. After all, as noted earlier, how does it make common sense or serve the national purpose for state and local school districts to go their own way over what students learn and how to measure whether they have learned it? Are the foundational skills of reading, 'riting and 'rithmetic different in one state than another? Is science different in red states and blue states? (Well at least until the age of Trump, it wasn't.)

And with particular focus on struggling learners, is there any rhyme or reason why different states should have different definitions of learning disabilities and different percentages of students in special education?

Zealots for state rights are also wrong by posing the issue of local control as an all or nothing proposition. Inequalities nationwide, many of which particularly discriminate against poor and minority children, can be remedied without eliminating much of the role of state and local educators. Federal laws need only set a floor, not a ceiling, for state and local standards, tests and instructional best practices. Compared to how other countries govern schools, the U.S. is an educationally underdeveloped nation. According to the leading international authority on comparisons between U. S. schools and high-performing schools in other countries, other countries have far more centralized governance.[6]

And let's not forget that it is not just our national experience with K-12 policy that is so instructive and appalling. Consider the national track record on any basic rights of poor and minority families and children. Think about Social Security. Think about Medicare. Think about Medicaid, Food Stamps and Unemployment Insurance. Think about laws that protect the environment, occupational safety and voting rights. Think about laws that prevent discrimination on the basis of gender, sexual preference, disability and age.

Then try to think of which, if any, of these, did not come about as a result of federal legislation or federal court decisions that overcame the inaction of state and local governments.

This is a short chapter but federal action is a tall order that must be clearly understood and embraced. If the educational abuse of struggling learners is to be stopped, there must be a federal right to an education that will enable struggling learners to succeed. The next chapter lays out various means to bring this about.

Chapter 9

· ·

A Civil Right to End the Wrongs, and the Reinvention of Special Education

From a decision of the U.S. Supreme Court: "Illiteracy is an enduring disability. The inability to read and write will handicap the individual deprived of a basic education each and every day of his life. [Its denial violates] the framework of equality embodied in the Equal Protection Clause [of the U.S. Constitution]."[1]

A student we'll identify as "B" is in the fourth grade and reading between a first and second grade level. B did not receive adequate RTI interventions in general education and was found eligible for special education services in the first grade as a student with a Specific Learning Disability and ADHD. But, despite a succession of Individual Education Programs (IEPs), he failed to improve in reading. At the same time, his behavior deteriorated, owing in part to academic frustration.

So what's special about B? He doesn't appear that much different from other struggling learners described throughout this book who have been educationally abused. And he's not, except in one crucial respect. B, alone among the students whose stories are sketched in the book, is not a student I represented. Rather, B is one of the plaintiffs in a class action lawsuit filed in May 2017 in a U.S. district court claiming a constitutional right to be taught to read.

The lawsuit alleges that the Berkeley, California school district had systematically failed to educate students suspected of having reading disorders.[2] As the lead attorney for the plaintiffs stated, "Students with reading disorders in [the Berkeley schools] and every public school in this country have the fundamental right to learn to read and participate fully with their peers."[3]

B's illiteracy is a terrible cross for him to bear, but he may help save millions of struggling learners from similar fates. The Berkeley lawsuit is one of the strategies—legislative as well as judicial—that could lead to federal action that ends the educational abuse of struggling learners. The strategies are not pie in the sky. The key to them all is the establishment of a federal right to read.

To backtrack a bit, we have learned that state and local school governments aren't up to the job of providing RTI interventions so that B and other struggling learners can learn to read and succeed in higher education and in the workforce. And it is wishful thinking that the education establishment—within state and local school systems and professional organizations including teachers unions—will ever police and reform itself. But in fairness, educators couldn't reform the system by themselves if they wanted to. They don't have the political authority to transform laws governing school policy and funding.

But who does? Responsibility for education policy is dispersed and disguised by a crazy quilt of overlapping policymakers. They include, from the top down, the president, Congress and U.S. Department of Education; 50 state governors, legislatures and departments of education; and at the local level, countless mayors, county commissioners, elected or appointed school boards, and school administrators.

The previous chapter pointed out the need to sort out this hodgepodge. Federal policymakers must play a lead role but how can we—parents, educators (not shackled by the education establishment) and other citizens—take political action to pressure them to act?

The struggle must be waged first and foremost in the halls of Congress and in federal courtrooms. Amendments to the Every Student Succeeds Act (ESSA) and/or the Individual with Disabilities Act (IDEA) could bring about change. At the same time, judicial rulings in the Berkeley case or others could mandate or spur legislative action. We now examine these strategies in more depth.

AMENDMENTS TO ESSA

ESSA is probably the best place to start. It could be amended to explicitly require that struggling learners receive adequate opportunity to succeed in school. States would be required, as a condition of receiving federal aid, to provide instruction that is reasonably calculated to enable all students (except students with the most severe disabilities) to meet the same state standards as their non-disabled peers. Such a mandate, let's recall, was intended under the No Child Left Behind Act. NCLB's Statement of Purpose was "to ensure that all children have a fair, equal, and significant opportunity to obtain a high-quality education and *reach, at a minimum, proficiency on challenging State academic achievement standards and tests. . . ."*[4] (Italics added.)

ESSA, which replaced NCLB, waters this down. Its Statement of Purpose says only that the purpose "is to provide all children significant opportunity to receive a fair, equitable, and high-quality education, and to close educational achievement gaps." "Close educational gaps" is a lower standard than "reach, at a minimum, proficiency." It significantly reduces the likelihood that struggling learners will receive sufficient RTI interventions and meet state standards.

ESSA doesn't come right out and admit the retreat. Under ESSA, states still have a responsibility to enable students to achieve "challenging State academic standards" through the "[e]stablishment of long-term goals." The goals are to be "ambitious." But these requirements are largely window dressing. Other ESSA provisions allow states to dumb down the standards and tests and drag out the timetable for meeting the goals.

It is noteworthy that in the bill passed by the Senate that preceded the final version of ESSA, there was bi-partisan support to include language to ensure that students who did not meet state standards for two years or more would be provided targeted intervention along the lines of RTI requirements. This requirement didn't make its way into ESSA, and it fell short anyway: for example, RTI would not be triggered until a student has fallen behind for two years, which is much too long to wait.[5]

But it shows bipartisan awareness that ESSA might have gone farther. If we politically demand it, ESSA could be amended to unequivocally compel states to provide struggling learners with RTI-like interventions that are reasonably calculated to enable them to learn to read and to meet state standards.

AMENDMENTS TO IDEA

Another well-marked path to reform can be found in the history of IDEA. IDEA could be amended to make clear, once and for all, that most struggling learners should no longer be misidentified, mislabeled and misserved as students with disabilities. That, as this book has revealed, is already the intent of the current law. But the law has been ignored or circumvented nationwide, inflicting grave harm on millions of students who are disproportionately poor and minority.

However, let's suppose there was the political will for reform. Suppose the Congress wanted to make certain that students would not be found eligible for special education unless they received adequate instruction in general education. Two prime avenues are open.

One is for the Congress and the U.S. Department of Education to put some sharper teeth into the current statute, regulations and monitoring. The law and regulations could make crystal clear that most students now found eligible under the Specific Learning Disability, Other Health Impaired (attention deficit disorders), Emotional Disability, and Speech and Language classifications, and sometimes Autism, should not be found eligible for special education without compelling proof that they had been afforded RTI interventions in general education. Federal funds could be withheld for non-compliance, same as with ESSA.

With these amendments in place, federal, state and local education administrators would have much less room to bury their bureaucratic heads in the sand. The burden would fall on federal officials to monitor compliance by state and local school districts. Of note, if this occurred, special education monitoring could redeem itself from the disrepute it deserves because of its almost exclusive focus on procedural compliance, rather than on student academic achievement.

Compliance monitoring could be re-engineered to emphasize scrutiny of student goals, outcomes and the sufficiency of instructional services. In its waning days, the Obama administration took steps in this direction. A shift in emphasis was to focus monitoring on "results driven accountability," that is, academic performance.[6] But the initiative never got going and is already in the Trump and DeVos educational dustbin.

There is, however, hope for the future. The political winds will change course sooner or later, and if they blow with zeal for reform of special education, there is an even bolder political pathway to reform. That would be to reinvent special education altogether, with IDEA being restructured to serve only students with severe cognitive and other limitations.

SEPARATION AND REINVENTION OF SPECIAL EDUCATION

Reinvention of special education so that it serves only students with the most severe disabilities might seem a big policy leap over the deep-rooted practices of the past 40 years. Most students in special education, those mislabeled as disabled, would be gone. Yet, actually, it would be less reinvention and more restoration of what IDEA was supposed to be in the first place.

Recall, as discussed in Chapter 2, the fear of mission creep at the time of passage of the original version of IDEA in 1975. Congress tried to put in safeguards to prevent special education from being overwhelmed by students without legitimate disabilities. However, the safeguards were feeble and ineffective.

Thus, special education was inundated with students who were illegally mislabeled as disabled. As struggling learners fell farther and farther behind in general education and overwhelmed general education teachers, they were labeled with pseudo disabilities and dumped into special education. Little thought was given to RTI in general education as an appropriate and cost-effective alternative.

But we now know better, and it's not too late. Amendments to IDEA and ESSA could mandate the reinvention. The Truly Disabled should be substantially separated from the Mainly Mislabeled. And the case for it is as compelling as it is urgent. Margaret J. McLaughlin, a professor of special education at the University of Maryland, has perhaps said it best. There is an acute need to

> alter the current construct of "disability" under the IDEA and take special education policy back to its roots as an educational law that pertains only to students with clear and evident disabilities. . . . This could focus the resources on those students most in need of specialized long term education and related services as opposed to having special education programs provide compensatory services for students whose only "disability" has been poor or insufficient general education.[7]

Law professor Robert Garda seconds the motion. He writes that the next reauthorization of IDEA "should reclaim special education from over-represented African-Americans and instructional casualties and place it back in the hands of the genuinely disabled by having 'special education' relinquish its exclusive grip on individualized instruction. . . ."[8]

What would such a back-to-the-future reinvention look like? First, general education would be expected to provide timely and effective assistance for *all* struggling learners. The idea of such a unified system has been evolving since the early 1980s. The groundbreaking article on the subject was titled, "Beyond Special Education: Toward a Quality System for All Students," and extolled the concept of "Rights without Labels."[9] The vehicle to accomplish it, though not identified as such, would be RTI with its early and intensive interventions. Struggling learners would no longer be arbitrarily and illegally deposited into special education. They would be spared the stigma, segregation and negative self-fulfilling prophecies of special education.

Some proponents of separation have even gone so far as to call for special education to be abolished in its entirety. As conceptualized in the "Beyond Special Education" article:

> The assumptions underlying separate programs have produced a system that is both segregated and second class. . . .
>
> In a merged or unitary system, effective practices in classrooms and schools would characterize education for all students. . . . Nor would blame be placed on students or on family characteristics. Rather, the focus would be on effective instruction for all students. . . .[10]

The unitarians are spot-on in their diagnosis. Yet, their prescription is an overdose of idealism. Special education should be preserved for students with the most severe disabilities. If so, special education would be truly specialized for truly special populations. Still, it is fair to ask: is it feasible to draw a line along the continuum between students with severe and profound learning problems and struggling learners?

The difference between the two populations has life-shaping consequences. Remember, struggling learners can be expected to meet regular academic standards if they receive adequate instruction in general education. Students with severe disabilities can't; they are only expected to meet alternative (lesser) standards at the highest level possible based on their individual needs and abilities.

Yet, the distinction is sometimes difficult to pinpoint. Disability classifications in IDEA are not educationally and medically precise. For example, there are heated debates about the validity of definitions and diagnoses of Specific Learning Disability and Other Health Impairment (attention deficit disorders). And within some classifications, there are students with and without severe cognitive limitations. That is generally understood for students on the autism spectrum. But it less understood for students with intellectual limitations including those with Down syndrome; some of these students—if they receive the best evidence-based instruction—are able to achieve at or near regular state standards and earn regular high school graduation diplomas.

Unfortunately, school systems are tempted to erroneously label students as severely disabled because schools are held to lesser accountability standards for their performance. ESSA and IDEA allow school systems too much leeway in the development of less-demanding alternate academic achievement standards for students "with the most significant cognitive disabilities."[11]

Nonetheless, despite all the difficulties in separating struggling learners from severely disabled students, a practical demarcation is do-able. In fact, current practice under NCLB, ESSA, and IDEA has paved the way. Most severe disabilities emerge at a young age and are medically well recognized. As two authorities have put it, "For these children, there is no need for an elaborate identification process within the schools. Long before they enter kindergarten, we know who they are, and to a large extent, we know their medical, rehabilitation, and educational needs."[12]

Parents still have to be on alert. Sometimes the decision is made prematurely, before developmental conditions are sufficiently known. Sometimes the decision is made before appropriate instructional interventions have been provided. Sometimes, as noted above, schools err on the side of determining students to be severely disabled in order to invoke lower standards and inflate test scores.

Still, the potential gains far outweigh the possible dangers. Most important would be the prospective benefits to classroom instruction. Special education teachers would be more specialized and better trained to meet the academic and life-skills challenges of truly disabled students. Another big benefit would be simplification of the eligibility determination process, allowing for reduction of the procedural paperwork that drives teachers nuts and out of special education. And management competence all-around would be strengthened by the tighter mission.

Yes, separation is a daunting challenge. But it's worth the struggle, which can be won with smart and dedicated political action as proposed in Chapter 10.

THE FEDERAL COURTROOM AND A CONSTITUTIONAL RIGHT TO BE TAUGHT TO READ

Class action lawsuits, particularly on behalf of struggling learners—inside and outside of special education—could speed up the reform process. We earlier met student "B," a plaintiff in the class action lawsuit pending in federal court in Berkeley. The Berkeley case is based on violations of IDEA, many of which were exposed in Chapter 2. A key one is that the Berkeley school system failed to provide B with "appropriate RTI," defined as "intensive early and research-based intervention."[13]

B, in effect, represents literally millions of struggling learners across the U.S. Among them are Jesse, Christopher, Isaias, Esmeralda, Paul, Gary and Jamie. They are students in the Detroit public schools who are in general education. not in special education. And, as alleged in a class action lawsuit filed in U.S. district court in 2016, "have been denied access to literacy by being deprived of evidence-based literacy instruction and by being subject to school conditions that prevent them from learning."[14] The denial, according to the class action complaint, violates the Due Process and Equal Protection clauses of the 14th amendment of the U.S. Constitution.

The complaint quotes a 1982 decision of the U.S. Supreme Court:

> The inability to read and write will handicap the individual deprived of a basic education each and every day of his life. The inestimable toll of the deprivation on the social, economic, intellectual, and psychological well-being of the individual, and the obstacle it poses to individual achievement, make it most difficult to reconcile the cost or the principle of a status-based denial of basic education with the framework of equality embodied in the Equal Protection Clause.[15]

The complaint contends that those who fail to learn are doomed to constitute "a discrete underclass in our society."[16] The "appalling outcomes in Plaintiffs' schools . . . would be unthinkable in schools serving predominantly white, affluent student populations."[17]

Both the Berkeley and Detroit lawsuits plant the seeds of a constitutionally mandated right to be taught to read. The Detroit case covers broader ground as it would protect all struggling learners, while the Berkeley case covers only students who have been illegally treated under IDEA.

Regardless of the distinction between them, both lawsuits face long and uncertain futures. The suits may or may not succeed. In 2013 a class action case was filed in Michigan, claiming that the state was legally obligated to ensure that all students learn to read. Plaintiffs lost that case but it was decided in a state, not a federal, court.[18]

The prospects in federal courts are a whole new and more promising ballgame. Lawsuits that copycat the Berkeley and Detroit causes of action are sure to follow in other states and cities. It will take many years for the cases to be decided, and then an even longer time to weigh the impact of the decisions. Still, the movement towards a federal constitutional right to literacy seems inevitable.

It is in the federal courts that other longstanding, basic denials of equal educational opportunity were eventually recognized. *Brown v. Board of Education*, the landmark Supreme Court decision that outlawed racial segregation in public schools, was a forerunner. The Detroit suit, in particular, follows closely in its hallowed footsteps.

Lawrence Tribe, an eminent constitutional law scholar at Harvard University, expects the Detroit case to make history "much as Brown v. Board of Education did." "If you think of Brown v. Board as one shoe that dropped, this is the other shoe . . . because though it eliminated, technically, inferior schools for blacks, and eliminated de jure segregation, it didn't achieve one of its basic goals. And that is a decent educational opportunity for all kids, regardless of race, regardless of class, regardless of geography. That's become a more elusive goal." "The legal theory, behind the suit," he says, is "creative and rock-solid."[19]

ANOTHER LEGAL APPROACH: MALPRACTICE

Another legal channel that could lead to a right to learn to read and meet state academic standards is laid out in an illuminating 2010 paper, "New Life for Educational Malpractice: Decades of Policy Revisited."[20] Do educators—unlike doctors, lawyers and accountants—have civil immunity from malpractice? Are school systems not liable civilly for harm to students when they act negligently and fail to follow evidence-based instructional practices?

For many years, it was dogma that educators were a privileged class and immune from malpractice standards. "Long ago," the paper recounts, "legal scholars held a funeral service for the tort of educational malpractice."[21] The nails in the coffin included "the inability of the courts to identify an educational professional standard of care, and an underlying belief that courts should not intrude on the 'educational expertise' of educational institutions."[22]

In a famous 1976 case, a California high school graduate—with normal intelligence and average grades—had achieved only a fifth grade reading level. Nonetheless, the California Supreme Court rejected the claim of malpractice, emphasizing the lack of a workable standard of care and the fear of burden on public schools.[23]

But over the years, workable standards of care have been solidly crafted. Federal and state laws since the early 1980's—including ESSA and IDEA—have mandated state academic standards. In an article titled, "A Crack in the Educational Malpractice Wall," the authors asked whether "With performance standards in place, will courts soon recognize an individual's right to competent instruction in the classroom?"[24] The standards have been part of an overall accountability movement, and we now have extensive data showing how struggling learners—whether in special or general education—are far below meeting the standards.

Another old justification for immunity from liability for malpractice is also long gone. There is now a growing body of evidence-based instructional best practices that school systems should prescribe for academically-ailing students, a point emphasized in the Detroit class action case. RTI can work if given the chance and done right. School systems that don't use it should be sued for malpractice.

It also bears notice that the students who have not mastered basic reading skills because of lack of evidence-based instruction are, more than ever, disproportionately from poor and minority families. Thus, the pressure continues to build for a constitutional right to read that would force schools to come out from under the old, tattered cloak of malpractice immunity.

MISSION POSSIBLE, OR IMPOSSIBLE?

This Chapter has tried to post starters in the race to end the educational abuse of struggling learners. Most likely to get to the finish line is federal action in the Congress and in the courts. But how much money are you willing to bet on the race?

In the next chapter we survey the political odds. U.S. history makes reform a longshot. Yet, to switch metaphors, the worm (in the apple on the teacher's desk) will turn. Sooner or later, we the people will take political action to end the abuse of struggling learners in general education and special education. And it will happen sooner than later if the political will to make it happen is matched with political muscle. That's the book's last lesson, and the next and final chapter is a campaign blueprint.

Chapter 10

···

A Political Call to Action

Parents—Unite and Fight!

"I'm mad as hell and I'm not going to take this anymore."[1]

Struggling learners aren't the only ones who have a lot to learn. So do their most passionate advocates, most of all parents. I hardly need tell parents how much they suffer when their children are mislabeled as disabled and under-educated. There's even a recent study that shows the "psychological fallout" on parents of children with learning problems.[2]

Yet, parents are not as aware as they should be. A leading researcher in the field, who is also a parent of a student with a true disability, has lamented, "I am afraid that students with disabilities have been facing systemic and institutionalized low expectations for so long that these low expectations are internalized even by their advocates."[3]

To be more effective advocates, parents need to learn that:

- low expectations lead to poor instruction and low achievement.
- struggling learners can achieve grade level standards if they receive timely, adequate instruction in general education through the RTI process.
- because of the lack of that instruction, the overwhelming majority of students in special education are mislabeled as disabled; and

- ironically, it is up to them as parents to teach these lessons to most educators.

Parents who learn these lessons will become enraged and hopefully insurgent, like the television newscaster in the movie Network who couldn't take it anymore. But that's not enough either. As their children struggle and suffer in school, they must channel their anger and heart-break into advocacy for their own child and political action to change the system altogether.

It won't be easy. The parents of struggling learners—whether their children languish in general education or special education—are, as a general rule, politically disabled, particularly since so many are poor and minority.[4] So what can parents do about it? And with what allies?

This chapter looks at the obstacles that stand in the way of empower-ment of parents. Parents must overcome the deep political inequality in our country. The political deck is stacked against them when they try individu-ally to get assistance for their children. And it's stacked against them when they try to organize and collectively campaign for system-wide reform.

As if that were not enough, parents of struggling learners sometimes splinter into factions that are more politically competitive than cohe-sive. And even when they do get their act together, they do not get as much support as they should from those who should be their strongest allies—like educators, including teachers unions, and political liberals.

Still, a campaign to end educational abuse can be mobilized and won if parents and allies unite and fight. This chapter tells how it can be done.

PARENTS ARE STYMIED IN TRYING TO ADVOCATE FOR THEIR OWN CHILDREN

The environment for parent advocacy is so inhospitable that even the wealthiest parents of struggling learners are disadvantaged.[5] School systems conceal the lack of student progress. Timely interventions are delayed or denied in general education. And the elaborate parental rights contained in IDEA for students in special education exist far more on paper than in practice.

The Void in Legal Protections for Parents of
Struggling Learners in General Education

As ineffectual as the procedural protections are under IDEA (as we will shortly see), there are no comparable protections, even on paper, for parents of struggling learners in general education. When parents raise concerns about their child's lagging progress, and when they are dissatisfied with the school's unresponsiveness, they have no practical place to turn. They have no explicit legal rights or remedies.[6] While some state or local regulations call for some elements of RTI, these provisions are typically not monitored or enforced, and any requirement for parental participation is either non-existent or token.

In Baltimore, local regulations call for school "problem-solving teams" prior to referral to special education and for individual remediation plans when students are in danger of failing courses and not being promoted to the next grade. These processes sound good, but they are generally ignored.

Even when schools claim to be providing some interventions through the framework of RTI, parents have little to no clue that there is such a thing and their children are entitled to it. Minimally, parents should receive more information than is contained on regular report cards about their child's skills deficits, any research-based interventions that have been tried, progress reports, and recourse to some kind of appeal if they are dissatisfied. The procedural protections afforded parents and children under IDEA—if they were meaningfully enforced—should be models for procedures during RTI and before referral to special education.

The Myth of Parents' Rights in Special Education

There are countless good intentions and high-sounding phrases in IDEA about parents being equal partners every step along the way in the determination of Individual Education Programs (IEPs). The steps include: consent to have their child evaluated by school staff and initial determination of eligibility; access to evaluations and other reports on the student's performance and problems; full participation in meetings at which eligibility is determined and when an IEP is developed or revised; periodic progress reports; regular re-evaluations of eligibility; and appeal procedures if parents disagree with IEP team decisions.

That all sounds well and good except for the overriding realities. School systems prevent parents from meaningfully exercising the rights.

IDEA's procedural protections have been called an "empty ritual."[7] That may be too strong a term but parents are under-resourced and over-matched in dealing with schools.

These facts of life for parents are brilliantly captured in a 2011 law journal article "Special Education, Poverty, and the Limits of Private Enforcement."[8] Peel away the legalese and the footnotes (373 in all), and the point is indisputable: only highly-educated and wealthy parents have a realistic chance to take advantage of parental rights under IDEA, and even they are up against formidable odds.

All parents, and even their advocates, must confront the technical jargon of instructional specialists, psychologists, speech and language pathologists and other school staff. Moreover, parents and their advocates are rarely privy to all that school members of the IEP team know and think. School staff—at least when the student has an advocate—almost invariably meet beforehand to discuss the IEP and make tentative decisions. Countless times, a parent and I have been made to wait outside the meeting room for a long time while the school team members finished their private pre-discussions.

Worse, school team members are under intense pressure to only discuss and recommend services that they think the school can afford. Many of them know that this violates the letter and spirit of IDEA: students are supposed to be guaranteed the services they need, not what the school or school system thinks it can afford. Yet, the system pretends otherwise, and parents are denied crucial information such as the range of options for evidence-based instruction and related services like counseling and speech and language therapy.[9]

All told, in the so-called partnership, schools hold decisive cards: parents can participate in the IEP team deliberations but can't control most of the final decisions.[10] Team decisions are supposed to be made by consensus, but when necessary, the school members on the team simply steamroller the parent. Parental consent is primarily required only for evaluations and the first IEP. Otherwise, IEP teams have pretty free rein to revise IEPs without a parent's approval.

Indeed, parents aren't even that much better off if they have an advocate. I know from my own frustrating experience as an advocate at hundreds of meetings that frequently IEP teams resent the presence of an advocate and may double down on their defensiveness. IEP teams have flat out said to me in clear violation of IDEA, "we're not going to give

[Marcus or Kimberly or Arianna or others] more services just because you are here . . . we'd have to give it to everybody and that's impossible." Well, it isn't impossible but parents don't know that.

Appeal Rites and Wrongs

But at least parents have the right under IDEA to appeal team decisions, don't they? Not really. Parents are even more at a loss after they've struck out with the IEP team. It says in IDEA and it says on the written notice they are given at the end of the IEP meeting that they have various options for other turns at bat to reverse the team decision. These options for "conflict resolution," as the appeals stage is called, sound promising.[11] But they are largely illusory.

Central is the right to a due process hearing, which means a trial before an administrative law judge (ALJ). And before the trial, the parent can request mediation. However, school systems do not have to agree to mediation, and even if they do, the mediation process is hard for a parent to access without an advocate.

Also, in lieu of mediation, the parent can opt for what is misnamed "resolution." Resolution is a conference that the school system must convene to consider the parent's grievance.[12] But it is solely within the control of the system. Typically, the resolution meeting resolves nothing; the school system goes through the motions and defends the IEP team's decision.

If the parent, with or without an advocate, does go all the way to an administrative law trial, ALJs almost always rule in favor of the school system. A public interest law group under the auspices of the Maryland Center for Developmental Disabilities at the Kennedy Krieger Institute examined the results of ALJ decisions in Maryland over a four year period ending in late 2017. Parents prevailed in only about 10 percent of the trials.[13] The odds weren't much better even if they were represented by an attorney.

The main reason for these lopsided results is Deference. The capital "D" is to underscore its almost insurmountable effect. The ALJ mantra is that they must defer to—they cannot substitute their judgment for—the expertise of the professionals on the IEP team. Deference is a fundamental principle that courts apply in rulings on challenges to the decisions of all administrative agencies, including public school systems.

But should it apply to schools when, as detailed in this book, IEP teams engage in so many illegal and one-sided practices? Like underestimating the cognitive potential of most students with IEPs? Like misunderstanding or ignoring the standard for students' progress? Like failing to use evidence-based best practices and tailoring IEPs to fit the school's budget rather than the student's needs? Like limiting information provided to parents? Of course not. But Deference still holds sway.

In partial defense of the ALJs, they are barely if at all trained to grasp these issues. In Maryland ALJs are not specialized; they conduct at most a handful of special education trials per year. So it's unrealistic to expect them to know enough to penetrate the intricacies of special education law and school systems' lack of transparency. Thus, Deference is their escape hatch.

An Extra Burden on the Backs of Parents
On top of all that, the ALJs can take advantage of the fact that in some states parents have the burden of proof. Meaning, that if the ALJ thinks a ruling could go either way, the ALJ is bound to find for the school system. You would think that with school systems having so many advantages to begin with, it would be only natural and fair for them to shoulder the burden of proof on appeals. But it ain't necessarily so.

This issue made its way to the U.S. Supreme Court in the case of *Schaffer v. Weast*, decided in 2005.[14] The Court held that states were individually free to impose the burden of proof on school systems. Numerous states do. But the Court balked at interpreting IDEA to require that the burden should always rest on school systems. Justice John Paul Stevens in a concurring opinion stated the rationale: "we should presume that public schools are properly performing their difficult responsibilities" under special education laws.[15]

That presumption was skewered by Justice Ruth Bader Ginsburg in dissent. School systems command huge advantages, she wrote: "the school has better access to relevant information, greater control over the potentially more persuasive witnesses (those who have been directly involved with the child's education), and greater overall education expertise than the parents." Further, she noted, "school districts striving to balance their budgets . . . will favor educational options that enable them to conserve resources."[16] In other words, in violation of their legal responsibilities, schools will balance budgets in part on the backs of vulnerable students in special education.

Fortunately, for the reasons expressed by Justice Ginsberg, a majority of states have opted to impose the burden of proof on the school system. Unfortunately, my own Maryland is not one of them. I have testified at legislative hearings and lobbied for changes in the Maryland law. Attempts, however, have failed because of the powerful opposition of local school systems who want to preserve their substantial advantages. They realize that the burden of proof is more than a minor legalistic matter. It has the power to tip the scales of justice in their favor and against parents.

The same kind of handicap attaches to the parent's right to appeal an ALJ ruling to the courts. The court review involves even more time and expense, including the practical necessity of a lawyer.

Because schools recognize that the appeal system is rigged in their favor, they have less reason to be receptive to parents' concerns. IEP teams can sound reasonable, even sympathetic in dismissing the concerns. "Don't worry, you can always appeal." Since I am often on the losing side of IEP team decisions, I have heard this party line innumerable times. But it is disingenuous, if not downright dishonest, for all but the wealthiest parents.

No one would deny wealthy parents the chance to spend as much as it takes for their children to gain adequate educational opportunity and escape educational abuse. But it is not just that other parents are far less likely to obtain equal opportunity for their children. There is another downside to the superior wherewithal of wealthy parents. When they can afford legal assistance and get the system to fix their child's individual situation, these parents have no reason to join less endowed parents and engage in advocacy for system-wide change. Moreover, there is the perception (sometimes well-founded) that the children of wealthy parents may be able to buy their child more than the law requires. Sometimes school systems give preferential treatment to avoid public controversy and enormous legal bills. These occurrences and perceptions create a backlash that undermines wide political support for system–wide reform.

Parents Need Advocacy Assistance But They Don't Receive It
To turn their rights from empty promises to viable realities, parents of struggling learners must have help in gaining appropriate RTI in general education and stronger IEPs in special education.[17] But it's nearly

impossible for them to get the help. Only upper income parents can afford private attorneys and educational and other experts. Middle class parents are typically priced out, although some take a second job or eat into their savings to scrape up the money. According to a legal scholar on parental rights, "the evidence suggests that children from wealthier families enforce their rights . . . at higher rates than children in poverty and that the enforcement disparity has a negative effect on the amount and quality of services children in poverty actually receive."[18] Duh.

So where does this leave other families and the poor in particular? As the saying goes, when Americans as a whole catch a cold, the poor catch pneumonia. With the double whammy of having a child who is a struggling learner and not having the means to pay for private assistance, call it double pneumonia. Nationwide, a smattering of free or reduced price lawyers or lay advocates can only meet a minuscule fraction of the need.

The powerlessness is all the more unjust because it is poor and minority families that not just need assistance most, but want it most. Conservatives often try to minimize the urgency of school reform by citing research that shows that most Americans give their own local schools a high grade. Yet, a poll reported in early 2018 revealed a huge economic and racial divide on the issue. Under the headline "New survey of minorities adds dissenting view to public satisfaction with schools," a Brookings summary of the report noted:

> 64 percent of African-Americans, 45 percent of Latinos, and 40 percent of Native Americans agree that children in their own racial or ethnic group don't have the same chances to get a quality education as white children. While many African-Americans, Latinos and Native Americans see their children as disadvantaged by the school system as a consequence of their race or ethnicity, most white Americans and Asian Americans do not share this concern.[19]

Most higher income families (and not exclusively white ones) would not stand for the deplorable schooling in low-wealth school districts and neighborhoods. In Baltimore in early 2018, frigid weather conditions caused water pipes to break and heating systems to crash in many dilapidated school buildings, resulting in school closings. Bravo to the parents for the outrage that followed. Yet, a vital point is lost: While kids can't learn in freezing classrooms, they also can't learn in classrooms where the research-based instruction is subzero. Parents must register comparable outrage at the horrible learning conditions inside schools even when the weather outside is perfect.

Ways to Enhance the Power of Parents

This chapter chiefly focuses on empowering parents to spur political action that will end the abuse of struggling learners. That will never happen unless, as spelled out in Chapter 9, there is a clear legislative or judicial right to adequate opportunity to learn to read. The biggest idea and best hope is national reform.

Still, there are significant ways to bulk up the muscle of parents of struggling learners in their individual dealings with schools. Almost invariably, parents must go it alone without the assistance of an advocate. Yet, self-help resources are very scarce too.

Parents of students in special education receive some information that school systems are required to provide under IDEA, and there are some commercial guidebooks on the market. However, these usually fall short and in any event are usually too late to do students mislabeled as disabled much good. Still, this information for parents of students in special education is light-years ahead of the guidance available for parents of struggling learners in general education.

School system guidelines may purport to assure parental involvement in the RTI process (if it exists). Yet, the guidance offered to parents is almost invariably long on words and short on practical usefulness. It's rarely written in words that are easy for parents to understand. And it is rarely provided to parents when they need it the most: that is, as soon as their child starts to fall behind and they are seeking explanations and assistance.

The basic remedies for these wrongs are straightforward enough. They are included in standard RTI protocols and require parental notification and involvement at every step in the process. Schools should be required to schedule meetings to fit the parents' schedules and send out advance notices that include a summary of the child's difficulties, efforts to provide extra assistance, and options for further interventions. The advance notices should also include a clear statement of the school system's legal duty to provide adequate instructional interventions so the child can close achievement gaps before referral to special education; and this statement should be explained orally to the parent at the start of any meeting.

And two more parental possibilities should be added at the end of any RTI decisions. One, school systems should establish some form of internal "complaint" procedures for parents that are less forbidding than the legalistic due process appeal rights under special education. For example, a school system ombudsperson or real resolution specialist should be available to review the parent's concerns. Two, some kind of external review—perhaps a last resort administrative appeal remedy—should also be established for parents before RTI is exhausted and their child is destined for special education.

In theory, parents can turn to various "parent centers," largely federally funded, that train parents to better navigate the IEP process.[20] However, these centers are few and far between. And even the best trained parent is likely to be overwhelmed by the technical subject matter. Further, if the parent is too assertive, the school system is likely to send in one of its lawyers to prop up the school IEP team.

Some Specific Tips for Parents

As noted, school systems are supposed to provide parents with guidance, and there are many commercial guidebooks for parents on understanding and navigating the IEP process. But none expose the educational abuse that occurs before and after referral to special education. Bewildered parents are offered few practical do's and don't's. Therefore, let me share a few that I think can make a difference. They are gleaned from my experience on the frontlines and are tips that most school systems would not want you to know.

- Keep written notes of what school staff say and do.

School teachers sometimes say the darndest things, like the plain truth about how and why your child is struggling, and why they can't provide more instructional help. Innumerable times, parents have told me that Teacher Jones admitted to them in casual conversation that Marcus or Kimberly wasn't getting the instruction that they needed. For example, that the extra help wasn't really helping much, or that the pull-out intervention was occurring only two days per week, not four days as it was supposed to, or that the instruction was the same old stuff that hadn't worked before. These admissions are often recanted or covered up in meetings, but parents should insist that the information in their notes be made a part of the student's file.

Even with a paper trail, it can be hard to hold the school system to its word. Nonetheless, something is better than nothing and parents should keep a paper trail of every communication with the school.

- Don't take the school system's word, particularly for how much progress your child is making.

Schools tend to exaggerate student progress. Recall grade inflation and "social promotion." So don't buy at face value claims that Marcus "is coming along well," or Arianna "is improving." And don't rely on teacher-made tests. Insist on seeing curriculum-embedded and/or standardized test data that substantiates measurable progress in narrowing the achievement gap.

A corollary piece of advice: go see for yourself. Naturally, parents should be closely attentive to and engaged in their child's progress. Help with homework. Communicate regularly with teachers. Volunteer at the school if you can and participate in the PTA. But, also, don't forget to visit the classroom, even though some schools are not as welcoming as they should be. You may be able to see whether your child is really in tune with the classroom instruction as reports of his or her progress may indicate.

- Don't be intimidated by fear that, if you advocate too persistently, the school will take it out on your child and do less not more.

For all my bouts with schools, I've never seen this happen. I have too much respect for educators to think it would happen. School officials may stop returning your phone calls or make you feel unwelcome, but they will do the very best they can for Kenny or Kimberly with the institutional hand they have been dealt.

And need it be said, not all parents are pitch-perfect either. Some parents can be downright rude and unreasonable. Still, they endure much more than they inflict, and will almost certainly be outgunned by school officials if they don't have the assistance of an advocate.

Is any advocacy assistance within reach? It is common practice at IEP meetings for parents to receive the names of non-profit organizations, including legal aid societies, which provide some form of help along the continuum between a lawyer and a trained volunteer. But what is left out of the notice is that these organizations are extremely underfunded and inaccessible.

The same holds true for "independent IEP facilitators," who are beginning to appear in school systems across the country.[21] The facilitators are supposed to improve relationships between parents and school staff. But they are not only in very short supply. They are a mixed bag in terms of training, and their role in IEP meeting is minimal because of their strict neutrality.

More robust models for assistance are highlighted in an article in the Yale Law Journal, "When Parents Aren't Enough: External Advocacy in Special Education."[22] One model is based on the public defender advocates appointed for children in child neglect and abuse cases. Another would fund well-staffed legal aid organizations. In both, trained community volunteers could supplement lawyers and paralegals.

And here's one more idea that comes to mind. How about if conservatives who so fervently advocate for school vouchers would propose vouchers so parents can pay for private assistance in IEP meetings? Ok, that's fanciful.

To sum up, the prospects that parents will be individually empowered to stand up for their own struggling learner, with or without an advocate at their side, are far-fetched. Even the best possibilities are, by no stretch of the imagination, probabilities. Each would more or less have to surmount general resistance to more government funding and the all-out determination of school systems to preserve their upper hand over parents.

Which brings us to the urgent imperative of collective political action by parents and their allies.

POLITICAL ACTION FOR SYSTEM-WIDE REFORM

As we've just seen, advocacy for parents in individual IEP meetings and appeals is a long way off. But even if it were more available and many students benefited, individual advocacy would not reform the system. School systems under pressure in individual student situations—whether the pressure comes from a parent or advocate or political official—can "fix" the individual complaint while deflecting attention from the urgency of system-wide change.

The Baltimore school system trumpets its Special Education Parents Response Unit which is supposed to investigate parent complaints. But its historical tendency has been to side with the school system while sweeping under the rug whether any violation is evidence of a system-wide pattern. The Maryland State Department of Education also has a unit to investigate parent complaints. Its investigations are more thorough and competent than the city's, and its findings not infrequently call upon the school or school system to review whether the individual complaint is evidence of a larger pattern. Yet again, there could be much more follow up to see whether there is a pattern and, if so, whether it has been meaningfully addressed.

The cold truth is that the educational abuse of struggling learners will never be halted without laws that explicitly guarantee system-wide rights. And such laws—whether federal or state—will never be enacted without forceful political action.

But how will parents get the force to be with them? How can parents be organized? And who will march arm-in-arm with them?

The Education Establishment Is a Non-Starter

For all the reasons that permeate this book, the education establishment will be AWOL from the battle. Its institutional allegiance is to the status quo. Witness the enduring folly of state and local control and the "race to the bottom" to undermine the reform goals of the No Child Left Behind Act. Chester E. Finn, Jr., a longtime school reform warrior, concludes, "In my experience, it's a system that bends—and then not nearly enough—only when powerful force is applied from outside. As soon as that force eases, the system resumes its previous shape."[23]

The system will be particularly unyielding in owning up to the abuse of struggling learners, especially students in special education. To illustrate, in 2013 the national School Superintendents Association issued a report that flew in the face of all the obstacles that parents face in exercising their appeal rights.[24] The report actually called for restricting parents' rights to due process, while trying to cover its tracks with weaker proposals. A national advocacy organization, the Council of Parent Attorneys and Advocates, called the report "nothing more than a shameful attack on parent and student civil rights."[25]

Usually the education establishment is not so brazen; it's able to cover its flanks through concealed tactics. The biggest special education scandal in recent memory erupted in Texas in 2016 when a Houston newspaper exposed deliberate attempts over many years by the state education agency to suppress eligibility for special education.[26] The state did so not on the grounds that students were mislabeled as disabled, but solely to save money. The misconduct was so blatant that even the inert U.S. Department of Education launched a prompt investigation that confirmed the wrongdoing and ordered corrective action.

But where were state and local educators while all of this was going on? Why were state officials silent except when, finally caught in the act, they put all the blame on the Texas legislature? And why didn't local special educators blow the whistle on the state? Obviously, bureaucratic fear or inertia reigned at all levels. Local special education administrators offered various excuses. The excuses ranged from "limited resources, limited training, and inconsistent guidance" to "it is not a dereliction of duty to follow a directive from your state regulatory agency."[27] Bottom line: there is nothing in the public record that any part of the spineless Texas education establishment spoke up.

Texas has been outsized in its wrongdoing. But when it comes to the educational abuse of struggling learners, there is silence all across the land. National, state and local associations of elementary school principals, secondary school principals, superintendents and school boards have been virtually silent. None of this, as this book has unveiled, is a surprise. It's even no surprise that associations of special educators—for example, teachers, state directors of special education, psychologists and speech and language pathologists—have not blown the whistle on the system's illegalities and injustices.

And so the fight for reform will have to be led by outsiders. But alas, that is not as straightforward as it would seem. The potential reformers—among them parents, their advocacy organizations and liberal Democrats—not as poised for the battle as they should be. We next look at what's behind this unexpected political foot-dragging.

Lack of Unity among Parents of Struggling Learners

To start with, the parents of struggling learners are difficult to organize cohesively despite their vast numbers. A primary reason is that the educational abuse their children suffer is largely hidden from their view. They recognize their children are struggling, but they don't realize how much better the children could and should be doing. They aren't aware how school systems cover up failure with fake grades, "social promotion" from grade to grade, and bogus high school diplomas.

At the same time, the parents of struggling learners who lag in general education and the parents of struggling learners who are mislabeled as disabled and dumped in special education don't realize their common cause. They aren't aware of their legal rights and mutual needs for early instructional interventions through the framework of RTI.

And even if they did, they don't have a bigger education reform movement to latch on to. Instructional reform in the classroom, let's not forget, is lost in the sound and fury of the nation's most polarized and raging crusades, such as school choice, privatization, testing, and local control.

And there's still more to the lack of unity. While all the parents of struggling learners should recognize they're more or less in the same boat, differences often arise that keep them from steering in the same political direction. The biggest difference is the tension, if not outright competition, between the two main groupings of students in special education.

Recall that the first group, mainly those we have called the Mainly Mislabeled, may comprise as many as 85 percent of all students in special education, usually under the classifications of Specific Learning Disability (including dyslexia), Other Health Impairment (predominately ADHD) and Speech or Language impairments. They are able to achieve regular state standards with adequate interventions.

The second group, mainly those we've called the Truly Disabled, are students with severe disabilities like Intellectual Disabilities, severe Autism and visual and hearing impairments. Not all but most of these students cannot be expected to meet the same academic standards as nondisabled peers.

Parents and other advocates for the Mainly Disabled and Truly Disabled could more successfully accomplish their complementary purposes if they were pulling together politically. But that is often not the case.

I have worked little on the national stage of disability politics. But I have interacted with many of the leading players who work for national organizations and with their state and local chapters in Maryland. Most represent the Truly Disabled, such as several groups that advocate for children with Down syndrome, the Arc for persons with intellectual and developmental disabilities, and the National Federation of the Blind. A smaller number represent the Mainly Mislabeled, including several groups representing students with dyslexia, the Learning Disabilities Association of America, and CHADD (Children and Adults with Attention-Deficit/Hyperactivity Disorder). Several organizations that advocate for students along the autism spectrum tend to pitch their tents in both camps, though most of the focus is on the severe end of the spectrum. And many more disability-specific groups could be listed.

What is to be made of this array? There is some common purpose and blood, sweat and tears but it's mixed with disarray. Some national coalitions attempt to play a unifying role. Among them, the Leadership Conference on Civil and Human Rights, the National Disability Rights Network, and the Consortium for Citizens with Disabilities. There are also state and local councils such as Councils on Developmental Disabilities and special education citizens' advisory committees. Yet, these tend to show little stomach or muscle for taking on the establishment. And the web of professional organizations of general and special educators, mentioned earlier, rarely makes its presence felt.

This is a cursory scan of the political landscape, but it shows clearly enough that strong and cohesive political resistance to the educational abuse of struggling learners is usually hard to find. Its most prominent feature is the tension between the Mainly Disabled and Truly Disabled organizations, but friction sometimes pops up between different groups that represent the same population.

I've encountered this first-hand in the rough and tumble of my own efforts in Maryland and nationally over the past decade, both to campaign for RTI and for Baltimore's One Year Plus policy described in Chapter 5. These policies would raise the bar for the goals and services for the Mainly Mislabeled and Truly Disabled, but their chief impact would be on the first group. For that reason, advocates for the Truly Disabled have done relatively little to join the causes. Even Maryland's coalition of advocates for students in special education, in which I have actively participated, has given relatively little support. It's dominated, as are most umbrella organizations in the field of special education, by parents and advocates for Truly Disabled students. And advocacy for the Truly Disabled has tended to center on issues other than instruction—like expulsion, restraint and seclusion, transportation and transition planning.

These are worthy concerns, and none of this means that advocates for the Truly Disabled are uncaring about all struggling learners. Instead, it mainly reflects competition for money and attention in a political environment that is inhospitable and unjust to all. Frequently, attorneys and other advocates for the Truly Disabled are themselves parents of children with severe disabilities. I understand the pain and passion that drives them. I would do the same if I were in their shoes.

Still, the competition between the Mainly Disabled and the Truly Disabled over inadequate resources sets back reform overall. Even before the first version of IDEA in 1975, there was, as an education historian has found, "disunity among the different organizations representing children who were deaf, crippled, blind, mentally retarded, and otherwise handicapped."[28] This flared up over the decades as special education rolls swelled with students who were Mainly Disabled, especially the students who were classified with a Specific Learning Disability (LD). A scholar has noted that "Students with LDs were viewed as competing for scarce resources with other 'deserving' groups."[29]

Over the years, some of the disability nomenclature has been changed but not much of the disunity. The reaction to the Supreme Court decision in the Endrew F case reflected this. Advocates for the Truly Disabled tended to see it in a positive light (for reasons that are mystifying to me as discussed in Chapter 8), while advocates for the Mainly Mislabeled were more skeptical and muted. Another fairly recent example arose in late 2015 when the national organization Decoding Dyslexia sought certain amendments to IDEA that were opposed by organizations representing students with the most severe disabilities. The head of a group devoted to students with intellectual limitations said the dyslexia advocates "give the impression, whether it's intended or not, that students with a certain type of learning disabilities have more pressing needs than other students with disabilities."[30]

One more sign of discord requires mention, I'm sorry to say. It isn't just advocates for the Truly Disabled and Mainly Disabled who often go their separate ways. Within advocacy groups for the Mainly Mislabeled, there are some unspoken differences too. What I call "the politics of dyslexia" sheds light on this.

The Invisible Politics of Dyslexia

Dyslexia is an endlessly fascinating and instructive subject. It embodies much that is good, but a little that is troublesome, about the plight of struggling learners. It has its own political dynamics, and discussion of it carries special risks. I am skating on thin, politically incorrect ice with the analysis that follows. Nonetheless, I think it's vital to note that many parents of students with dyslexia, while understandingly zealous in their advocacy, could play a more pivotal role in ending the abuse of a more broadly defined population of struggling learners.

To begin with, dyslexia commands a special resonance in the public mind. It garners great media attention. It has savvy and influential advocates. The online publication of the NASET (National Association of Special Education Teachers) Week in Review contained this item:

QUESTION: Tom Cruise, Keanu Reeves, Whoopi Goldberg, Cher, Selma Hayek, Richard Branson, Henry Winkler, Tim Tebow, and Magic Johnson. What do all of these famous people have in common?
ANSWER: They all reported having DYSLEXIA.[31]

Notice there is nary a postal worker, or home health aide, or clerk, or dishwasher among them. But so what? Isn't the success of celebrities inspiring to all struggling learners? My answer to that question is: this kind of publicity is not nearly as beneficial as it should be, and it can be counterproductive. It's too restricted and laden with adverse consequences for political reform.

A few years ago a foundation report supporting more services for students with dyslexia stated, "Multiple and sometimes competing constituencies," in the Specific Learning Disability field that includes dyslexia, "are divided and disorganized more often than they are unified, and it's usually children with LD who pay the price."[32] The way I see it is that sometimes advocates for dyslexia limit their reforms—usually state laws that call for screening and interventions and teacher training—without broader reference to RTI for all struggling learners.

These parent-advocates are typically well-educated and well-off financially. They pick up fairly early that their children are struggling to learn to read, and that school systems are missing or delaying the identification of dyslexia and timely instructional assistance. These parents may be able to hire private experts who document phonological processing deficits and other markers of dyslexia with a depth and expertise that public school systems lack. With evaluations in hand, the parents fight fiercely for services for their children, and if all else fails, they hire private lawyers. They are also the founders of dyslexia-only advocacy organizations.

But their view can be narrow. They tend to miss the "invisible dyslexics" that I wrote about in a report published by the Abell Foundation in 2003. The full title of my report was "The Invisible Dyslexics: How Public Schools in Baltimore and Elsewhere Discriminate Against Poor Children in the Diagnosis and Treatment of Early Reading Difficulties."[33] These "invisible dyslexics," first brought to light in Chapter 2, don't have high IQs, or exceptional ability in the arts or sports or anything else. They aren't lucky enough to have parents who can afford—through pricey private psychologists, reading specialists and lawyers—to establish their "dyslexia." Yet, they, by most common definitions, have dyslexia too.

This disservice to the reform cause happens when the reading problems of poor children are typically attributed not to dyslexia but to low-average IQs and poverty backgrounds. This is flat-out wrong, a triumph of stereotypical blaming the victim over the science of reading. Reading scientists have established that "invisible dyslexics" struggle to become proficient readers because of the same underlying causal factors as students from better-off families whose dyslexia is more visible, and they can benefit equally from the same evidence-based instruction. Dyslexia-only advocates tend to ignore or downplay these facts, narrowing and weakening overall political support for RTI and IEP reforms.

My own experience illuminates the danger of this happening, though it has a happy ending. A grass roots movement in a small county in Maryland founded a vibrant Maryland chapter of the national network Decoding Dyslexia. Its stellar accomplishments in a short period of time include pushing through state legislation to create a Dyslexia Task Force which proposed significant steps to increase diagnosis and treatment. Yet, for a while, a smaller band of advocates, including me, had trouble enlisting them in more inclusive attempts to address struggling learners.

Now, to their credit, that's changed. We are allied in efforts to increase funding and accountability for RTI in general education and One Year Plus-like IEPs in special education.

Still, just the fact that there was some distance for a while between our efforts seems symptomatic of the national failure of the popular dyslexia movements of the day to embrace struggling learners defined more broadly. Dyslexia organizations can bring potent political support when they fight on behalf of reforms to end the educational abuse of all struggling learners. Decoding Dyslexia of Maryland is showing the way.

Liberal Fratricide

The political tensions among advocates for different disabilities, as troubling as they are, are far more defensible than the educational free-for-all among political liberals. Nothing seems more in the natural political order of things than liberals leading the charge to establish a civil right to an adequate education, thereby laying the foundation for ending the abuse of struggling learners. The civil right would include guarantees of RTI-like interventions and the money to pay for them.

The opposition of conservatives is certain. Conservative orthodoxy holds that privatization and emasculation of teachers unions would do the job without legal guarantees or more money. Yet, over the past decade or so, some liberals have spent too much time warring against each other rather than against conservatives. This stems from the tendency of some liberals (not all!) to agree with conservatives that school reform cannot be accomplished without larger economic and social transformations outside of school.

The tendency goes back to the famous 1966 Coleman report findings that school resources meant less in determining student achievement than family economic and educational background. Still, there is a world of difference in why odd liberal and conservative bedfellows climb into the same political sack.

These liberals dwell mainly on the conviction that society at large is at fault. Inequality of opportunity—poverty, un- and under-employment, poor housing and neighborhoods, crime and the scourge of drugs, and other economic and social circumstances—are the root causes of student failure in school. Conservatives believe it is not society but individual parents who are most to blame. Family culture, they think, counts more than teachers or other school resources. In their view, homework doesn't get done, absences and latenesses pile up (reading instruction is often the first class in the morning), and teachers are disrespected.

While liberals are unified in fighting for more funding, they splinter on strategy.[34] One camp argues that the primary focus must be on fighting poverty and inequality *outside* of the schools. As articulated by Richard Rothstein, a brilliant researcher and political progressive, "The influence of social class characteristics is probably so powerful that schools cannot overcome it, no matter how well-designed are their instructional programs and climates."[35] That doesn't mean schools can't do anything by themselves. Rothstein would "never say public schools can't do better ... [but] they can't do much better" without first redressing the social and economic ills of the poor.[36]

Other liberals—and I am staunchly one of them—believe that this focus on economic and social programs outside the schools lets educators too easily off the hook. The former reform-minded superintendent of the Baltimore city schools preached a "no excuses" culture: "we take kids the way we find them and educate them well no matter what." I agree.

In a sense, that's a bottom line message of this book. Notwithstanding all the social and economic problems that disadvantage struggling learners, and all the policy and political obstacles to reform, public schools can improve mightily. Student achievement can rise. And in particular, we can end the educational abuse of struggling learners if more money and better management were devoted to RTI and related programs.

There is one further significant division in what should be a united liberal front: conflicting priorities between low and upper income parents, usually over budget priorities.

One telltale example is whether pre-kindergarten programs for four and three year olds should be available for all children (the universal approach) or only for "at-risk" poor children (the targeted approach). Research shows that the advantages of pre-k programs accrue generally to at-risk children but not others. Yet, parents across the economic spectrum seek the programs for their children too. Without the votes of legislators representing middle income and up constituents, it is more difficult to enact targeted programs, even when funds are lacking for the universal approach.

Other examples of competition for scarce funding range from smaller class sizes, to summer school, to programs for gifted and talented children—all of which provide greater benefits for low- than high-achieving students. It's political triage really. As a member of the Baltimore school board, I was the lone dissenting vote against providing extra funds for gifted and talented programs because I felt, given the system's threadbare budget, the funds in question would be more cost-effective if spent on interventions for struggling learners. Proponents of the gifted and talented funding argued less on its academic merits and more on its importance in keeping the dwindling public school population of middle class children. People can rightly differ in making such damned-if-you-do, damned-if-you-don't decisions. What's clear, however, is that the budget competition strains political unity among liberals.

Still, the point should be kept in context. The differences among liberals are nowhere near as dangerous to school reform as monolithic conservative doctrine is. Nonetheless, given the prevailing conservative political supremacy, liberals can be much more politically astute and victorious if they heal the breaches in their ranks.

Enlisting Teachers Unions in the Campaign

And here's one more big political "if:" there is a much greater chance to end educational abuse if teachers unions can be fully engaged in the campaign. Unions are an admirable mainstay of liberal politics in many respects. I usually admire and defend them. In particular, they are the backbone of political efforts to increase school funding. Yet, they have almost exclusively linked the need for more money to higher teacher salaries.

True, teacher compensation definitely lags behind comparable professions. And unions have every right to campaign for higher pay and benefits. Yet, they have done relatively little to flex their muscles behind more funding for other reforms, notably RTI for struggling learners. This shortsightedness does their membership a disservice since it neglects other factors that are essential to teacher recruitment and retention. To underscore a point made many chapters ago, teachers rank working conditions ahead of pay. Few conditions are more demoralizing to general education teachers than having so many struggling learners in their fairly large classes. Job satisfaction suffers when teachers are unable to boost far-behind struggling learners or bring out the best in students who aren't struggling. And pity most of all beleaguered and abandoned special educators who must cope with so many students who are even farther behind (and mislabeled as disabled).

Teachers unions need to get this message and place it high up on their political agenda.

CALL TO ACTION

As this book comes to a close, I have left you my dear readers with a balancing task of your own. First, I have hardly pulled punches in indicting public education. I've also tried to be open and honest in not glossing over the many ideological and political obstacles to reform. As a nation, we are divided over causes and cures for inequality, including unequal educational opportunity. And educators themselves are institutionally resistant to change.

Still, I hope that I have left you with another strong impression: the conviction that reform is possible. I have shown how there is a credible and feasible way to elevate student achievement to a higher plateau. Struggling learners can be taught to meet grade level standards. It's a matter of ways (RTI and better management) and means (resources). And it's up to all of Us including Educators to deliver them.

Don't let the Trump-era politics discourage you. Yes, present prospects for change for the common good including public education are bleak. And they look worst at the federal level, where the prime foundations for reform must be laid. The U. S. Department of Education is now in reverse overdrive, crushing even modest reform roots.[37] The same is true for K-12 policy in many red states. But in blue states like my Maryland, there are near-term opportunities. Best of all could be passage of legislation that incorporates the recommendations of the Kirwan Commission whose work has been profiled earlier.

In any and all events, be of stout resolve. Our nation's politics run in cycles, and the current one shows signs of running out. Take heart too from the Winston Churchill's maxim that we Americans do the right thing only after we've exhausted all the other possibilities.

Some day we the American people will look back on the educational abuse of struggling learners. On our failure to enable our children to learn to read and have a fair shot at higher education and the workplace. On the particular discrimination against poor and minority children. And on the self-inflicted decline in our nation's economic and social well-being.

We and future generations will say: how could we let it happen and go on for so long? Shouldn't the educational abuse of struggling learners stir up some of the same emotions and shame as our national past on school segregation? Shouldn't we end once and for all the education abuse of struggling learners, who are predominantly poor and minority children?

The answers should be self-evident. Let's unite and organize to end this national disgrace. We owe it legally and morally to our children, and we owe it to ourselves. Our standing as a just nation is at stake.

Notes

CHAPTER 1

1. This was said to me by a Baltimore special education teacher who did not want to be identified for fear of retribution by administrators.
2. Here is one general statement of the law across the states: "When a child is negligently, recklessly, intentionally, or knowingly injured by an act or mission by any person, then that person can be charged with felony child abuse." "Felony Child Abuse," FreeAdvice, n.d., https://criminal-law.freeadvice.com/criminal-law/violent_crimes/felony-child-abuse.htm. And see, for example, "the term 'child abuse' means a crime committed under any law of a State that involves the physical or mental injury, sexual abuse or exploitation, negligent treatment, or maltreatment of a child by any person." 34 U.S. Code, Sec. 40104(3).
3. Throughout the book, struggling learners are sometimes described as being "in" special education. That is not technically true because special education is not a place but a continuum of services, and most of those services are in fact delivered in "inclusionary" general education settings. Still, it sometimes strengthens the book's narrative if reference is made to students "in" special education—particularly to contrast students in special education who are mislabeled as disabled with those who are truly disabled.
4. Janie Scull and Amber M. Winkler, "Shifting Trends in Special Education," Thomas B. Fordham Institute, May 25, 2011, https://edexcellence.net/publications/shifting-trends-in-special.html; Daniel Koretz, *Measuring Up: What Educational Testing Really Tells Us* (Cambridge, MA: Harvard University Press, 2008), 283–86.
5. Alan Gartner and Dorothy Kerzner Lipsky, "Beyond Special Education: Toward a Quality System for All Students," *Harvard Educational Review* 57, no. 4 (November 1987): 367–95, 372.
6. Claire Raj, "The Misidentification of Children with Disabilities: A Harm with No Foul," *Arizona State Law Journal* 48 (Summer 2016): 373–437, esp. 374; Thomas M. Skrtic, "The Special Education Paradox," in *Special Education for a New Century*, ed. Lauren I. Katzman et al. (Cambridge, MA: Harvard Educational Review, 2005), 204; Rebecca O. Zumeta et al., "Identifying Specific

Learning Disabilities," *Topics in Language Disorders* 34, no. 1 (January–March 2014): 8–24, esp. 21.

7. See Scull and Winkler, "Shifting Trends"; also Raj, "Misidentification of Children," 382.

8. "Number and Percentage of Children Served under Individuals with Disabilities Education Act (IDEA), Part B, by Age Group and State or Jurisdiction: Selected Years, 1990–91 through 2013–14," National Center for Education Statistics (NCES), December 2015, https://nces.ed.gov/programs/digest/d15/tables/dt15_204.70.asp?current=yes.

9. Candace Cortiella and Sheldon H. Horowitz, *The State of Learning Disabilities: Facts, Trends and Emerging Issues*, 3rd ed. (New York: National Center for Learning Disabilities, 2014), https://www.ncld.org/wp-content/uploads/2014/11/2014-State-of-LD.pdf.

10. 34 CFR 200.1(d). Students with the "most significant cognitive disabilities" are not defined under IDEA. Those intended to be covered are students whose "cognitive impairments may prevent them from attaining grade-level achievement standards, even with the very best instruction." Eric D. Lomax and Ann Lordeman, *The Education of Students with Disabilities: Alignment between the Elementary and Secondary Education Act and the Individuals with Disabilities Education Act* (Washington, DC: Congressional Research Service, 2011), 5.

11. Wade F. Horn and Douglas Tynan, "Time to Make Special Education 'Special' Again," in *Rethinking Special Education for a New Century*, ed. Chester E. Finn Jr. et al. (Washington, DC: Thomas B. Fordham Foundation and Progressive Policy Institute, 2001), 40.

12. For a breakdown of students in disability categories, see "Children and Youth with Disabilities," NCES, last updated April 2018, https://nces.ed.gov/programs/coe/indicator_cgg.asp.

13. G. Reid Lyon et al., "Rethinking Learning Disabilities," in *Rethinking Special Education*, ed. Finn Jr. et al., 260. See also expert estimates that between 50 and 75 percent of struggling learners end up unnecessarily in special education. Allan R. Odden and Lawrence O. Picus, *School Finance: A Policy Perspective*, 5th ed. (New York: McGraw-Hill, 2014), 97.

14. Martha L. Thurlow et al., "Meeting the Needs of Special Education Students: Recommendations for the Race to the Top Consortia and States," National Center on Education Outcomes, Minneapolis, Minnesota, 2011, https://nceo.umn.edu/docs/OnlinePubs/Martha_Thurlow-Meeting_the_Needs_of_Special_Education_Students.pdf, 5.

15. Arne Duncan, "Fulfilling the Promise of IDEA," U.S. Department of Education, November 18, 2010, http://www.ed.gov/news/speeches/fulfilling-promise-idea-remarks-35th-anniversary-individuals-disabilities-act.

16. For citations and further data, see chapter 3.
17. E. D. Hirsch Jr., *The Schools We Need and Why We Don't Have Them* (New York: Doubleday, 1996), 15.
18. The study is reported in Pamela Darr Wright, "The Blame Game! Are School Problems the Kids' Fault?," *Wrightslaw* (blog), 2010, http://www.wrightslaw.com/advoc/articles/ALESSI1.html.
19. Margaret J. McLaughlin, "Closing the Achievement Gap and Students with Disabilities: The New Meaning of a 'Free and Appropriate Public Education'" (paper presented at the Second Annual Symposium on Educational Equity, Teachers College, Columbia University, New York, November 13–14, 2006), http://www.equitycampaign.org/events-page/equity-symposia/2006-examining-americas-commitment-to-closing-achievement-gaps-nclb-and-its-a/papers/McLaughlin_Edited[1].Closing-the-Achievement-Gap-11-29.pdf, 34.
20. Cited in Gartner and Lipsky, "Beyond Special Education," 384.
21. *Student A v. the Berkeley Unified School District*, U.S. District Court (Northern District of California), complaint for injunctive and declaratory relief, May 2, 2017, https://dredf.org/wp-content/uploads/2017/05/dredf-busd-complaint-5-2-17.pdf.
22. *Gary B. v. Richard D. Snyder*, U.S. District Court (Eastern District of Michigan, Southern Division), civil action no. 16-CV-13292, class action complaint, September 13, 2016.
23. Ryan Felton, "Detroit Civil Rights Lawsuit Attempts to Assert a Constitutional Right to Literacy," *Guardian*, September 14, 2016, https://www.theguardian.com/us-news/2016/sep/14/detroit-civil-rights-lawsuit-constitutional-literacy-education.

CHAPTER 2

1. G. Reid Lyon et al., "Rethinking Learning Disabilities," in *Rethinking Special Education for a New Century*, ed. Chester E. Finn Jr. et al. (Washington, DC: Thomas B. Fordham Foundation and Progressive Policy Institute, May 2001), 260.
2. Jack M. Fletcher et al., *Learning Disabilities: From Identification to Intervention* (New York: Guilford Press, 2007), 5.
3. Allan R. Odden and Lawrence O. Picus, *School Finance: A Policy Perspective*, 5th ed. (New York: McGraw-Hill, 2014), 97; Lyon et al., "Rethinking Learning Disabilities," 260.
4. Claire Raj, "The Misidentification of Children with Disabilities: A Harm with No Foul," *Arizona State Law Journal* 48 (Summer 2016): 373–437, esp. 374;

Thomas M. Skrtic, "The Special Education Paradox," in *Special Education for a New Century*, ed. Lauren I. Katzman et al. (Cambridge, MA: Harvard Educational Review, 2005), 204; Rebecca O. Zumeta et al., "Identifying Specific Learning Disabilities," *Topics in Language Disorders* 34, no. 1 (January–March 2014): 8–24, esp. 21.

5. CFR 3000.550.

6. James McLeskey and Nancy L. Waldron, "Educational Programs for Elementary Students with Learning Disabilities: Can They Be Both Effective and Inclusive?," *Learning Disabilities Research & Practice* 26, no. 1 (February 2011): 48–57, esp. 49. See also Nathan Levenson, "Something Has Got to Change: Rethinking Special Education" (working paper 2011-01, American Enterprise Institute), 7. For a positive perspective on inclusion, see generally "The Segregation of Students with Disabilities," National Council on Disability, February 7, 2018, https://ncd.gov/sites/default/files/NCD_Segregation-SWD_508.pdf.

7. Zumeta et al., "Identifying Specific Learning Disabilities," 11.

8. "President Gerald R. Ford's Statement on Signing the Education for All Handicapped Children Act of 1975," Ford Library and Museum, last updated August 3, 2000, https://www.fordlibrarymuseum.gov/library/speeches/750707.htm.

9. Wade F. Horn and Douglas Tynan, "Time to Make Special Education 'Special' Again," in *Rethinking Special Education*, ed. Finn Jr. et al., 23.

10. "Children 3 to 21 Years Old Served under Individuals with Disabilities Education Act (IDEA), Part B, by Type of Disability: Selected Years, 1976–77 through 2014–15," National Center for Education Statistics (NCES), July 2016, https://nces.ed.gov/programs/digest/d16/tables/dt16_204.30.asp.

11. See, for example, Richard Peterson, "The Persistence of Low Expectations in Special Education Law Viewed through the Lens of Therapeutic Jurisprudence," *International Journal of Law and Psychiatry* (November–December 2010): 2, https://www.ncbi.nlm.nih.gov/pubmed/20923716.

12. See the No Child Left Behind Act of 2001, Pub. L. No. 107-117, 115 Stat. 1425 (2002), https://www2.ed.gov/policy/elsec/leg/esea02/107-110.pdf.

13. George W. Bush, "Executive Order 13227: Presidents Commission on Excellence in Special Education," October 2, 2001, American Presidency Project, http://www.presidency.ucsb.edu/ws/index.php?pid=61508.

14. 34 CFR 300.307–11.

15. "Number and Percentage of Children Served under Individuals with Disabilities Education Act (IDEA), Part B, by Age Group and State or Jurisdiction: Selected Years, 1990–91 through 2013–14," NCES, December 2015, https://nces.ed.gov/programs/digest/d15/tables/dt15_204.70.asp?current=yes.

16. "Fostering Motivation in Kids with Learning and Attention Problems," Great Schools Staff, March 14, 2016, https://www.greatschools.org/gk/articles/motivating-kids-learning-attention-problems/.

17. Bryan Goodwin, "Reading: The Core Skill," *Educational Leadership* 69, no. 6 (March 2012): 80–81, esp. 81.

18. Keith Stanovich, "Matthew Effects in Reading: Some Consequences of Individual Differences in the Acquisition of Literacy," *Reading Research Quarterly* 22 (Fall 1986): 360–407, https://rsrc.psychologytoday.com/files/u81/Stanovich__1986_.pdf.

19. The phrase "soft bigotry of low expectations" is generally attributed to President George W. Bush. "Excerpts From Bush's Speech on Improving Education," *New York Times*, September 3, 1999, https://www.nytimes.com/1999/09/03/us/excerpts-from-bush-s-speech-on-improving-education.html.

20. Candace Cortiella and Sheldon H. Horowitz, *The State of Learning Disabilities: Facts, Trends and Emerging Issues*, 3rd ed. (New York: National Center for Learning Disabilities, 2014), https://www.ncld.org/wp-content/uploads/2014/11/2014-State-of-LD.pdf, 11.

21. G. Alessi, "Diagnosis Diagnosed: A Systemic Reaction," *Professional School Psychology* 3, no. 2 (1988): 145–51, esp. 149, http://dx.doi.org/10.1037/h0090554.

22. Dr. Alessi's study is highlighted in an excellent article by Pamela Darr Wright, "The Blame Game! Are School Problems the Kids' Fault?," *Wrightslaw* (blog), 2010, http://www.wrightslaw.com/blog/?tag=galen-alessi. The quotes above are from page 3 of the article. See the full study at http://www.wrightslaw.com/advoc/articles/alessi.article.pdf.

23. Kalman R. Hettleman, *The Invisible Dyslexics: How Public School Systems in Baltimore and Elsewhere Discriminate against Poor Children in the Diagnosis and Treatment of Early Reading Difficulties* (Baltimore, MD: Abell Foundation, 2003), https://www.abell.org/sites/default/files/publications/ed_invisible_dyslexics.pdf.

24. For a convenient summary, see "The Thirty Million Word Gap," School Literacy and Culture, Rice University, 2011–12, http://childrenshousepreschool.org/wp-content/uploads/2014/08/Rice-University-School-Literacy-and-Culture-The-Thirty-Million-Word-Gap-1.pdf.

25. Janie Scull and Amber M. Winkler, "Shifting Trends in Special Education," Thomas B. Fordham Institute, May 25, 2011, https://edexcellence.net/publications/shifting-trends-in-special.html; Daniel Koretz, *Measuring Up: What Educational Testing Really Tells Us* (Cambridge, MA: Harvard University Press, 2008), 283–86.

26. Alan Gartner and Dorothy Kerzner Lipsky, "Beyond Special Education: Toward a Quality System for All Students," *Harvard Educational Review* 57, no. 4 (November 1987): 367–95, esp. 372.

27. Education for All Handicapped Children Act of 1975, Pub. L. No. 94-142, 89 Stat. 773 (1975), https://www.gpo.gov/fdsys/pkg/STATUTE-89/pdf/STATUTE-89-Pg773.pdf.

28. Fletcher et al., *Learning Disabilities*, 20.

29. "Children 3 to 21 Years Old."

30. Fletcher et al., *Learning Disabilities*, 20.

31. Catherine E. Snow, M. Susan Burns, and Peg Griffin, eds., *Preventing Reading Difficulties in Young Children* (Washington, DC: National Academy Press, 1998), 91. See also Lyon et al., "Rethinking Learning Disabilities," 260.

32. Sally E. Shaywitz, "Dyslexia," *Scientific American*, November 1996, 98–104, esp. 103.

33. Joseph K. Torgesen, "Catch Them before They Fall," *American Educator*, Spring–Summer 1998, 32–39, esp. 34.

34. Lyon et al., "Rethinking Learning Disabilities," 266. For an excellent and more recent review of the evidence debunking the discrepancy gap, see North Carolina Department of Public Instruction Exceptional Children Division, *Proposed Policy Revisions: Specific Learning Disabilities*, report from the Specific Learning Disability Task Force, April 2015, https://ec.ncpublicschools.gov/gcs04-taskforce-report.pdf, 2.

35. Gartner and Lipsky, "Beyond Special Education," 383.

36. Vance L. Austin, "Learning Disabilities Today: An Examination of Effective and Not-So-Effective Interventions," *Journal of the American Academy of Special Education Professionals*, Spring–Summer 2015, 7–28, esp. 7.

37. Lyon et al., "Rethinking Learning Disabilities," 264.

38. John D. E. Gabrieli, "A New Synergy between Education and Cognitive Neuroscience," *Science* 325 (July 2009): 280–83, esp. 281.

39. Gabrieli, 282.

40. CFR 300.309(a)(2)(ii).

41. Fletcher et al., *Learning Disabilities*, 48.

42. Sharon Vaughan and Sylvia Linan-Thompson, "What Is Special about Special Education for Students with Learning Disabilities?," *Journal of Special Education* 37, no. 3 (2003): 140–47, esp. 141.

43. Daniel J. Reschly, "Response to Intervention and the Identification of Specific Learning Disabilities," *Topics in Language Disorders* 34, no. 1 (2014): 39–58, esp. 53.

44. Fletcher et al., *Learning Disabilities*, 5.

45. See the definitions of the disability categories in CFR 300.8(c).

46. Letter from acting director, Office of Special Education Programs, U.S. Department of Education, November 28, 2007, https://www2.ed.gov/policy/speced/guid/idea/letters/2007-4/redact112807eligibility4q2007.pdf.

47. The special education legal expert Perry A. Zirkel shed some light on this in a 2017 journal article. The specific case he discusses focuses on whether students who are succeeding academically in general education can be found eligible for special education because of nonacademic problems such as behavior and mental health. In other words, do the nonacademic problems have an "adverse affect" on the student's "educational performance" that justifies eligibility for special education? Zirkel, "A Major New Court Decision: Are Blurred Boundaries Worth the Price on the Eligibility Side?," *Exceptionality* 25, no. 1 (2017): 1–8.

48. Perry A. Zirkel, "The Legal Dimension of RTI: Part II. State Laws and Guidelines," RTI Action Network, 2013, http://www.rtinetwork.org/learn/ld/the-legal-dimension-of-rti-part-ii-state-laws-and-guidelines, 2.

49. Maryland State Department of Education, "Using the Response to Intervention (RtI) process for Identifying Specific Learning Disabilities (SLD)," *Technical Assistance Bulletin* 16 (2009): 6.

50. "Related Disorders of a Learning Disability: What You Should Know," Learning Disability Association of America, October 2013, https://ldaamerica.org/what-you-should-know-about-related-disorders-of-learning-disability/. The conditions that most commonly occur with dyslexia include speech and language disorders and ADHD. Mark Seidenberg, *Language at the Speed of Sight: How We Read, Why So Many Can't, and What Can Be Done about It* (New York: Basic Books, 2017), 166.

51. Fletcher et al., *Learning Disabilities*, 7.

52. Cortiella and Horowitz, *State of Learning Disabilities*, 5.

CHAPTER 3

1. Caleb Stewart Rossiter, *Ain't Nobody Be Learnin' Nothin': The Fraud and the Fix for High-Poverty School* (New York: Algora, 2015).

2. Thomas M. Skrtic, "The Special Education Paradox: Equity as the Way to Excellence," in *Special Education for a New Century*, ed. Lauren I. Katzman et al. (Cambridge, MA: Harvard Educational Review, 2005), 204. See also Claire Raj, "The Misidentification of Children with Disabilities: A Harm with No Foul," *Arizona State Law Journal* 48 (Summer 2016): 373–437, esp. 374. I know of no study that compares the achievement of struggling learner who winds up in special education with those who don't, but we know that there is often no great difference in the nature and degree of their learning struggles. So the enormous disparity between the test scores of students who do and don't receive special education services—later documented—is at least a rough marker that the students who don't receive special education services are relatively better off.

3. Lee Funk, "Stats Show That Few Special Ed Students Fully Re-enter General Education," *Cabinet Report*, August 29, 2011, https://www.cabinetreport.com/special-education/stats-show-that-few-special-ed-students-fully-re-enter-general-education.

4. "2017 NAEP Mathematics and Reading Assessments: Highlighted Results at Grades 4 and 8 for the Nation, States, and Districts," National Center for Education Statistics (NCES), April 2018, https://nces.ed.gov/pubsearch/pubsinfo.asp?pubid=2018037.

5. "Mathematics and Reading Assessments," Nation's Report Card, 2015, https://www.nationsreportcard.gov/reading_math_2015/#?grade=4.

6. Candace Cortiella and Sheldon H. Horowitz, *The State of Learning Disabilities: Facts, Trends and Emerging Issues*, 3rd ed. (New York: National Center for Learning Disabilities, 2014), https://www.ncld.org/wp-content/uploads/2014/11/2014-State-of-LD.pdf, 15.

7. David R. Johnson et al., *Diploma Options, Graduation Requirements, and Exit Exams for Youth with Disabilities: 2011 National Study*, National Center on Educational Outcomes, technical report no. 62, Minneapolis, Minnesota, 2012.

8. Unpublished documents. Please contact the author to obtain copies.

9. Emily Workman, "Third-Grade Reading Policies," Education Commission of the States, Denver, Colorado, December 2014, https://www.ecs.org/clearinghouse/01/16/44/11644.pdf, 2.

10. Workman, 2.

11. Motoko Rich, "A Summer of Extra Reading and Hope for Fourth Grade," *New York Times*, August 4, 2014, https://www.nytimes.com/2014/08/05/us/a-summer-of-extra-reading-and-hope-for-fourth-grade.html.

12. Robert E. Slavin, "Reading by Third Grade—or Else," *HuffPost* (blog), updated December 6, 2017, https://www.huffingtonpost.com/robert-e-slavin/reading-by-third-grade_b_5677958.html.

13. Catherine Gewertz, "Pressure to Graduate Failing Students Is Felt Nationwide," *Education Week*, February 28, 2018, https://www.edweek.org/ew/articles/2018/02/09/dcs-scandal-and-the-nationwide-problem-of.html.

14. Rossiter, *Ain't Nobody Be Learnin'*, 42.

15. Gewertz, "Pressure to Graduate"; and see Mark Dynarski, "Is the High School Graduation Rate Really Going Up?," Brookings, May 3, 2018, https://www.brookings.edu/research/is-the-high-school-graduation-rate-really-going-up/.

16. Valerie Strauss, "Why High School Exit Exams Are a Waste of Time," *Washington Post*, April 18, 2017, https://www.washingtonpost.com/news/answer-sheet/wp/2017/04/18/why-high-school-exit-exams-are-a-waste-of-time/?utm_term=.96ee633759fc.

17. Donna St. George and Lynh Bui, "Probe Finds Late Grade Changes for 5,500 in Prince George's," *Washington Post*, November 3, 2017, https://www .washingtonpost.com/local/education/probe-finds-late-grade-changes-for-5500 -in-prince-georges/2017/11/03/5e54e10c-be62-11e7-959c-fe2b598d8c00_story .html?utm_term=.8523921efd68l.

18. Perry Stein, "Report Calls into Question Validity of Hundreds of Diplomas," *Washington Post*, January 29, 2018, https://www.washingtonpost.com/local/ education/report-calls-into-question-validity-of-hundreds-of-diplomas/ 2018/01/29/d86e5c82-0513-11e8-8777-2a059f168dd2_story.html?utm _term=.e28d88f82325.

19. Maryland State Department of Education, *Bridge Plan for Academic Validation Administrative Manual*, rev. ed. (Baltimore: Maryland State Department of Education, 2017), http://mdk12.msde.maryland.gov/share/pdf/bridge_final.pdf.

20. School officials told me this off the record; I couldn't obtain an official count.

21. Robert E. Slavin, "On High School Graduation Rates: Want to Buy My Bridge?," *Robert Slavin's Blog*, February 15, 2018, https://robertslavinsblog.wordpress .com/2018/02/15/on-high-school-graduation-rates-want-to-buy-my -bridge/.

22. 34 CFR 300.26(b)(3); 34 CFR 300.347(a)(2). A good primer on accommodations is Joanne Karger and Charles Hitchcock, *Access to the General Curriculum for Students with Disabilities: A Brief Legal Interpretation* (Wakefield, MA: National Center on Accessible Instructional Materials, 2003).

23. Sandra J. Thompson et al., *Accommodations Manual: How to Select, Administer, and Evaluate Use of Accommodations for Instruction and Assessment of Students with Disabilities*, 2nd ed. (Washington, DC: Council of Chief State School Officers, 2005), https://osepideasthatwork.org/sites/default/files/ AccommodationsManual.pdf, 15.

24. Miriam Kurtzig Freedman, "Special Education: Its Ethical Dilemmas, Entitlement Status, and Suggested Systemic Reforms," *University of Chicago Law Review* 79, no. 1 (2012): 13, http://lawreview.uchicago.edu/sites/lawreview .uchicago.edu/files/Freedman.pdf.

25. "Suspicious Test Scores across U.S. Raise Questions of Cheating," *Washington Post*, March 25, 2012, A11; Greg Toppo, "Schools Marred by Testing Scandals in 2011," *USA Today*, December 29, 2011, http://usatoday30.usatoday.com/ news/education/story/2011-12-29/schools-test-scandal/52274708/1.

CHAPTER 4

1. That's what a group of researchers on RTI say they heard from teachers. Amanda VanDerHeyden et al., "Four Steps to Implement RTI Correctly,"

Education Week, January 5, 2016, https://www.edweek.org/ew/articles/2016/ 01/06/four-steps-to-implement-rti-correctly.html.

2. Two websites devoted essentially to RTI principles and practices are the National Center on Intensive Intervention, https://www.intensiveintervention.org, and the RTI Action Network, https://www.rtinetwork.org. For a sample of the literature that overviews RTI, see "Response to Intervention, Next Generation," *Education Week*, December 14, 2016, https://www.edweek.org/ew/ toc/2016/12/14/index.html; "Assisting Students Struggling with Reading: Response to Intervention (RtI) and Multi-tier Intervention in the Primary Grades," What Works Clearinghouse, Institute of Education Sciences, U.S. Department of Education, 2009; and Paula Burdette and Pontea Etemad, "Response to Intervention: Select State Programs," National Association of State Directors of Special Education, Forum Policy Analysis, September 2009. See also Russell Gersten et al., "What Is the Evidence Base to Support Reading Interventions for Improving Student Outcomes in Grades 1–3?," National Center for Education Evaluation and Regional Assistance, Institute of Education Sciences, U.S. Department of Education, April 2017, https://files.eric .ed.gov/fulltext/ED573686.pdf. A particularly provocative critique of RTI is Douglas Fuchs et al., "Smart RTI: A Next-Generation Approach to Multilevel Prevention," *Exceptional Children* 78, no. 3 (Spring 2012): 263–79, https:// www.ncbi.nlm.nih.gov/pmc/articles/PMC3380278/.

   Many state departments of education have issued RTI manuals. Two examples are "Implementation Guide: Response to Instruction and Intervention Framework," Tennessee Department of Education, updated February 2016, https://www.tn.gov/content/dam/tn/education/special-education/ rti/rti2_implementation_guide.pdf; and "A Tiered Instructional Approach to Support Achievement for All Students: Maryland's Response to Intervention Framework," Maryland State Department of Education, 2008, http:// marylandpublicschools.org/NR/rdonlyres/D182E222-D84B-43D8-BB81 -6F4C4F7E05F6/17125/Tiered_Instructional_ApproachRtI_June2008.pdf. Much of the recent literature has been prompted by the connection between RTI and determination of eligibility for the special education classification of "specific learning disability." See, for example, Daniel J. Reschly, "Response to Intervention and the Identification of Specific Learning Disabilities," *Topics in Language Disorders* 34, no. 1 (2014): 39–58; and Joseph F. Kovaleski et al., *The RTI Approach to Evaluating Learning Disabilities* (New York: Guilford Press, 2013).

3. VanDerHeyden et al., "Four Steps to Implement RTI."

4. G. Reid Lyon, "Learning Disabilities and Early Intervention Strategies" (testimony before the Subcommittee on Education Reform, Committee on

Education and the Workforce, U.S. House of Representatives, June 2, 2002), http://www.cdl.org/wp-content/uploads/2003/01/Testimonies-to-Congress .pdf, 7.

5. See generally the Positive Behavioral Interventions and Supports (PBIS) web-site, https://www.pbis.org/.

6. For a short overview, see Stacy Hurst, "What Is the Difference between RTI and MTSS?," *Reading Horizons* (blog), January 6, 2014, https://www .readinghorizons.com/blog/what-is-the-difference-between-rti-and-mtss.

7. Russell Gersten et al., *Assisting Students Struggling with Mathematics: Response to Intervention (RtI) for Elementary and Middle Schools*, NCEE 2009-4060 (Washington, DC: Institute of Education Sciences, 2009), https://ies.ed.gov/ ncee/wwc/Docs/PracticeGuide/rti_math_pg_042109.pdf.

8. Susanna Loeb, "A Counterintuitive Approach to Improving Math Education: Focus on English Language Arts Teaching," Brookings, April 6, 2017, https:// www.brookings.edu/research/a-counterintuitive-approach-to-improving -math-education-focus-on-english-language-arts-teaching/.

9. Martin R. West, "From Evidence-Based Programs to an Evidence-Based Sys-tem: Opportunities under the Every Student Succeeds Act," Brookings, Feb-ruary 5, 2016, https://www.brookings.edu/research/from-evidence-based -programs-to-an-evidence-based-system-opportunities-under-the-every -student-succeeds-act/.

10. West.

11. CFR 300.309(a)(1)(2)(3).

12. West, "Evidence-Based Programs."

13. Joseph K. Torgesen, "Avoiding the Devastating Downward Spiral: The Evi-dence That Early Intervention Prevents Reading Failure," *American Educator*, Fall 2004, 6.

14. Torgesen, 17.

15. Allan R. Odden and Lawrence O. Picus, *School Finance: A Policy Perspective*, 5th ed. (New York: McGraw-Hill, 2014), 97.

16. For an overview of prekindergarten programs in top-performing countries and U.S. states, see Center on International Benchmarking, *How Does Mary-land Stack Up: Gap Analysis Comparing Maryland to International and Domes-tic Top Performers* (Washington, DC: National Center on Education and the Economy, 2018), 13–15.

17. For a convenient summary, see "The Thirty Million Word Gap," School Lit-eracy and Culture, Rice University, 2011–12, http://childrenshousepreschool .org/wp-content/uploads/2014/08/Rice-University-School-Literacy-and -Culture-The-Thirty-Million-Word-Gap-1.pdf.

18. Ariane Baye et al., "A Synthesis of Quantitative Research on Reading Programs for Secondary Students," Best Evidence Encyclopedia, 2018, http://www.bestevidence.org/word/Secondary-Reading-01-31-18.pdf. And see Philip J. Cook et al., "Not Too Late: Improving Academic Outcomes for Disadvantaged Youth," Institute for Policy Research, Northwestern University, 2015, https://www.ipr.northwestern.edu/publications/docs/workingpapers/2015/IPR-WP-15-01.pdf.

19. See chapter 4, note 2.

20. Center on International Benchmarking, *How Does Maryland Stack Up*, 25–37.

21. David Steiner, "Curriculum Research: What We Know and Where We Need to Go," StandardsWork, March 2017, https://standardswork.org/wp-content/uploads/2017/03/sw-curriculum-research-report-fnl.pdf.

22. Chester E. Finn Jr., "Curriculum Becomes a Reform Strategy," Thomas B. Fordham Institute, April 5, 2017, https://edexcellence.net/articles/curriculum-becomes-a-reform-strategy.

23. James R. Delisle, "Differentiation Doesn't Work," *Education Week*, January 7, 2015, https://www.edweek.org/ew/articles/2015/01/07/differentiation-doesnt-work.html.

24. David Griffith, "Differentiated to Death," Thomas B. Fordham Institute, February 4, 2015, https://edexcellence.net/articles/differentiated-to-death.

25. "What Is Universal Design for Learning?," SWIFT Center, n.d., http://www.swiftschools.org/sites/default/files/What%20is%20Universal%20Design%20%20for%20Learning.pdf.

26. For example, see "ESSA: Key Provisions and Implications for Students with Disabilities," Council of Chief State School Officers (CCSSO), July 20, 2016, https://ccsso.org/sites/default/files/2017-10/ESSA_Key_Provisions_Implications_for_SWD.pdf, 5.

27. Michael B. Horn, "Now Trending: Personalized Learning, Can a Buzzword Deliver on Its Promises?," *Education Next* 17, no. 4 (Fall 2017), https://www.educationnext.org/now-trending-personalized-learning-buzzword-promise-innovation/.

28. APA Consulting, *Final Report of the Study of Adequacy of Funding for Education in Maryland*, prepared for the Maryland State Department of Education, November 30, 2016, http://www.marylandpublicschools.org/Documents/adequacystudy/AdequacyStudyReportFinal112016.pdf.

29. A sampling of the research and literature includes Robert E. Slavin et al., "Effective Programs for Struggling Readers: A Best-Evidence Synthesis," *Education Research Review* 6 (2011): 1–26; Allan Odden and Lawrence O. Picus, *Appendix F: Full Report and School Case Studies for the Evidence-Based Approach to Estimating a Base Spending Level and Pupil Weights for Maryland*, prepared for the Maryland State Department of Education, November 30,

2016, http://www.marylandpublicschools.org/Documents/adequacystudy/ AppendixFSchoolCaseStudies113016.pdf; R. Barker Bausell, *Too Simple to Fail: A Case for Educational Change* (New York: Oxford University Press, 2011); Roseanna Ander, "Improving Academic Outcomes for Disadvantaged Students: Scaling Up Individualized Tutorials," Hamilton Project, March 2016, http://www.hamiltonproject.org/papers/improving_academic_outcomes_for _disadvantaged_students_scaling_up_individua; and Roland G. Fryer, "The Production of Human Capital in Developed Countries: Evidence from 196 Randomized Field Experiments," Scholars at Harvard, March 2016, https:// scholar.harvard.edu/files/fryer/files/handbook_fryer_03.25.2016.pdf, 38–42.

30. Slavin et al., "Effective Programs."
31. Bausell, *Too Simple to Fail*, 190.
32. Noah Smith, "Want to Fix Education? Just Give a Kid a Tutor," *Bloomberg View*, April 20, 2016, http://www.chicagotribune.com/news/opinion/commentary/ ct-give-kids-tutors-to-fix-education-20160420-story.html.
33. Odden and Picus, *Appendix F*, 34.
34. Recent research, called "shocking" by a leading scholar, found "tutoring by paraprofessionals (teaching assistants) was at least as effective as tutoring by teachers." Robert E. Slavin, "New Findings on Tutoring: Four Shockers," *Robert Slavin's Blog*, April 5, 2018, https://robertslavinsblog.wordpress.com/ 2018/04/05/new-findings-on-tutoring-four-shockers/.
35. See chapter 4, note 29.
36. "Tiered Instructional Approach."
37. A recent expert opinion on the most effective tutoring models and their tutor-to-student ratios is Robert E. Slavin, "Achieving Proficiency for *All*: Maryland's Opportunity" (presented to the Maryland Commission on Innovation and Excellence in Education, October 2017), http://mgaleg.maryland .gov/pubs/commtfworkgrp/2017-innovation-excellence-in-education -commission-2017-10-12.pdf.
38. Reschly, "Response to Intervention," 44–47; Douglas Fuchs, "The 'Blurring' of Special Education in a New Continuum of General Education Placements and Services," *Exceptional Children* 76, no. 3 (Spring 2010): 301–23, esp. 309–15.
39. Ander, "Improving Academic Outcomes," 6.
40. Fuchs et al., "Smart RTI," 13.
41. A sharp insight into effective implementation is provided by leading reading expert Louisa Moats, "Can Prevailing Approaches to Reading Instruction Accomplish the Goals of RTI?," *Perspectives on Language and Literacy* 43, no. 3 (Summer 2017): 15–22, https://mydigitalpublication.com/publication/?i= 425075&article_id=2836403&view=articleBrowser&ver=html5#{"issue_id": 425075,"view":"articleBrowser","article_id":"2836403"}.

42. "Assessing Progress: Four Years of Learnings from RTI2 Implementation in Tennessee," Tennessee Department of Education, February 2018, https://www.tn.gov/content/dam/tn/education/reports/rpt_rti_report_assessing_progress.pdf.

43. "Implementation Guide."

44. Education—Specialized Intervention Services—Reports, S. Bill 1, Chap. 728 (2017), https://legiscan.com/MD/text/SB1/2017, accessed August 1, 2018.

45. "Tiered Instructional Approach."

46. Emily Workman, "Third-Grade Reading Policies," Education Commission of the States, Denver, Colorado, December 2014, https://www.ecs.org/clearinghouse/01/16/44/11644.pdf, 1.

47. See a summary of Beverley Holden Johns, James M. Kauffman, and Edwin W. Martin, "The Concept of RTI: Billion-Dollar Boondoggle," January 26, 2017, at "Response to Intervention: Response from Bev Johns, Jim Kauffman, and Ed Martin," Learning Disabilities Association of SC, March 26, 2017, http://ldasc.blogspot.com/2017/03/rti-discussion.html. See also "Alternative Facts Are Alive in Education as Well: A Response to Johns, Kaufman and Martin," Consortium for Evidence-Based Intervention, n.d., https://www.hdc.lsuhsc.edu/tiers/docs/Alternative%20Facts%20Are%20Alive%203-23B.PDF, 1.

48. "Alternative Facts."

49. Rekha Balu et al., *Evaluation of Response to Intervention Practices for Elementary School Reading*, NCEE 2016-4000 (Washington, DC: Institute of Education Sciences, 2015), https://ies.ed.gov/ncee/pubs/20164000/pdf/20164000.pdf.

50. Balu et al., 1.

51. Balu et al. 3.

52. Johns et al., "Concept of RTI," 5.

53. Johns et al., 5.

54. "Alternative Facts," 1.

55. "Alternative Facts," 2.

56. Sarah D. Sparks, "Study: RTI Practice Falls Short of Promise," *Education Week*, November 11, 2015, https://www.edweek.org/ew/articles/2015/11/11/study-rti-practice-falls-short-of-promise.html. For a much longer version of his views on the study and RTI in general, see Douglas Fuchs and Lynn S. Fuchs, "Critique of the National Evaluation of Response to Intervention: A Case for Simpler Frameworks," *Exceptional Children* 83, no. 3 (April 2017): 244–54.

57. See generally National Center for Learning Disabilities, "RTI-Based SLD Identification TOOLKIT," RTI Action Network, http://www.rtinetwork.org/toolkit.

58. Cecil R. Reynolds and Sally E. Shaywitz, "Response to Intervention: Ready or Not? Or, from Wait-to-Fail to Watch-Them-Fail," *School Psychology Quarterly* 24, no. 2 (June 2009): 130–45.

59. Matt Cohen, "Response to Intervention Policy Statement," Council of Parent Attorneys and Advocates, adopted June 16, 2016, https://www.copaa.org/general/custom.asp?page=RTI.

60. Melody Musgrove, memorandum to the state directors of special education, OSEP 11-07, January 21, 2011, https://www2.ed.gov/policy/speced/guid/idea/memosdcltrs/osep11-07rtimemo.pdf.

61. Tina Marlene Hudson and Robert G. McKenzie, "The Impact of RTI on Timely Identification of Students with Specific Learning Disabilities," *Learning Disabilities: A Multidisciplinary Journal* 21, no. 2 (2016): 46–58, esp. 55, https://js.sagamorepub.com/ldmj/article/view/7722.

62. Tina M. Hudson and Robert G. McKenzie, "Evaluating the Use of RTI to Identify SLD: A Survey of State Policy, Procedures, Data Collection, and Administrator Perceptions," *Contemporary School Psychology* 20, no. 1 (March 2016): 31–45, https://eric.ed.gov/?id=EJ1090019.

63. Martha L. Thurlow et al., "Meeting the Needs of Special Education Students: Recommendations for the Race to the Top Consortia and States," National Center on Education Outcomes, Minneapolis, Minnesota, 2011, https://nceo.umn.edu/docs/OnlinePubs/Martha_Thurlow-Meeting_the_Needs_of_Special_Education_Students.pdf, 5.

    For the number of students in special education by disability, see "Digest of Education Statistics," National Center for Education Statistics (NCES), https://nces.ed.gov/pubs2017/2017094.pdf, 115.

64. "2017 NAEP Mathematics and Reading Assessments: Highlighted Results at Grades 4 and 8 for the Nation, States, and Districts," NCES, April 2018, https://nces.ed.gov/pubsearch/pubsinfo.asp?pubid=2018037.

65. "NAEP Mathematics and Reading Assessments," Nation's Report Card, 2017, https://www.nationsreportcard.gov/reading_math_2017_highlights/.

CHAPTER 5

1. Said by an angry parent at a community meeting I attended in January 2017.

2. 34 CFR 300.320(a)(2)(i).

3. 34 CFR 300.39(a)(3)ii.

4. No Child Left Behind Act of 2001, Pub. L. No. 107-117, 115 Stat. 1425 (2002), https://www2.ed.gov/policy/elsec/leg/esea02/107-110.pdf.

5. Sandra J. Thompson et al., *Accommodations Manual: How to Select, Administer, and Evaluate Use of Accommodations for Instruction and Assessment of Students with Disabilities*, 2nd ed. (Washington, DC: Council of Chief State School Officers, 2005), 10, https://osepideasthatwork.org/sites/default/files/AccommodationsManual.pdf.

6. Eileen Ahearn, *Standards-Based IEPs: Implementation Update*, Forum Brief Policy Analysis (Alexandria, VA: NASDE, 2010), 1, 2.

7. Daniel J. Losen and Kevin G. Welner, "Legal Challenges to Inappropriate and Inadequate Special Education for Minority Children," in *Racial Inequity in Special Education*, ed. Daniel J. Losen and Gray Orfield (Cambridge, MA: Harvard Education Press, 2002), 167–94, esp. 185.

8. *Board of Education v. Rowley*, 458 U.S. 176 (1982), pp. 176–218.

9. *Rowley*, 202.

10. Martha L. Thurlow et al., "Meeting the Needs of Special Education Students: Recommendations for the Race to the Top Consortia and States," National Center on Education Outcomes, Minneapolis, Minnesota, 2011, https://nceo .umn.edu/docs/OnlinePubs/Martha_Thurlow-Meeting_the_Needs_of_Special _Education_Students.pdf, 5.

11. Perry A. Zirkel, "The Aftermath of *Endrew F.* One Year Later: An Updated Outcomes Analysis," *West's Education Law Reporter* 352 (April 2018): 448–55, esp. 454, https://docplayer.net/87540335-A-special-section-of-west-s-education -law-reporter-sponsored-by-the-education-law-association-the-aftermath -of-endrew-f.html.

12. I received the memorandum in 2006, when I was a member of the Baltimore school board.

13. For a full discussion of the development and content of the One Year Plus policy, see Kalman R. Hettleman, *Students with Disabilities Can Succeed! How the Baltimore City Public Schools Are Transforming Special Education* (Baltimore, MD: Abell Foundation, 2013).

14. Email communications to me, published in Hettleman, 5.

15. "Dear Colleague Letter," U.S. Department of Education, Office of Special Education and Rehabilitative Services, November 16, 2015, https://www2.ed.gov/ policy/speced/guid/idea/memosdcltrs/guidance-on-fape-11-17-2015.pdf.

16. Arne Duncan, "Fulfilling the Promise of IDEA," U.S. Department of Education, November 18, 2010, http://www.ed.gov/news/speeches/fulfilling-promise -idea-remarks-35th-anniversary-individuals-disabilities-act.

17. "Dear Colleague Letter," 1.

18. "Dear Colleague Letter," 5.

19. Maryland State Department of Education, "Improving Outcomes for Students with Disabilities: Curriculum, Instruction, and Assessment," technical assistance bulletin, updated April 2018, http://www.marylandpublicschools.org/programs/ Documents/Special-Ed/TAB/MarylandTABImprovingOutcomesforSWD.pdf.

20. Anna Medaris Miller, "A Patient's Guide to ADHD," *U.S. News*, n.d., https:// health.usnews.com/health-conditions/brain-health/adhd/overview.

21. 34 CFR 200.1(d)(3), U.S. Department of Education Non-regulatory Guidance, August 2005, 21.

PART III

1. About two-thirds in one poll. Valerie Strauss, "Poll: What Americans Say about Public Education," *Washington Post*, August 22, 2012, https://www .washingtonpost.com/blogs/answer-sheet/post/poll-americans-views-on -public-education/2012/08/22/37203c5a-ebcf-11e1-aca7-272630dfd152 _blog.html?utm_term=.eea943d6f3b2. And see Dana Goldstein and Ben Casselman, "Teachers Find Public Support as Campaign for Higher Pay Goes to Voters," *New York Times*, May 31, 2018, https://www.nytimes.com/2018/05/ 31/us/politics/teachers-campaign.html.

CHAPTER 6

1. Adapted from a familiar bumper sticker advocating more money for schools.
2. Maria Danilova, "Teachers Dig Deep into Their Own Pockets to Pay for Supplies, Study Finds," *Christian Science Monitor*, May 16, 2018, https://www .csmonitor.com/USA/Education/2018/0516/Teachers-dig-deep-into-their -own-pockets-to-pay-for-supplies-study-finds.
3. See, for example, Bruce Baker et al., *Is School Funding Fair? A National Report Card*, 6th ed. (New Brunswick, NJ: Education Law Center and Rutgers Graduate School of Education, 2017), http://www.edlawcenter.org/assets/files/ pdfs/publications/National_Report_Card_2017.pdf; and Matthew M. Chingos and Kristin Blagg, "Do Poor Kids Get Their Fair Share of School Funding?," *Urban Institute*, May 2017, https://www.urban.org/sites/default/files/ publication/90586/school_funding_brief.pdf.
4. Jonathan Kozol, *Savage Inequalities: Children in America's Schools* (New York: Crown Press, 1991).
5. Coleman, James S. Equality of Educational Opportunity (COLEMAN) Study (EEOS), 1966. Ann Arbor, MI: Inter-university Consortium for Political and Social Research [distributor], 2007-04-27. https://doi.org/10.3886/ ICPSR06389.v3.
6. *San Antonio Independent School District v. Rodriguez*, 411 U.S. 1 (1973).
7. For a historical perspective, see Allan R. Odden and Lawrence O. Picus, *School Finance: A Policy Perspective*, 5th ed. (New York: McGraw-Hill, 2014).
8. Baker et al., *Is School Funding Fair?*, 4.

9. Baker et al., 5. See also Chingos and Blagg, "Poor Kids," 7.

10. William S. Koski, "Beyond Dollars? The Promises and Pitfalls of the Next Generation of Educational Rights Litigation," *Columbia Law Review* 117 (November 2017): 1898–1931.

11. Kevin Carey and Elizabeth A. Harris, "It Turns Out Spending More Probably Does Improve Education," *New York Times*, December 12, 2016, https://www.nytimes.com/2016/12/12/nyregion/it-turns-out-spending-more-probably-does-improve-education.html.

12. Eric Hanushek, "Money Matters After All?," *Education Next Blog*, July 7, 2015, https://www.educationnext.org/money-matters-after-all/.

13. Maryland Commission on Innovation and Excellence in Education, *Preliminary Report*, January 2018, chap. 1, "A Call to Action," http://dls.maryland.gov/pubs/prod/NoPblTabMtg/CmsnInnovEduc/2018-Preliminary-Report-of-the-Commission.pdf.

14. Robert E. Slavin, "Achieving Proficiency for *All*: Maryland's Opportunity" (presented to the Maryland Commission on Innovation and Excellence in Education, October 2017), http://mgaleg.maryland.gov/pubs/commtfworkgrp/2017-innovation-excellence-in-education-commission-2017-10-12.pdf.

15. Baker et al., *Is School Funding Fair?*, 7.

16. David P. Gardner et al., "A Nation At Risk: The Imperative for Educational Reform," National Commission on Excellence in Education, Wash. D.C., 1983. https://files.eric.ed.gov/fulltext/ED226006.pdf.

17. Kalman R. Hettleman, *It's the Classroom, Stupid: A Plan to Save America's Schoolchildren* (Lanham, MD: Rowman & Littlefield Education, 2010), 9.

18. Maryland Commission, *Preliminary Report*, 89.

19. Hettleman, *It's the Classroom*, 87–136.

20. Charles M. Payne, *So Little Change: The Persistence of Failure in Urban Schools* (Cambridge, MA: Harvard Education Press, 2008), 192.

21. David Tyack, "School Reform Is Dead (Long Live School Reform)," *American Prospect*, November 7, 2001, http://prospect.org/article/school-reform-dead-long-live-school-reform.

CHAPTER 7

1. Tom Watkins, "Everyone Has a Plan for Education Reform, Except Educators," *Education News*, February 5, 2013, http://www.educationviews.org/everyone-has-a-plan-for-education-reform-except-educators/.

2. Robert Epstein, "Why High School Must Go: An Interview with Leon Botstein," *Phi Delta Kappan* 88, no. 9 (May 2007): 659–63, esp. 663.

3. Maggie Severns, "How Congress Finally Killed No Child Left Behind," *Politico*, December 11, 2015, https://www.politico.com/story/2015/12/paul-ryan-congress-no-child-left-behind-216696.

4. Emma Brown, "What Should America Do about Its Worst Public Schools? States Still Don't Seem to Know," *Washington Post*, August 7, 2017.

5. Brandon L. Wright and Michael J. Petrilli, "Good News for Students and Federalism: Most States Step Up on Accountability under ESSA," Thomas B. Fordham Institute, November 15, 2017, https://edexcellence.net/articles/good-news-for-students-and-federalism-most-states-step-up-on-accountability-under-essa.

6. Institute for a Competitive Workforce, *Leaders and Laggards: A State-by-State Report Card on Educational Effectiveness* (Washington, DC: U.S. Chamber of Commerce, 2007), 7.

7. Richard M. Ingersoll, *Who Controls Teachers' Work? Power and Accountability in America's Schools* (Cambridge, MA: Harvard University Press, 2005), 168.

8. Mary Kennedy, *Inside Teaching: How Classroom Life Undermines Reform* (Cambridge, MA: Harvard University Press, 2005), 186–90.

9. Stacy Childress, Richard Elmore, and Alan Grossman, "How to Manage Urban School Districts," *Harvard Business Review* 84 (November 2006): 55–68, esp. 58.

10. National Council on Teacher Quality, "What Education Schools Aren't Teaching about Reading and What Elementary Teachers Aren't Learning," executive summary, revised June 2006, 8.

11. Dana Goldstein, *The Teacher Wars: A History of America's Most Embattled Profession* (New York: Doubleday, 2014), 242.

12. Douglas Fuchs, Lynn B. Fuchs, and Pamela Stecker, "The 'Blurring' of Special Education in a New Continuum of General Education Placements and Services," *Exceptional Children* 76, no. 3 (2010): 301–23, esp. 309.

13. Richard F. Elmore, "The Limits of Change," *Harvard Education Letter*, January–February 2002, 2.

14. Marc Tucker, "Differences in Performance within Schools: Why So Much Greater Than in Other Countries?," *Education Week*, September 6, 2017, http://blogs.edweek.org/edweek/top_performers/2017/09/differences_in_performance_within_schools_why_so_much_greater_than_in_other_countries_1.html.

15. Robert Pondiscio, "Failing by Design: How We Make Teaching Too Hard for Mere Mortals," Thomas B. Fordham Institute, May 10, 2016, https://edexcellence.net/articles/failing-by-design-how-we-make-teaching-too-hard-for-mere-mortals.

16. Arthur Levine, *Educating School Leaders* (Washington, DC: Education School Project, 2006), 13.

17. Jane Hanaway and Andrew J. Rotherham, eds., *Collective Bargaining in Education: Negotiating Change in Today's Schools* (Cambridge, MA: Harvard Education Press, 2006), 263.

18. Chester E. Finn Jr. and Michael Petrilli, foreword to *The Leadership Limbo, Teacher Labor Agreements in America's Fifty Largest School Districts*, by Frederick M. Hess and Coby Loup (Washington, DC: Thomas B. Fordham Institute, 2008), 6.

19. Mark Seidenberg, *Language at the Speed of Sight: How We Read, Why So Many Can't, and What Can Be Done About It* (New York: Basic Books, 2017), 303.

20. Anthony S. Bryck et al., *Learning to Improve: How America's Schools Can Get Better at Getting Better* (Cambridge, MA: Harvard Education Press, 2015), ix.

21. Bryck et al., x.

22. Arthur Levine, *Educating School Teachers* (Washington, DC: Education School Project, 2006), 19.

23. National Council on Teacher Quality (NCTQ), *2014 Teacher Prep Review* (Washington, DC: NCTQ, 2014), 3.

24. NCTQ, *2011 State Teacher Policy Yearbook: National Summary* (Washington, DC: NCTQ, 2012), https://www.nctq.org/publications/2011-State-Teacher-Policy-Yearbook:-National-Summary.

25. NCTQ.

26. Fuchs, Fuchs, and Stecker, "'Blurring' of Special Education," 318.

27. Fuchs, Fuchs, and Stecker, 305–8.

28. Robert Pondiscio, "The Problem with Current Efforts to Fix Teachers' Professional Development," Thomas B. Fordham Institute, June 22, 2016, https://edexcellence.net/articles/the-problem-with-current-efforts-to-fix-teachers-professional-development. See also Mark Dynarski and Kirsten Kainz, "Why Federal Spending on Disadvantaged Students (Title I) Doesn't Work," Brookings, November 20, 2015, https://www.brookings.edu/research/why-federal-spending-on-disadvantaged-students-title-i-doesnt-work/; Melissa Tooley and Kaylan Connally, "No Panacea: Diagnosing What Ails Teacher Professional Development before Reaching for Remedies," *New America*, June 2016, https://www.newamerica.org/education-policy/policy-papers/no-panacea/.

29. Chester E. Finn Jr., "Curriculum Becomes a Reform Strategy," Thomas B. Fordham Institute, April 5, 2017, https://edexcellence.net/articles/curriculum-becomes-a-reform-strategy.

30. Cited in Ted Mitchell and Jonathan Schorr, "Federal Education Innovation: Getting It Right," *Education Week*, October 29, 2008, https://www.edweek.org/ew/articles/2008/11/19/13letter-b1.h28.html.

31. Catherine E. Snow, M. Susan Burns, and Peg Griffin, eds., *Preventing Reading Difficulties in Young Children* (Washington, DC: National Academy Press, 1998).

32. Peter Baker, "Mikhail Gorbachev Brought Democracy to Russia and Was Despised for It," review of *Gorbachev: His Life and Times*, by William Taubman, *New York Times*, September 6, 2017, Sunday Book Review, https://www.nytimes.com/2017/09/06/books/review/william-taubman-gorbachev-his-life-and-times.html.

33. Childress, Elmore, and Grossman, "Urban School Districts," 58.

34. Robert E. Slavin, "Reading by Third Grade—or Else," *HuffPost* (blog), updated December 6, 2017, https://www.huffingtonpost.com/robert-e-slavin/reading-by-third-grade_b_5677958.html.

35. "Hire Expectations: Big-District Superintendents Stay in Their Jobs Longer Than We Think," Broad Center, May 2018, https://www.broadcenter.org/wp-content/uploads/2018/05/TheBroadCenter_HireExpectations_May2018.pdf.

36. David Tyack and Larry Cuban, *Tinkering toward Utopia: A Century of Public School Reform* (Cambridge, MA: Harvard University Press, 1995), 10.

CHAPTER 8

1. David P. Driscoll, *Commitment and Common Sense: Leading Education Reform in Massachusetts* (Cambridge, MA: Harvard Education Press, 2017), 4.

2. *Milliken v. Bradley*, 418 U.S. 717 (1974), 741.

3. Cited in Patrick J. McGuinn, *No Child Left Behind and the Transformation of Federal Education Policy, 1965–2005* (Lawrence: University Press of Kansas, 2006), 166.

4. Maggie Severns, "Congress Set to Dump No Child Left Behind," *Politico*, November 30, 2015, https://www.politico.com/story/2015/11/no-child-left-behind-education-bush-congress-216291.

5. William J. Bennett, "Feds' Role in Your Child's Education May Be Shrinking. Finally!," Thomas B. Fordham Institute, May 11, 2017, https://edexcellence.net/articles/feds-role-in-your-childs-education-is-shrinking-finally.

6. Maryland Commission on Innovation and Excellence in Education, *Preliminary Report*, January 2018, http://dls.maryland.gov/pubs/prod/NoPblTabMtg/CmsnInnovEduc/2018-Preliminary-Report-of-the-Commission.pdf, 79–82.

CHAPTER 9

1. *Plyler v. Doe*, 457 U.S. 202, 222 (1982).

2. *Student A v. the Berkeley Unified School District*, U.S. District Court (Northern District of California), complaint for injunctive and declaratory relief, May 2,

2017, https://dredf.org/wp-content/uploads/2017/05/dredf-busd-complaint-5-2-17.pdf.

3. "Students with Reading Disorders Sue Berkeley Unified School District (BUSD) for Failing to Educate Them," Disability Rights Education and Defense Fund, May 2, 2017, https://dredf.org/2017/05/02/students-with-reading-disorders-sue-berkeley-unified-school-district/.

4. "Title I: Improving the Academic Achievement of the Disadvantaged," U.S. Department of Education, last modified September 15, 2004, https://www2.ed.gov/policy/elsec/leg/esea02/pg1.html.

5. "ECAA Must Require Intervention When Students Struggle to Meet Reading and Math Goals," Council of Parent Attorneys and Advocates (COPAA), June 16, 2015, http://www.copaa.org/news/236976/ECAA-Must-Require-Intervention-When-Students-Struggle-to-Meet-Reading-and-Math-Goals.htm.

6. See discussion in chapter 5.

7. Margaret J. McLaughlin, "Closing the Achievement Gap and Students with Disabilities: The New Meaning of a 'Free and Appropriate Public Education'" (paper presented at the Second Annual Symposium on Educational Equity, Teachers College, Columbia University, New York, November 13–14, 2006), http://www.equitycampaign.org/events-page/equity-symposia/2006-examining-americas-commitment-to-closing-achievement-gaps-nclb-and-its-a/papers/McLaughlin_Edited[1].Closing-the-Achievement-Gap-11-29.pdf, 34.

8. Robert Garda, "A Fresh Look at IDEA Eligibility Criteria," AASA, April 26, 2016, http://www.aasa.org/idea-blog.aspx?id=39492&blogid=84005.

9. Alan Gartner and Dorothy Kerzner Lipsky, "Beyond Special Education: Toward a Quality System for All Students," Harvard Educational Review 57, no. 4 (November 1987): 367–95, esp. 387.

10. Gartner and Lipsky, 367. See also Thomas M. Skrtic, "The Special Education Paradox: Equity as the Way to Excellence," in Special Education for a New Century, ed. Lauren I. Katzman et al. (Cambridge, MA: Harvard Educational Review, 2005), 204–10; Douglas Fuchs, Lynn B. Fuchs, and Pamela Stecker, "The 'Blurring' of Special Education in a New Continuum of General Education Placements and Services," Exceptional Children 76, no. 3 (2010): 301–23, esp. 307–8.

11. "Every Student Succeeds Act and Students with Disabilities," National Council on Disabilities, February 7, 2018, https://ncd.gov/sites/default/files/NCD_ESSA-SWD_Accessible.pdf, 19–22.

12. Wade F. Horn and Douglas Tynan, "Time to Make Special Education 'Special' Again," in Rethinking Special Education for a New Century, ed. Chester E. Finn Jr. et al. (Washington, DC: Thomas B. Fordham Foundation and Progressive Policy Institute, 2001), 40.

13. *Student A v. the Berkeley Unified School District.*
14. *Gary B. v. Richard D. Snyder*, U.S. District Court (Eastern District of Michigan, Southern Division), civil action no. 16-CV-13292, class action complaint, September 13, 2016.
15. *Gary B. v. Snyder*, 15.
16. *Gary B. v. Snyder*, 41.
17. *Gary B. v. Snyder*, 2.
18. John Wisely, "Detroit School Lawsuit: Does U.S. Constitution Guarantee Literacy?," *Detroit Free Press*, October 1, 2016, https://www.freep.com/story/news/education/2016/10/01/literacy/90902874/.
19. Ryan Felton, "Detroit Civil Rights Lawsuit Attempts to Assert a Constitutional Right to Literacy," *Guardian*, September 14, 2016, https://www.theguardian.com/us-news/2016/sep/14/detroit-civil-rights-lawsuit-constitutional-literacy-education. The Berkeley and Detroit class action cases are also part of a trend in which state courts as well as federal courts are being called on to decide other challenges to equal opportunity, ranging from the adequacy of funding to the role of teachers unions. See Dana Goldstein, "How Do You Get Better Schools? Take the State to Court, More Advocates Say," *New York Times*, August 21, 2018, https://www.nytimes.com/2018/08/21/us/school-segregation-funding-lawsuits.html.
20. Hope Gray, "New Life for Educational Malpractice: Decades of Policy Revisited," Loyola University Chicago, Childlaw and Education Institute Forum, spring 2010, http://www.luc.edu/media/lucedu/law/centers/childlaw/childed/pdfs/2010studentpapers/Hope_Gray.pdf.
21. Gray, 3.
22. Gray, 3.
23. Gray, 4, 6.
24. Terri A. DeMitchell and Todd A. DeMitchell, "A Crack in the Educational Malpractice Wall," *School Administrator Article*, December 18, 2017, http://www.aasa.org/SchoolAdministratorArticle.aspx?id=6516. See also Mark Dynarski, "Can Schools Commit Malpractice? It Depends," Brookings, July 26, 2018, https://www.brookings.edu/research/can-schools-commit-malpractice-it-depends/.

CHAPTER 10

1. The primal scream of the fictional anchorman in the 1976 movie *Network*.
2. "Learning Disabilities: Kids and Families Struggle beyond the Academics," *Science Daily*, June 28, 2018, https://www.sciencedaily.com/releases/2018/06/180628120039.htm.

3. Rachel Quenomoen, "Civil Rights, No Child Left Behind, Assessments, Accountability, and Students with Disabilities," written comments, U.S. Commission on Civil Rights, February 6, 2003, https://nceo.umn.edu/docs/Presentations/usccr.pdf.

4. See generally M. Hannah Koseki, "Meeting the Needs of All Students: Amending the IDEA to Support Special Education Students from Low-Income Households," *Fordham Law Journal* 44 (July 2017): 793–831; Elisa Hyman et al., "How IDEA Fails Families without Means: Cause and Corrections from the Frontlines of Special Education," *Journal of Gender, Social Policy & the Law* 20, no. 1 (2011): 107–62; Eloise Pasachoff, "Special Education, Poverty, and the Limits of Private Enforcement," *Notre Dame Law Review* 86 (2011): 1413; Nicholas Gumas, "Socioeconomic and Racial Disparities in Public Special Education: Alleviating Decades of Unequal Enforcement of the Individuals with Disabilities Education Act in New York City," *Columbia Journal on Race and Law* 8 (2018): 398.

5. See generally Koseki, "Meeting the Needs"; Hyman et al., "How IDEA Fails Families"; Pasachoff, "Special Education"; and Gumas, "Socioeconomic and Racial Disparities."

6. Claire Raj, "The Misidentification of Children with Disabilities: A Harm with No Foul," *Arizona State Law Journal* 48 (Summer 2016): 373.

7. Kosecki, "Meeting the Needs," 6.

8. Pasachoff, "Special Education," 1417.

9. "Broken Promises: The Underfunding of IDEA," National Council on Disability, February 7, 2018, https://ncd.gov/sites/default/files/NCD_BrokenPromises_508.pdf, 35.

10. The problem has plagued parental rights under IDEA from the start. Alan Gartner and Dorothy Kerzner Lipsky, "Beyond Special Education: Toward a Quality System for All Students," *Harvard Educational Review* 57, no. 4 (November 1987): 367–95, esp. 378.

11. "Federal Monitoring and Enforcement of IDEA Compliance," National Council on Disability, February 7, 2018, https://www.ncd.gov/sites/default/files/NCD_Monitoring-Enforcement_508_0.pdf.

12. "IDEA Special Education Resolution Meetings: A Guide for Parents of Children and Youth (Ages 3–21)," Resolving Disputes with Parents Series, National Association of Special Education Teachers (NASET), n.d., https://www.naset.org/4890.0.html.

13. Unpublished data, Maryland Center for Developmental Disabilities at Kennedy Krieger Institute, Baltimore, 2018, available from the author upon request.

14. *Schaffer v. Weast*, 546 U.S. 49 (2005).

15. *Schaffer v. Weast*, 62.

16. *Schaffer v. Weast*, 64.
17. See generally Koseki, "Meeting the Needs"; Hyman et al., "How IDEA Fails Families"; Pasachoff, "Special Education."
18. Pasachoff, "Special Education," 1417.
19. Logan Casey and Elizabeth Mann, "New Survey of Minorities Adds Dissenting View to Public Satisfaction with Schools," Brookings, January 11, 2018, https://www.brookings.edu/blog/brown-center-chalkboard/2018/01/11/new-survey-of-minorities-adds-dissenting-view-to-public-satisfaction-with-schools/.
20. "$14 Million Awarded for 40 Special Education Parent Training and Information Centers," U.S. Department of Education, August 7, 2015, https://www.ed.gov/news/press-releases/14-million-awarded-40-special-education-parent-training-and-information-centers. And see the Center for Parent Information and Resources website, http://www.parentcenterhub.org/.
21. Center for Appropriate Dispute Resolution in Special Education (CADRE), *Individualized Education Program (IEP) Facilitation: A Guide for Parents of Children and Youth (Ages 3–21)* (Eugene, OR: CADRE, 2014), https://www.cadreworks.org/sites/default/files/IEP_Facilitation_ParentGuide_11.3.14.pdf.
22. Erin Phillips, "When Parents Aren't Enough: External Advocacy in Special Education," *Yale Law Journal* 117, no. 8 (June 2008): 1568–1957; Gumas, "Socioeconomic and Racial Disparities," 440.
23. Chester E. Finn Jr., "John Merrow's Flawed Plan to Rescue Public Schools," Thomas B. Fordham Institute, October 4, 2017, https://edexcellence.net/articles/john-merrows-flawed-plan-to-rescue-public-schools.
24. Sasha Pudelski, "Rethinking the Special Education Due Process System," School Superintendents Association, April 2016, https://www.aasa.org/uploadedFiles/Policy_and_Advocacy/Public_Policy_Resources/Special_Education/AASARethinkingSpecialEdDueProcess.pdf.
25. "AASA Document Nothing More Than a Shameful Attack on Parent and Student Civil Rights," Council of Parent Attorneys and Advocates (COPAA), April 4, 2013, https://www.copaa.org/news/121292/AASA-Document-Nothing-More-Than-A-Shameful-Attack-on-Parent-and-Student-Civil-Rights-.htm.
26. Christina A. Samuels, "Ed. Dept. Finds Texas Suppressed Spec. Ed. Enrollment," *Education Week*, January 17, 2018, https://www.edweek.org/ew/articles/2018/01/11/ed-dept-finds-texas-suppressed-enrollment-of.html.
27. Aliyya Swaby, "Special Education Caps Were the Texas Legislature's Idea, Educators Say," *Texas Tribune*, January 14, 2018, https://www.texastribune.org/2018/01/14/school-groups-special-education-texas-legislators/.
28. Diane Ravitch, *The Troubled Crusade: American Education 1945–1980* (New York: Basic Books, 1983), 306.

29. Susan Etscheidt, "'Truly Disabled'? An Analysis of LD Eligibility Issues under the Individual with Disabilities Education Act," *Journal of Disability Policy Studies* 24, no. 3 (2013): 81–192, esp. 182.

30. Christina A. Samuels, "Parent-Driven Group Wields Influence on Dyslexia Issues," *Education Week*, December 9, 2015, https://www.edweek.org/ew/articles/2015/12/09/parent-driven-group-wields-influence-on-dyslexia-concerns.html.

31. "Week in Review: February 16, 2018," *NASET* 4, no. 7 (2018), https://www.naset.org/index.php?id=4855.

32. Leila Fiester, "Don't 'Dys' Our Kids: Dyslexia and the Quest for Grade-Level Reading Proficiency," Emily Hall Tremaine Foundation, 2012, http://www.colettiinstitute.org/resources/4.4_Don%27t_Dys_our_kids.pdf, 53–54.

33. Kalman R. Hettleman, *The Invisible Dyslexics: How Public School Systems in Baltimore and Elsewhere Discriminate against Poor Children in the Diagnosis and Treatment of Early Reading Difficulties* (Baltimore, MD: Abell Foundation, 2003), https://www.abell.org/sites/default/files/publications/ed_invisible_dyslexics.pdf.

34. For an overview of the division of liberals, see Kalman R. Hettleman, *It's the Classroom, Stupid: A Plan to Save America's Schoolchildren* (Lanham, MD: Rowman & Littlefield Education, 2010), 196.

35. Richard Rothstein, *Class and Schools: Using Social, Economic, and Educational Reform to Close the Black-White Achievement Gap* (Washington, DC: Economic Policy Institute, 2003), 5.

36. Diane Jean Schemo, "It Takes More Than Schools to Close Achievement Gap," *New York Times*, August 9, 2006, https://www.nytimes.com/2006/08/09/education/09education.html.

37. Perry A. Zirkel, "Shift in Education Policy under the Trump Administration," *Perry Zirkel Files* (blog), January 15, 2018, https://perryzirkel.files.wordpress.com/2018/01/trump-shift-in-education-policy.pdf.

Index

Abell Foundation, 175
abuse: definition of, 3–4; educational, xvi, xvii, 3, 180
access to curriculum, 50
accommodations, 49–51, 93–94
accountability, 108–9, 117–20, 144, 150, 156
adequacy: definition of, 108; in education, 69; federal guarantee of, 110–11; in spending, 105; studies of, 107
ADHD. See attention deficit hyperactivity disorder (ADHD)
administrators, 52, 122–23
administrative law judge (ALJ), 161–62
advance notification, 165
adverse effect requirement, for disabilities, 39–40
advocacy assistance, 163–68
advocacy organizations, 19, 140, 170
advocates, 20, 157–80
Ain't Nobody Be Learnin' Nothin' (Rossiter), 47–48
Alessi, Galen, 32–33
ALJ. See administrative law judge (ALJ)
Alonso, Andres, 89–90
alternative assessments and standards, 97
American Institutes of Research, 132
anti-social behaviors, xii, 5, 58
appeal, of IEP decisions, 161–63
appropriate, meaning of word, 85
"Assessing Progress" (Tennessee Department of Education), 74–75
assessment instruments, 61
at-risk students, 69–70, 108

attention deficit hyperactivity disorder (ADHD), 28–29, 82, 95, 146
autism, 8, 39, 96, 152, 171
autonomy, professional, 117, 123–25

Baltimore, Maryland, xv, 9, 43–52, 68, 83, 89–95, 159, 164
Bausell, R. Barker, 70–71
behavioral causes of learning disabilities, 58
below basic performance, 43
Berkeley, California, 17, 147, 153, 154
Best Evidence Encyclopedia (Johns Hopkins University), 132
best practices, evidence-based, 61–70, 101, 128, 139, 156
"Beyond Special Education" (Gartner and Lipsky), 151
blaming the victims, 13, 28, 31–34, 175
Board of Education v. Rowley, 86–87
Botstein, Leon, 118
brain scans, 37–38
Bridge Plan for Academic Validation, 48
Brookings Institute, 59, 164
Brown v. Board of Education, 14, 16–17, 142, 154–55
bungling, 76–79
burden of proof, 162–63
bureaucracy, 105, 116–17
Burger, Warren, 141–42
Bush, George W., 26, 31, 119, 143
Buzzy clause, 113

calculators, 50
California, 110

California Supreme Court, 155
call to action, xvi, 4, 20–21, 57–58, 179–80. *See also* political action
career and technical education, 108
Center for American Progress, 120
centralized governance, 145
central offices, 122–23
certificates of completion, 96
chains of command, 125
Chamber of Commerce, U.S., 120
charter schools, 114
cheating on standardized tests, 52
Chesterton, G.K., 11
Churchill, Winston, 14, 179
civil rights: education as, 14–17, 139, 146–56, 176; movement, 142
class action lawsuits, 16–17, 139, 147, 153–56
Cleveland, Ohio, 43
coaching, on-the-job, 117, 125, 131
cognitive impairments, xviii, 7, 96, 152
Coleman Report, 105, 176
collective bargaining contracts, 126
collective political action, 19, 168–79
Colorado, 110
commercially produced intervention programs, 77
Commission on Innovation and Excellence in Education. *See* Kirwan Commission
Committee on the Prevention of Reading Difficulties in Young Children, 35
Common Core standards, 131–32, 143–44
community control of education, 113, 125. *See also* local control of education
competition for resources, 173, 177–78
complacency, xiii–xiv
complaint procedures, 166, 169
compliance monitoring, 150
"Concept of RTI: A Billion-Dollar Boondoggle, The" (Johns, Kauffman, and Martin), 76
consent, parental, 160

conservatives, political, 106, 114, 164–68, 176–78
Consortium for Evidence-based Early Intervention, 76–78
consultants, 107–8
content knowledge, 129
core instruction, 59, 64–69
costs: of services, xii–xiii, 160–63; of special education, 25; of tutoring, 109
Council of Chief State School Officers, 49–50, 85, 170
Council of Parent Attorneys and Advocates, 78
"Counterintuitive Approach to Improving Math Education, A" (Loeb), 59
cover-up, of underachievement, 45–52
"Crack in the Educational Malpractice Wall, A" (DeMitchell and DeMitchell), 155
crime, educational establishment guilty of, xiii, 118
Cruise, Tom, 104
culture wars, 66, 131. *See also* education wars
curricula: access to, 50; mismanagement of, 131; modified, 51; national, 66; reform of, 65–66
curriculum-embedded tests, 167

dance of the lemons, 125
data tracking, 93
day-to-day help for teachers, 127
decentralization, 125
Decoding Dyslexia, 173–75
deference to school authorities, 87, 161
de minimis standard, 87
demoralization of teachers, 68
desegregation, 14, 142
Deshler, Donald, 91
desperation, teacher, xv–xvi, 28–31, 37
Detroit, Michigan, 153–54
developmentally appropriate reading instruction, 133
DeVos, Betsy, 65, 92

differentiated instruction, 66–68
"Differentiation Doesn't Work" (Delisle), 67
diplomas, 47–49
disabilities: accommodations for students with, 50; adverse effect requirement, 39–40; advocacy organizations, 172; changing construct of, 16; classifications of, 7; illiteracy as, 146–47; medical, 6; multiple, 96; physical, 8; redefining, 151; and RTI, 78–79; severe, xviii, 96–97, 152–53, 171; teacher preparation and, 129
discrepancy gap, 28, 35–37, 77, 82. *See also* gaps in achievement
discriminatory attitudes and practices, 32
double retentions, 46
Down syndrome, 8, 152
downward spiral, 29, 62
Driscoll, David, 141
dropout rates, 45
due process clause, 17, 154
due process hearings, 161
dumbed down standards, 51–52
Duncan, Arne, 8–9, 143
dyslexia, 33–38, 173–76
Dyslexia Task Force, 175

EAHC. *See* Education for All Handicapped Children Act (EAHC)
early childhood practitioners, 133
early identification and intervention, 62–64, 101
economic class biases, 31–34
economic issues, 13, 28, 63, 164, 176
educational abuse, xvi–xvii, 3, 180
Education Commission of the States, 76
Education for All Handicapped Children Act (EAHC), 24, 142
Education Trust, 132
education wars, 104, 114–15, 125. *See also* culture wars
Education Week, 47, 78
effort, lack of, 95
egg crate schools, 124

Einstein, Albert, 141
elected school boards, 113
Elementary and Secondary Education Act, 14, 142
eligibility for special education, 4, 6, 22–28, 34, 60, 149, 153, 170
Elmore, Richard, 123
emotional disability, 5, 8, 39, 58
Endrew F. case, 173
equal educational opportunity, 139–42
equal opportunity funding, 105
equal protection clause, 17, 154
equity in spending, 105
ESSA. *See* Every Student Succeeds Act (ESSA)
establishment, educational, xvii–xviii, 12, 101–2, 118, 169–70
"Evaluation of Response to Intervention Practices for Elementary School Reading" (Balu), 77
evaluations of teachers, 125–26
Every Student Succeeds Act (ESSA), 7, 15, 61, 85, 117–20, 132–33, 144–52
evidence-based best practices, 61–70, 101, 128, 139, 156. *See also* research-based programs
Evidence for ESSA, 132
exaggeration of progress, 167
exit exams, high school, 48
experimental teaching, 73
expert instructors, 73
extended time accommodation, 50
external regulation, 117

failure: academic, 58; fear of, 29, 95; of system, xiv, xvi
falling behind, 30–31, 62, 83
falsifying achievement, 42
family culture, 13, 176–77
family support, 108
fear of failure, 29, 95
federal courts, 154
federal regulations, 111–14
federal role in education, 14–15, 92, 112, 139, 141–45
Finn, Chester E., 66, 131, 169

Fletcher, Jack M., 22
flunking. *See* retentions
Ford, Gerald R., 24
foundational reading, 128
14ᵗʰ amendment to U.S. Constitution, 17, 154
fraternities, 126
frontline teachers, 13, 101
frustration, feeling of, xvi–xvii
Fuchs, Douglas, 77–78
funding: competition for, 177–78; conservative views on, 106; disparities in, 105, 110–11; federal guarantee of, 110–11; inefficient spending of, 142; lack of, 11–12, 75, 102–15; liberal views on, 106; management of, 18, 101; review of, 107

Gabrieli, John, 37
gaps in achievement, 148. *See also* discrepancy gap
Garda, Robert, 151
general education: adequate instruction in, 7, 27, 39, 69; core instruction in, 64–68; failure of, 23; insufficient, 16; struggling learners in, 9, 41–43, 79–80, 159
gifted and talented programs, 177–78
Ginsburg, Ruth Bader, 162–63
Goldstein, Dana, 123
Gooding, Cuba, 103
governance of schools, 104
grade inflation, 10, 48, 167
grade level gaps, 44
graduation diplomas, 47–49
Gray, Freddie, 89
Great Society crusade, 142

Hanushak, Eric A., 106
Hart, Betty, 33–34
Head Start program, 63
helplessness, feelings of, xv–xvi
high-performance schools, 65, 124, 145
high school bridge projects, 48–49
high school diplomas, 47–49
home environment, 32
Houston, Texas, 170

IDEA. *See* Individuals with Disabilities Education Act (IDEA)
identification process, 57, 62–64
ideology, 114–15
IEPs. *See* Individual Education Programs (IEPs)
improvement of instruction, 65, 101, 134
inclusion, 23–24, 129
independent IEP facilitators, 168
independent proficiency, 88
independent skills, 50
Individual Education Programs (IEPs): appropriate instruction required by, 27; failure of, 146; goals for, 90; measurable goals, 82–85; parents as partners in, 19, 159–62; program modifications, 51; team meetings, xviii, 29, 89; tutoring added to, 5
individualized instruction, 67
Individuals with Disabilities Education Act (IDEA): amending, 147–53; classification of disabilities, 7; expediency prevailing over, 23; legal mandates of, 85; local districts ignoring, 141; loopholes in, 15, 34–39; 1997 amendments to, 26; procedural protections under, 159; requirements of, 22, 61–62; specially designed instruction required by, 28; 2004 amendments to, 26; unintended consequences of, 25
inequality of opportunity, 12, 104, 139, 158, 176, 179
inexperienced teachers, 127
inflation of achievement, 10, 42, 47, 94, 167
informal school policy, 32
innovation, 135
Inside Teaching (Kennedy), 122
Institute of Education Sciences, 77, 132
institutional attention deficit disorder, 134–36
institutional attitudes, 33
instructional materials, 124
intensive instruction, 71

international comparison of schools, 145

intervention process, 57, 62–64, 77. *See also* Response to Intervention (RTI)

Invisible Dyslexics, The (Hettleman), 33, 175

IQ, importance of, 33–36

It's the Classroom, Stupid (Hettleman), 65, 114

"It Turns Out Spending More Probably Does Improve Education" (Carey and Harris), 106

jargon, technical, 160

Jerry Maguire (movie), 103

Johns Hopkins University, 66, 132

Johnson, Lyndon B., 14, 142

Kame'enui, Edward, 91–92

Kennedy, Edward, 143

Kennedy Krieger Institute, 161

kindergarten, 63

King, Jr., Martin Luther, xix

Kirwan, Brit, 108

Kirwan Commission, 69, 106–9, 121, 135, 179

Kozol, Jonathan, 104

labor agreements, 126

language impairments, 39

large scale programs, 73–74

lawsuits, 16–17, 139, 147, 153–56

laziness, 32

learned helplessness, 29

learning disabilities: co-morbidities, 40; increase in number of students with, 35; manipulation of definition, 34–35; misconceptions about, 32; neuroscience of, 37–38; statutory definition of, 37

Learning Disabilities (Fletcher), 38–39

learning styles, 66

Learning to Improve (Bryck), 127

least restrictive environment (LRE), 23

legal aid societies, 168

legal decisions, 86–88

LEP. *See* Limited English Proficiency (LEP)

lesson plans, 65

Levine, Arthur, 125, 128

liberals, political, 18, 104–6, 114, 140–42, 158, 170, 176–78

Limited English Proficiency (LEP), 69

Linan-Thompson, Sylvia, 38

literacy: instruction, 63; lawsuits for denial of access to, 17; right to, 139, 153–56

local control of education, 14–15, 109–10, 121–24, 139–42. *See also* community control of education

local reforms, 141–45

local regulations, 111–14

loopholes, legal, 28, 34–39

low expectations, 13, 26, 31, 84, 87–88, 128, 157

LRE. *See* least restrictive environment (LRE)

Lyon, G. Reid, 22

mainly mislabeled students, xviii, 6–9, 27, 149–50, 171

mainstreaming, 23–24

malpractice, educational, 155–56

management failures, 102

management norms, 117–23

management training, 125–27

Manpower Demonstration Research Corporation, 132

Maryland, 39–40, 48, 70, 75–76, 92–93, 106–10, 162, 169, 179

Maryland Center for Developmental Disabilities, 161

Maryland Commission on Innovation and Excellence in Education. *See* Kirwan Commission

Maryland RTI Guidance Manual, 71–72

Maryland State Department of Education (MSDE), 75, 93, 169

Massachusetts, 141

math, RTI applications to, 59

Matthew effect, 30, 62, 83

McLaughlin, Margaret J., 15–16, 150–51

measurable goals, 82–84
mediation process, 161
mega-reforms, 65
mentors, 125
Michigan, 154
micro-management, 111–14
middle class parents, 164
mislabeling of students, xviii, 6–9, 27, 149–50, 171
mismanagement of instruction, 116–36
mission creep, 35, 150
Mississippi, 110
mobilizing political power, 17–20, 140, 157–80
modifications, 49–50, 51–52
money. *See* funding
motivation, loss of, 29, 83, 95
MSDE. *See* Maryland State Department of Education (MSDE)
MTSS. *See* Multi-tier System of Support (MTSS)
multiple disabilities, 96
Multi-tier System of Support (MTSS), 59

NAEP. *See* National Assessment of Educational Progress (NAEP)
narrowing the gap policy, 93
NASET. *See* National Association of Special Education Teachers (NASET)
National Assessment of Educational Progress (NAEP), 43, 79–80
National Association of Special Education Teachers (NASET), 174
National Association of State Directors of Special Education, 85
National Center and State Collaborative (NCSC), 97
National Center on Education and the Economy (NCEE), 65, 124
National Center on Educational Outcomes, 8, 88
National Center on Learning Disabilities, 32, 40

National Commission on Excellence in Education, 142
National Council on Teacher Quality, 123, 128, 129
national curriculum, 66, 131–32
National Research Council Committee on the Prevention of Reading Difficulties in Young Children, 133
Nation at Risk, A (National Commission on Excellence in Education), 110, 142
NCEE. *See* National Center on Education and the Economy (NCEE)
NCLB. *See* No Child Left Behind Act (NCLB)
NCSC. *See* National Center and State Collaborative (NCSC)
needless suffering, xvi–xvii
negligence, 4
neuroscience, 37–38
new education federalism, 112
"New Life for Educational Malpractice" (Gray), 155
New York Times, 106
No Child Left Behind Act (NCLB), 14, 26, 48, 61, 85, 117–19, 142–43, 148, 169
no excuses culture, 177
non-profit organizations, 167–68

Obama, Barack, 92, 119, 135, 150
observations, classroom, 117
obstacles to reform, 11, 55–56, 179
Office of Special Education Programs, 78
one-to-one instruction, xii, 5, 60, 71. *See also* tutoring
One Year Plus policy, 90–97
online education, 135
opportunity, inequality of, 12, 104, 139, 158, 176, 179
Orfield, Gary, 144
organization charts, 125
other health impairments, 8, 39, 82, 152, 171
oversight of schools, 104
over-testing, 63, 143

paper trail of communication, 166–67
paperwork, 117
parent centers, 166
parents: complaint procedures for, 166; conflicting priorities of, 177; consent of, 160; despair of, xv; disunity among, 171–74; dyslexia advocates, 175; empowering, 165; commercial guidebooks, 166; legal protections for, 158–59; lower income, 18–19; middle class, 164; mobilizing, 140, 157–80; notification of, 165; as partners, 159–61; poor, 164; restricting rights of, 169–70; rights of, 19, 159–61; role in educational reform, 17–19; RTI involvement, 165; socio-economic status of, 105; tips for, 166–68; wealthy, 163–64
parent-teacher associations (PTAs), 103
Payne, Charles M., 114–15
peer-reviewed research, 62
personalized learning, 67
personal relationships, 126
personnel evaluations, 117–18
Peter Principle, 123
Philadelphia, Pennsylvania, 43
phonics approach, 133
phonological processing, 36–38, 175
polarization, political, 114–15
policy guidance, 104
policymakers, 101, 147
political action, 17–20, 140, 165, 168–79. See also call to action
political expediency, 135
political inequality, 158
political polarization, 114–15
Pondiscio, Robert, 124
positive behavior support systems, 59
poverty, 10, 12, 164, 175
pre-kindergarten, 63, 108, 177
preparation of teachers, 108
Prince George's County, Maryland, 48
private schools, 114
privatization of schools, 65, 105, 114, 176

problem-solving approach, 73
problem-solving teams, 159
procedural protections, 159
professional autonomy, 117, 123–25
professional culture, 120
professional development, 130–31
professional organizations, 19–20
proficiency: independent, 88; percentage of students achieving, 43; as standard, 148
progress: exaggeration of, 10, 42, 47, 94, 167; standards for, 96–97
promotions to administrative offices, 123
proven practices, xii
psychological fallout, 157
psychological processing, 37–39
psychologists, school, 13, 32–33
PTAs. See parent-teacher associations (PTAs)
public defender advocates, 168
Public Education Leadership Project, 123
pupil support positions, 69

qualifications of tutors, 72
quality, teacher, 65
Quenemoen, Rachel, 91

race to the bottom, 119, 143–44, 169
racial biases, 28, 31–34, 164
random trials, 62
R&D. See research and development (R&D)
read-aloud accommodation, 50, 94
reading: assessments, 46; difficulties, 35; foundational, 128; instruction, 77, 128
reading wars, 114, 133
redefining disability, 151
reforms: advocacy for, xvi–xviii; of curricula, 65–66; federal role in, 139–45; implementation of, 135; local, 141–45; mega-reforms, 65; movements, 20–21, 171; obstacles to, 179; possibility of, 13–17, 179; potential reformers, 170; revolving

reforms (*continued*)
   door of, 135; road to, 9–11; stalemated politics of, 139; state, 14–15,
   141–45; system-wide, 163, 168–79;
   Tier 1 impacted by, 65; union support for, 178–79; urgency of, 164
remedial instruction, 91
replicating programs, 73–74
report cards, 47
Reschly, Daniel J., 38
research, educational, 62
research and development (R&D),
   109, 132–34
research-based programs, 28, 60–70,
   117, 128, 133. *See also* evidence-
   based best practices
resolution meetings, 161
Response to Intervention (RTI),
   57–80; adequacy of, 108–10; applications to math, 59; as appropriate
   instruction, 27; as boondoggle,
   76–78; components of, 10; denial
   about absence of, 74–76; exten-
   sion of process, 39–40; federal
   guarantees of, 139; framework for
   assistance, xvi; implementation of,
   74–79; lawsuits for failure to provide, 17; and learning disabilities,
   78–79; necessity of, 39; obstacles
   to, 11, 55–56; for older students,
   63; parental involvement in, 165;
   principal features of, 57; regulations,
   78; Tier 1, 59–60, 64–68; Tier 2, 60,
   68–70; Tier 3, 60, 68–70; tutoring as
   essential element of, 71–74, 108–10;
   waiting lists for, 79–80
"Response to Intervention: Ready or
   Not?" (Reynolds and Shaywitz), 78
results driven accountability, 150
retentions, 31, 45–47
review, of RTI process, 166
reviews of research, 132
rights: under IDEA, 83; without
   labels, 151; of parents, 169–70;
   reading as, 17, 153–56, 165;
   system-wide, 169
Risley, Todd R., 33–34

Roberts, John G., 87
Robinson, Brooks, 89
Rossiter, Caleb Stewart, 41, 47
Rothstein, Richard, 177
RTI. *See* Response to Intervention
   (RTI)

salaries, teacher, xvii, 108, 178
satisfaction with schools, 164
savage inequalities, 104
scandals, 170
scapegoating of teachers, 68
Schaffer v. Weast, 162
school-based management, 124
school boards, 112–13
school culture, 32
School Superintendents Association,
   169
Science magazine, 37
screening instruments, 59–61
scribes, 50
segregation: racial, 142, 154–55; of
   special education, 6, 23, 151
Seidenberg, Mark, 127
self-help resources, 165
separate-but-equal schooling, 142
severe disabilities, xviii, 96–97,
   152–53, 171. *See also* truly disabled
   students
Shaywitz, Sally E., 22, 36, 78
short-term solutions, 42, 134
size of instructional group, 72
Slavin, Robert, 46, 49, 108–9, 132, 135
small group instruction, xii, 5, 60,
   71–73
social class, 177
social connections, 126
social issues, 176
social promotion, 31, 47, 167
solo practitioners, educators as, 123–24
some benefit, meaning of term, 87
sororities, 126
special education, 81–97; abolition
   of, 151; associations of educators,
   170; costs of, 25; dumping students into, 3, 9, 23–25; eligibility
   for, 4, 6, 22–28, 34, 60, 149, 153,

170; paperwork for, 117; portrayal of, xviii; reinvention of, 15–16, 146–56; scandals, 170; segregation of, 6, 23, 151; as short-term service, 42; stigma of, 6, 23, 151; struggling learners in, 10, 41, 43; under-preparation of teachers, 129–30
"Special Education" (Pasachoff), 160
Special Education Parents Response Unit, 169
specialization of teachers, 129
specially designed instruction, 23, 28, 56, 85, 89
specific learning disabilities, 4, 7–8, 24–28, 45, 146, 152, 171, 174
speech impairments, 39
staff shortages, 75
standardized tests, 52, 167
standard of care, educational, 155–56
standards, academic, 26, 51–52, 85, 96–97, 110, 119
standard treatment protocol, 73
Stanovich, Keith, 30–31
states: academic standards, 155; boards of education, 113; control of education, 110; courts, 154; departments of education, 120–21; devolution of power to, 120; funding systems, 105; reforms, 141–45; regulations, 111–14; rights, 144–45; role in reform, 14–15
Steiner, David, 66
Stevens, John Paul, 162
stigma of special education, 6, 23, 151
strategic early interventions, 63
strategy, disagreement on, 177
strengths and weaknesses method, 38–39
structural changes, xiii
struggling learners: adequate instruction of, 152; definition of, 5–6, 69–70; educational abuse of, 3; in general education, 9, 41–43, 79–80, 159; mislabeling of, 8–9; problems faced by, xi–xii; in special education, 9, 41–43
student/teacher ratios, 60, 69

"Study of Promotion/Retention Policies in Urban School Districts" (Hettleman), 46
superintendents, 134–35
supervision of teachers, 125
supplemental instruction, 31
supplementary aids and services, 51
support for teachers, 117, 127–34
supportive services, 69
Supreme Court, California, 155
Supreme Court, U.S., 86, 105, 141–42, 146, 154, 162, 173
system-wide reforms, xiv, 163, 168–79

targeted programs, 177
tax credits, 114
teachers: altruism, 122; care deeply and work tirelessly, 12; collegiality, 118, 122; day-to-day help for, 127; demoralization of, 68; desperation of, xv–xvi, 28–31, 37; evaluations of, 125–26; expediency, 9, 23; frontline, 13, 101; heroes, xvii; inexperienced, 127; job satisfaction, 178–79; on-the-job training, 117, 125–31; preparation of, 52, 108, 125–34; prescribed instruction, 73–75, 124; quality of, 65; salaries of, xvii, 108, 178; scapegoating of, 68; specialization, 129; supervision of, 125; support for, 117, 127–34; training of, 52, 125–34; unions, 19–20, 102–5, 114, 126, 140, 158, 176–79; working conditions, 12, 178–79
teachers colleges, 123–30
Teacher Wars, The (Goldstein), 123
Tennessee, 74–75
tests: cheating on, 52; curriculum-embedded, 167; grade level and, 46; as graduation requirements, 48; inflation of scores, 10, 42, 94, 119; for learning disabilities, 38–39; over-testing, 63, 143; resistance to, 144; standardized, 167; teacher-made, 167; varying, 110

Texas, 110, 170
textbooks, 65–66
thirty million word gap, 33–34
Thomas B. Fordham Institute, 126, 132
Tier 1 of RTI, 59–60, 64–68
Tier 2 of RTI, 60, 68–70, 84
Tier 3 of RTI, 60, 68–70, 84
"Tiered Instructional Approach to Support Achievement for All Students, A" (MSDE), 75–76
time of tutoring sessions, 72
"Time to Make Special Education 'Special' Again" (Horn and Tynan), 25
Tinkering Toward Utopia (Tyack and Cuban), 135–36
tips for parents, 166–68
tools, teaching, 131–34
Too Simple to Fail (Bausell), 71
Torgesen, Joseph K., 36, 62
Tribe, Lawrence, 17, 155
truly disabled students, xviii, 7–8, 150, 171. See also severe disabilities
Trump, Donald, 21, 92, 101, 144
tutoring, xii, 31, 60, 68–74, 108–10, 134. See also one-to-one instruction
tutor/student ratios, 72–73, 109
Tyack, David, 115

UDL. See Universal Design for Learning (UDL)
underachievement, 41–52
under-preparation of special education teachers, 129–30
unions, teacher, 19–20, 102–5, 114, 126, 140, 158, 176–79

unitary system, 151–52
Unitas, John, 89
United States, comparison of school system with other countries, 65–66
unity, lack of, 171–74
Universal Design for Learning (UDL), 67
unrealistic goals, 117, 135, 143
urban school systems, 43, 89
U.S. Department of Education, 96–97, 132, 149, 170, 179
U.S. Educational Innovation Index, 135

variation in human populations, xii
Vaughan, Sharon, 38
verbatim reading. See read-aloud accommodation
visiting classrooms, 167
vouchers, 114, 168

waiting lists for RTI, 79–80
wait-to-fail approach, 36, 58, 78
Wall Street Journal, 120
"Want to Fix Education? Just Give a Kid a Tutor" (Smith), 71
Washington, D.C., 48
Washington Post, 120
waste, bureaucratic, 105
wealthy communities, 103, 163–64
What Works Clearinghouse, 132
"When Parents Aren't Enough" (Phillips), 168
whole class instruction, 71
whole language, 114, 133
written notes, 166–67

Acknowledgments

These acknowledgements can't do justice to all those to whom I am indebted. There are far too many of them. First are parents and teachers. The hundreds of parents I have represented have inspired me with their love for their children and their indomitable spirit. They won't give up the fight, and we shouldn't either.

Teachers are no less inspirational. I have been deeply moved and motivated by the thousands of them that I have interacted with over the years. They are heroic in their tireless efforts to overcome systemic barriers and do the best they can to enable their students to succeed.

I am also profoundly thankful to colleagues who have been unstinting in their help. Their assistance ranged from reading the whole manuscript, to reading parts of it, to consultation on a particular issue. That doesn't mean that colleagues have endorsed all of the book, or even key analyses or recommendations. Their feedback has sometimes been long on pushback. But I have benefited greatly from many informative exchanges.

Ulrich Boser has provided extensive, invaluable editorial consultation. Ulrich, an education policy expert and accomplished author outside the field of education, has been an unsparing source of encouragement and guidance in all facets of the book's development.

Others on the alphabetical honor roll of those who have helped in some way are: Meg Benner, Jarrod Bolte, Candace Cortiella, Alan Coulter, Donald Deshler, Robert Embry, Checker Finn, Marcella Franczkowski, Doug Fuchs, Eve Heyn, Laura Kaloi, Ed Kame'enui, Marcy Kolodny, Denise Marshall, Jay Mathews, Maggie McLaughlin, Mike Petrilli, and Rachel Quenemoen.

Sadly, one acknowledgement is in memoriam. David Schimmel, a lifelong friend and acclaimed professor of education, died as the book was nearing completion. But happily, we had many conversations about the book and he taught me many lessons over many years.

On the home front, my wife and four sons, Jeffrey, Neil, Daniel and Robert, were editors and supporters par excellence. In the family tradition, each, in a no-holds-barred way, was always there to help and humor Dad.

I also want to convey my appreciation to Mark Fretz and Evan Phail at Radius Book Group and Naomi Gunkel at Scribe Inc. I have benefited from their expert and patient assistance at every step along the long path to publication.

Finally, let me single out two persons for special expressions of gratitude. One, a dear family friend Sarajane Greenfeld, I was very lucky to have the benefit of her superb copy-editing skills as the book developed.

The other person is Robert Slavin, who is in a class by himself. He's an education scholar and program developer of wide renown. Even more remarkably, he is an outspoken advocate for reform, and I am inexpressibly honored by his generous Introduction to the book. What he omits, however, is his own role as a mentor and fountainhead for many ideas in the book about how to transform instruction for struggling learners.

Bob and I are sometimes side by side in challenging the education establishment. But it hardly need be said that I am not remotely in the same education league as he is. Which makes it all the more extraordinary that he has taken so much time to assist me. Of course, his professional reputation is so great that it can easily withstand any association with my work. With immeasurable admiration and appreciation, thanks Bob.

About the Author

Kalman "Buzzy" Hettleman has had a notable career on the frontlines of education policy and politics. He has represented pro bono over 200 students in special education, while developing systemic policy reforms and advocating for them at the state, local and national levels. His published reports on special education and struggling learners include: *Students with Disabilities Can Succeed!: How the Baltimore City Public Schools are Transforming Special Education; The Invisible Dyslexics: How Public School Systems in Baltimore and Elsewhere Discriminate Against Poor Children in the Diagnosis and Treatment of Early Reading Difficulties;* and *The Road to Nowhere: The Illusion and Broken Promises of Special Education.*

During 2016-2018, he was a member of the Maryland Commission on Innovation and Excellence in Education, charged by the governor and state legislature with recommending comprehensive, statewide K-12 school reform. In Baltimore, he has been a member of the school board twice, deputy mayor/executive assistant for education (and other social programs) under two mayors, and executive director of a large dropout prevention project.

His acclaimed book *It's the Classroom, Stupid: A Plan to Save America's Schoolchildren* was published in 2010. Other published articles have appeared in *The Nation, Education Week,* the *Washington Post* and the *Baltimore Sun.*

He has further served as Maryland cabinet secretary for social welfare programs, and director of the Baltimore department of social services, taught social policy at several universities, been a public interest attorney, and managed state and local political campaigns.

CPSIA information can be obtained
at www.ICGtesting.com
Printed in the USA
BVHW070723210519
548670BV00002B/5/P